Central Asia and the Rise of Normative Powers

Central Asia and the Rise of Normative Powers

Contextualizing the Security Governance of the European Union, China, and India

EMILIAN KAVALSKI

BLOOMSBURY
NEW DELHI • LONDON • OXFORD • NEW YORK • SYDNEY

First published in India 2017
First published 2012

Bloomsbury and the Diana logo are trademarks of Bloomsbury Publishing Plc
This edition published with permission from Bloomsbury Publishing Plc
50 Bedford Square, London WC1B 3DP

Library of Congress Cataloging-in-Publication Data
A catalog record for this title is available from the Library of Congress.

ISBN: 978 93 86349 46 0
10 9 8 7 6 5 4 3 2 1
For sale in the Indian subcontinent only

Bloomsbury Publishing India Pvt. Ltd
Second Floor, Building No. 4
DDA Complex LSC, Pocket C – 6 & 7
Vasant Kunj, New Delhi 110070
www.bloomsbury.com

Typeset by Deanta Global Publishing Services, Chennai
India Printed and bound in India by Thomson Press

Contents

Acknowledgments

This book took three months to write and three years to complete. I would like to thank my commissioning editor Marie-Claire Antoine for taking on this project when I was already thinking of giving it up and supporting it so enthusiastically. During this period, a number of individuals contributed both directly and unwittingly to the shape and trajectories of this book, and I would like to thank them all. I would like to start with my fellow denizens of the research haven generously provided for us by the Rachel Carson Center (Münich, Germany). Without their knowing, the complexity of our intellectual conversations and collective "fremdschämen" provided an important lifeline for this project. Thanks are also due to the participants at the workshop on "Comparative Approaches to Regionalism in the Asia-Pacific" at Deakin University (Australia), where many of the ideas developed in the following pages were first articulated. In particular, I am grateful to David Hundt, David Walker, Baogang He, Chengxin Pan, and Philomena Murray for their thoughtful comments. Finally, the Taiwan Fellowship offered by the Ministry of Foreign Affairs of the Republic of China (Taiwan) and my hosts at the Institute of Political Studies, Academia Sinica provided an extremely hospitable environment for completing this project. I would especially like to thank Wu Yu-Shan, Chu Chin-peng, Tsai Tung-Chieh, Hung Ming-Te, Liu Tai-Ting, Liu Kuang-hua, Tai Wan-chin, David Lin, and Tom Wilkins for making my stay in Taiwan so worthwhile. Last but not least, the vibrant conversations with my fellow ASIR-ists at the University of Western Sydney sustained this project despite all the frustrations.

Some of the ideas presented in this book offer much revised versions of arguments that have been developed earlier in *India and Central Asia: The Mythmaking and International Relations of a Rising Power* (I. B. Tauris, 2010); "The international politics of fusion and fissure in the awkward states of post-Soviet Central Asia," in E. Kavalski (Ed.), *Stable outside, fragile inside? Post-Soviet statehood in Central Asia* (Ashgate, 2010); "Shanghaied into cooperation: Framing China's socialization of Central Asia," *Journal of Asian and African Studies* 44 (2010); "'Do as I Do': The global politics of China's regionalization" in E. Kavalski (Ed), *China and the global politics of regionalization* (Ashgate, 2009); "The complexity of global security governance: An analytical overview," *Global Society* 22 (2008); and *Extending the European security community: Constructing peace in the Balkans* (I. B. Tauris, 2008). I would like to thank these journals and publishers for permitting me to use the arguments that first appeared in their publications. I am also grateful to Vladimir Bessarabov from the UN Cartographic Section for granting permission to reproduce the map of Central Asia included in this volume.

Finally, there are more personal thanks to Raycho Kavalski for skyping-in reality on a daily basis and to Magdalena Zolkos both for putting up with and supporting "all this," and with apologies that this is not the "ostrich-and-chicken" book that she would want.

List of abbreviations

CFSP	Common Foreign and Security Policy
DCECI	Development Cooperation and Economic Cooperation Instrument
EIR	European International Relations theory
ENP	European Neighbourhood Policy
ESDP	European Security and Defence Policy
ESS	European Security Strategy
EU	European Union
EUSR	European Union Special Representative
ICG	International Crisis Group
IOM	International Organization for Migration
NATO	North Atlantic Treaty Organization
NGO	nongovernmental organization
NIS	Newly Independent States
OSCE	Organization for Security and Cooperation in Europe
PCA	Partnership and Cooperation Agreement
PFP	Partnership for Peace Program
RATS	Regional Anti-Terrorist Structure
RSP	Regional Strategy Paper
SCO	Shanghai Cooperation Organization
TACIS	Technical Assistance to the Commonwealth of Independent States

TRACECA	Transport Corridor Europe–Caucasus–Asia
UN	United Nations
UNDP	United Nations Development Program
USA	United States of America
USSR	Union of Soviet Socialist Republics

List of figures and map

Introduction: Framing the normative foreign policy agency of the European Union, China, and India in Central Asia

Central Asia has always been different.

Ahmed Rashid (1994, p. 9)

The attention to the region-building agency of international actors such as the European Union (EU), China and India are of fairly recent provenance in the study of world affairs. Framed under the label of "new regionalism," its discussions have tended to investigate the institutions, policies, and economic relations that underpin such externally promoted region-building approaches. Yet, little attention seems to have been accorded to the strategic storytelling that marks the global politics of new regionalism. If one were to undertake such an exploration, the narrative underpinning of new regionalism would reveal attitudes about self and other that do not transpire in conventional accounts of trade figures, geopolitical interests, and security threats. In particular, the account of the EU's, China's, and India's engagement in various regional contexts uncovers the role of othering as a central feature of the nascent processes of region-building. Indicative of who is positioned inside a community of regional interactions and who is excluded from it, the other provides a tangible frame of reference for the simultaneous recognition and projection of the identity of international actors undertaking the practice of regionalization.

Thus, as the epigraph to this chapter suggests, post-Soviet Central Asia (encompassing the countries of Kazakhstan, Kyrgyzstan, Tajikistan, Turkmenistan, and Uzbekistan) has been one of those perennial others in the global politics of regionalization. Its difference in the eyes of external actors has urged them to assert (and only occasionally reflect upon) their own international identity through incursions in the region. Thus, more often than not, the external engagement with Central Asia has been a projection of the perceptions, attitudes, and feelings of international actors about who they think they are, rather than about the objective reality of the region.

In short, Central Asia has consistently been denied its subjectivity in international life. Thus, extending Ahmed Rashid's claim from the epigraph, the contention of this study is that because it has been perceived as different, Central Asia has always been treated the same—as the *context* for the agency of external actors.[1] Ever since the days of the "great game," the region's difference has become eponymous with otherness.[2] The Central Asian self in this respect has tended to be framed by the external actor undertaking the regionalization process. It is in this sense that the so-called Oriental/Third World/developing nations with which Central Asia has often been bundled emerge as the plaything of the whims of external actors—either as mere spectators (at best) or victims (at worst). In both instances, however, *agency* (the ability to control one's own fate) was not a recognized feature of their international identity. Instead, Central Asian actors were assumed to be the passive recipients of the external gaze/rule/aid as scripted by the templates of colonialism, Cold War bipolarity, and—now—democratization.

The proposition then is that the current dynamics of the regionalization of Central Asia are an instance of this trend. Thus, the Central Asian agency of the EU, India, and China reveals the treatment of the region as a context for their "struggle for recognition." Admittedly, as it will soon be explained, the content of such treatment might have changed (especially in terms of the relational character of the assumed otherness of Central Asia in international life), but not the form—that is, Central Asia continues to be treated as a context for the agency of extraregional actors.

The reference to context is not coincidental. It intimates that Central Asia has been positioned as an explanatory environment which simultaneously serves as a "cause," a "barrier," and a "changing meaning" for the regional agency of international actors (Goertz, 1994). Thus, the strategic storytelling underpinning the Central Asian agency of the EU, China, and India suggests that the region is construed as an intersubjective background of expectations, dispositions, and language that give meaning to the material reality of external actors and helps explain the constitutive and causal mechanisms that participate in the construction of their security governance (Adler, 2006). Thus, as Chapter 1 will reveal, Central Asia is not merely an "old idea taking on a new life" (Rashid, 1994, p. 209). Instead, its treatment as a *context* for the agency of external actors turns the region into a "vague idea," whose concreteness emerges from the iterated practices of such international involvement.

It is for this reason that this book explores the attitudes of normative foreign policy actors in Central Asia. Such an outside-in approach is not intended to deny the individuality and autonomous agency of regional actors. On the contrary, both the dynamics of the "new great game" (discussed in Chapter 1) and the processes of socialization (discussed in Chapter 3) indicate that Central Asian states are "active subjects" capable of articulating their own interests.[3] Such regional agency notwithstanding, the claim here is that the "outside-in" dynamic of regionalization is not only "the more powerful one," but also "drives" the domestic responses of Central Asian actors, because regional states "tend to establish objectives and strategies to pursue these objectives reactively or opportunistically in response to their perception of the larger actors' strategies" (Wimbush, 2011, p. 263). For this reason, this study asserts that external actors are actively engaged in the deliberate construction of the region as a context for their own policies (very often at the expense of the subjectivity of Central Asian states). Therefore, the outside-in perspective of this study allows for interrogating the continuities, changes, and innovations in the security governance practices extended to the context of Central Asia by the EU, China, and India.

The outside-in analysis of the Central Asian agency of normative foreign policy actors demands a qualification about their treatment as unitary/corporate actors. All three of them—the EU, China, and India—reflect complex institutional, historical, cultural, political, and economic patterns of relations (which are detailed in Part II). Yet, such complexity cannot be experienced in any other way, but through the stories that their actorness tells (Kavalski, 2008a, p. 13). It is for this reason that thinking about complex international actors—such as the EU, China, and India—in terms of unitary entities is "so deeply embedded in our common sense that it is difficult to imagine how international politics might be conceptualized and conducted" outside of the "anthropomorphized" perception of world politics which operates according to "the same psychological principles that govern interactions between individuals" (Greenhill, 2008, p. 346; Wendt, 1999, p. 196).

Confirming such tendencies toward individuation, this study often uses Brussels, Beijing, and New Delhi as shorthand for the agency of the EU, China, and India. It should not be assumed, however, that such treatment offers an exhaustive analysis of their external affairs, nor should it be taken as an indication of the homogeneity of either the EU, China, or India.[4] Instead, the research merely concurs with the suggestion that it is impossible to know about the practices of the EU's, China's, and India's security governance in Central Asia except by their cumulative effect—that is, they are analyzable only in light of "what we perceive to be the impact of [unitary] actor choices on events" (Kolodziej, 2005, p. 19).

Prior to embarking on its investigation of the international affairs of Central Asia, this introductory chapter demarcates the notion of "rising normative powers." It also explains why this study zooms-in on the region-building agency of the EU, China, and India and not that of other actors. The discussion draws attention to the dynamics that have allowed the fledgling normative foreign policy agency of Brussels, Beijing, and New Delhi to articulate security governance mechanisms for Central Asia—a region that is traditionally perceived as Russia's "backyard." This introductory chapter also offers an overview of the eclectic methodology of this study, which rests on recent developments in European International Relations (EIR) theory and the research program of "narrative splicing." The dynamic analytical environment provided by these approaches underpins the conceptual architecture of this book. In particular, the parallel assessment of normative foreign policy agency contends that the security governance projects of the EU, China, and India in Central Asia are motivated by a desire to be recognized as actors that are not only capable, but should also be allowed to set the ramifications of the "normal" in global life.

What rise of normative powers?

The reference to a "rise of normative powers" in the title to this volume might sound like a misnomer. To begin with, it can be argued that the behavior of all international actors—whether they be states, international organizations, or nonstate actors—is embedded in certain rules, standards, and principles of behavior. As Hans Morgenthau (1967, p. 10) has discerned, "all nations are tempted—and few have been able to resist the temptation for long—to clothe their own particular aspirations and actions in the moral purposes of the universe." While not everyone need agree with the significance of this normativity to the agency of particular actors, it nevertheless indicates certain value-based judgment underpinning their international interactions. Yet, the point of departure for this investigation is much more straightforward—just because any international behavior can be labeled as normative should not be taken as an indication that in fact all actors are normative powers.

On the contrary, following Ian Manners' oft-quoted definition, normative powers are only those actors that have the ability to "shape what can be 'normal' in international life" (Manners, 2002, p. 253). Manners' framing of normative power intends a distinction from its conceptual sibling—"soft power." Joseph Nye (2004, p. 5) defines soft power as "getting others to want the outcomes that you want."[5] While many will argue that the notions of soft power and normative power are twin concepts, the claim here is that the ramification of the normal implies a more comprehensive leadership in international life than merely getting others to want the same outcomes as you. Thus, while soft power is about making others support ideas and positions that they did not previously share, the impact of normative power is more encompassing and goes beyond co-optation. In short, others do not perceive to be following somebody else's goals, but their own. This is what defining the ramifications of the normal entails—it alters the perceptions and attitudes of target states, so that they internalize the perspectives of the normative power in their daily practices.[6]

Since Chapter 2 will expand on the import and the content of the term "normative power" and its application to (and implications for) the extraregional involvement in Central Asia, it would suffice here to say that the designation of normative power reflects an ability to frame the strategic narratives of target states through nonviolent means. At the same time, it has to be acknowledged from the outset that normative power is strategic. Influence—even if normative in character—is never altruistic. In this sense, "what makes normative power practices different. . . is that they are bent on transcending modern power politics" (Adler, 2010, p. 77). Yet, the expression of what is "normal" invokes a certain agenda and entails power relations.

The claim, therefore, is that the EU, China, and India offer some of the most conspicuous indications of the different degrees of normative power in global life (not just in Central Asia). The suggestion is that the particular understanding of Central Asia that the EU, China, and India engender is not necessarily a reflection of some objective reality, but the particular exercise of normative power that Brussels, Beijing, and New Delhi extend to the region. It needs to be declared from the beginning that such a designation of the international agency of Brussels, Beijing, and New Delhi does not distinguish between the notions of "normative power" and "normative foreign policy actor," and instead treats them interchangeably—as stylistic variations. Thus, both these terms are assumed to reveal "what an actor wants (its goals), how it acts (the deployment of its policy means), and what it achieves (its impact)" (Tocci, 2008, p. 5).

On an instrumental level, therefore, the reference to a "rise of normative powers" in Central Asia aims to distinguish between the proliferation of international agency in the region and the practices of security governance extended by normative foreign policy actors. Substantively, however, the proposition of a "rise of normative powers" in Central Asia suggests the emergence of alternative (and oftentimes) contending conceptualizations of political goods in global life and the appropriate way(s) for their achievement. The contention of a regional rise of normative powers can be interpreted as a contemporary twist on the age-old inquiry into what a multipolar theory of international relations might look like (Holsti, 1991, p. 19). If one is to pursue such a study, the parallel investigation of normative powers promises to open the doors to a contextual exploration of the intellectual foundations not only of multipolarity, but also to the proliferation of a cacophony of normative languages in global life.

The focus on the normative foreign policy agency of the EU, China, and India in Central Asia also intends to overcome the "deadlock" in the current literature on actors struggling for or claiming a "great power" status. Brock Tessman indicates that such a deadlock arises from (i) the growing tendency for status quo-oriented behavior among emerging powers and (ii) the increasingly confrontational attitudes that emerging powers hold about each other (Tessman, 2009, p. 298). How then can we come to terms with the complexity attendant in the global rise to prominence of the EU, China, and India? The response provided in this volume is fairly uncomplicated: through a contextual assessment of their normative power. This contention follows from Morgenthau's suggestion that all power is contextual—that is, "its content and the manner of its use are determined by the political and cultural environment [of its application]" (Morgenthau, 1967, p. 9).

Thus, Central Asia provides the context for the parallel assessment of the agency of Brussels, Beijing, and New Delhi in the region. In this process, the "deadlock" provoked by the simultaneity of accommodating and confrontational tendencies in their behavior—which seems to befuddle the current analyses of rising powers—gains its relevant explanation through the comparative assessment of the EU's, China's, and India's actorness in particular global locales. The suggestion here is that by looking for (if not merely *guessing* who will be) the next "great power", analysts miss the point and overlook the emerging patterns of global politics. Instead, it is the practices which become prominent in a particular region that offer the tell-tale signs of a superpower in the making.

The attention needs to be on the different *practices* that the EU, China, and India promote in Central Asia.[7] Thus, the rise of normative powers in Central Asia suggests the *layered disconnect* between their regionalizing agency. This term refers to the distinct "layers of practical regions" (Adler and Greve, 2009, p. 81) that Brussels, Beijing, and New Delhi enact in Central Asia. In other words, the EU, China, and India enact through their foreign policy behavior distinct modes of Central Asian *regionness* which, while spreading over the same geographic expanse, refers to distinct region-building strategies (and ultimately spaces). What transpires in this simultaneous regionalization is a "balance of practices" (Adler, 2008, p. 203) in Central Asia. Thus, the label of layered disconnect suggests that the concurrent dynamics of accommodation and confrontation between Brussels, Beijing, and New Delhi in Central Asia should not be perceived as a sign of the analytical impossibility of their coexistence, but as an indication of the empirical reality of global complexity (Kavalski, 2009b). Central Asia, therefore, emerges as a context of overlapping practices and patterns of relations enacted simultaneously through the interactions between different external and regional actors.

The disconnect between the distinct "repertoires of practices" (Adler and Greve, 2009, p. 65) enacted by Brussels, Beijing, and New Delhi in the Central Asian context ensures that their regional interactions do not escalate to warlike behavior. As the investigations in Part II will demonstrate, while the EU, China, and India offer equally vociferous proclamations of their commitment to the values of region-building, not all of them backstop these statements with actual *deliberate* policy *practice* of regionalization.

As the following sections will indicate, the unevenness underpinning the regional security governance strategies promoted by Brussels, Beijing, and New Delhi becomes a defining feature of the layered disconnect characterizing their concomitant agency in Central Asia. The unevenness emerges from the distinct logics of action informing their regional agency. Such agency requires both ideas and materiality: (i) ideas, "because without thought as motivation, there is no agency, there is only inertia and reaction"; and (ii) materiality, "because ultimately one cannot dispense with assumptions about human material psychology" (Barkin, 2010, p. 36). Informed by their distinct strategic cultures, the EU's normative power tends to prioritize ideas through the "logic of appropriateness" of its security governance; India, on the other hand, stresses the materiality of its agency through the "logic of consequences"; while China seems to be the only one of the three normative foreign policy actors to combine both ideas and materiality in its security governance of Central Asia through the "logic of relationships."

Thus, while the patterns of security governance are usually circumscribed by the territoriality of the specific geographic locales, this investigation articulates them through the practices and, in particular, the "generative relationships" initiated by normative powers. It also indicates that the pertinent question to ask is not which normative foreign policy actor is likely to become the next "great power," but which practices gain intelligibility in the particular regional context to which they are applied. Consequently, for a normative power to shape, influence, and change the preferences of its intended target, it "must be able to interact with that target in something that functions like a marketplace of ideas;" if the target is never exposed to the message that the normative power sends, then it can obviously never be influenced by it (Kroenig at al., 2010, p. 414). Therefore, it should not be surprising that the parallel assessment of the agency of the EU, China, and India in Central Asia in the concluding chapter indicates Beijing as the most effective of the three in developing a meaningful intersubjective "marketplace of ideas" in the region.

As the analytical framework of the volume in Part I will make explicit, the effectiveness of the security governance practices of normative foreign policy actors rests on the relational ability to make externally promoted norms "echo and adequately monitor the strategic aspects of the identity and social realms to be socialized" (Coicaud, 2001, p. 70). Such contextual localization of the practices of security governance initiated by normative foreign policy actors also suggests that the actions of normative powers are not necessarily always premeditated, but in fact are oftentimes contingent on the practices in which they engage. In this respect, Part II of the volume will reveal that more often than not "a practice can be oriented toward a goal without being consciously informed by it" (Pouliot, 2008, p. 261).

Thus, concurring with the proposition that the "basic parameters of international politics are a collective achievement," the dynamic interactions between Brussels, Beijing, and New Delhi in Central Asia suggest that their normative foreign policy agency in the region constitutes "the structural contexts" within which the awkward Central Asian states operate.[8] However, the context itself also impinges on the agency of normative powers, and the effectiveness of their security governance emerges from its intersubjectivity—namely, the capacity to foster "generative relationships" and collective knowledge that "persists beyond the lives of individual social actors embedded in social routines and practices as they are reproduced by interpreters who participate in their production and workings" (Adler, 1997, p. 321).

Before proceeding further with this investigation, it is necessary to demonstrate why other actors—such as Russia or the United States for instance—must be excluded from this analysis. The reason is fairly simple—no one else fits the bill of (let alone gestures toward) normative power. Apart from Brussels, Beijing, and New Delhi, no one else seems intent on influencing conceptualizations of the "normal" in Central Asia. Instead, other international actors are in the region either purely for the extraction of resources or as part of projects for (usually, military) domination. For instance, the United States is excluded from this analysis because of the failure of its Central Asian agency to meet the requirements of a normative foreign policy actor on both counts. In fact, to the extent that there is an American policy in the region, it remains an appendage to its post-2001 involvement in Afghanistan (Fumagalli, 2009). For very similar reasons, Russia is also excluded from this study. However, since Moscow's role in Central Asia has a longer (and more idiosyncratic) provenance than that of Washington, it is necessary to indicate how and why has the fledgling normative foreign policy agency of the EU, China, and India managed to seep through to Russia's Central Asian "backyard."

And how about Russia?

Since the rise of normative powers in Central Asia is perceived to be largely at the expense of Russia—the traditional "big brother" of the region—this point needs some elaboration. The claim here is that the proliferation of agency in Central Asia is an outcome of a contingent combination of factors, most of which refer to either intended or unintended outcomes of Moscow's own policies. Thus, as one conservative Russian foreign policy pundit has suggested, the current pattern of Central Asian affairs reflects the Kremlin's understanding that the presence of other actors in Central Asia "stabilizes the situation, which Russia is too weak to control alone."[9] These claims notwithstanding, the rise of normative powers in Central Asia "has also raised the specter of growing geopolitical pluralism" in the former Soviet space (Allison, 2004, p. 477).

On the one hand, reflecting the broader pattern of Russia's foreign policy inconsistencies during the tenure of President Boris Yeltsin, Moscow's preoccupation with the Caucasus (mainly the conflict in Chechnya) during the 1990s has led to the attenuation of its position in Central Asia. Such inconsistency in the maintenance and exercise of regional leadership has led to the degradation of the Kremlin's influence and power (Frazier and Stewart-Ingersoll, 2010, p. 743). Moreover, owing to the severe economic decline in the wake of Soviet dissolution, Russia underwent a profound retrenchment, which led it to redistribute limited resources away from peripheral commitments and toward its core interests. Some have even ascertained that this development has produced a "power vacuum in the East" (Lambridis and Koukoulis, 2005, p. 479).[10] Russian observers have noted that in the context of such confusion and disengagement, "it would be simply foolish for our foreign partners not to take advantage of this circumstance."[11] At the same time, Russia has been able to establish a pragmatic basis for its relations with the normative foreign policy agency of the EU, China, and India in the region. While the regional relations between Brussels and Moscow are subject to the lukewarm EU-Russia bilateral relations,[12] it would appear that China and India have been able to establish much more convincing ties with the Kremlin than the EU did.

In the case of Beijing, the sense of shared threat perceptions has led China and Russia to view the other as its "strategic rear" (Ovchinnikov, 2000). In this respect, although they compete for Central Asia's energy resources, the coincidence of interests between Moscow and Beijing has facilitated the recognition of the benefits from their cooperation—that is, they are "positioning themselves to define the rules under which the USA, the EU, Iran and Turkey will be allowed to participate in the region" (Cohen, 2001, p. 2).[13] Confirming this proposition, the Russian President Vladimir Putin has declared that the two countries "have set a solid foundation for friendship, trust, and cooperation. . . for a long time to come;" while his Chinese counterpart, Hu Jintao asserted that Moscow and Beijing "are increasing coordination and cooperation on important regional and international issues such as guaranteeing stability in Central Asia and the SCO" (*USA Today*, 2005).

In the instance of New Delhi, the suggestion has been that the "convergence of Russian and Indian geopolitical interests in the peace and security of Central Asia [is] historical" (Kaushik, 1997, p. 52). Thus, building on the experience of Cold War collaboration, New Delhi and Moscow have found themselves on the same side in the struggle against "Muslim fundamentalism" (Chopra, 1997, p. 26)—well before the start of the so-called global war on terror. It is this cooperation, which (as Chapter 6 reveals) has assisted India in establishing its military presence in Tajikistan (Kavalski, 2010a). Indian commentators have, therefore, asserted that "Russia would like India to become a big player in the region as a balancing factor for both the American and Chinese presence" (Jain, 2008, p 214–5).

Finally, and this is again related to the regional agency of China (but can also be used as an explanation of why Central Asian states have not been averse to the regional involvement of other international actors). Thus, what appears to have won Beijing significant street credit in Central Asia is its lack of overt conditionality and commitment to the practice of noninterference in the domestic affairs of states. This perception seems to have been reinforced as a result of China's response to both the so-called color revolutions in the early 2000s supported (and sponsored) by the West and, especially, Russia's military invasion of Georgia in 2008. In both instances, Beijing was critical of what it perceived as external meddling in the domestic affairs of sovereign states (Kavalski, 2010e). With regard to Georgia, Chinese commentators have gone as far as to assert that Russia's military action in South Ossetia confirms Moscow's internalization of the Western practices of hegemonism (Yan, 2011, p. 246).[14]

Statements like this have urged leading Russian commentators to acknowledge that Beijing has not only "managed to quietly displace Moscow from the region without provoking Russia's ire and open resentment," but also that Russia is effectively becoming a "political client of China" (Trenin, 2011, pp. 228–34). The conclusion seems to be that "the Kremlin lacks either the strength or willingness to put up a fight for Central Asia" (Gabuyev, 2009). This context has assisted the Central Asian agency of normative foreign policy actors. Such an overview, however, is not intended as a challenge to Russia's legacy in the region and its idiosyncratic significance as "an outsider, though one possessing an insider's feel for the leitmotifs of societies it once ruled and for the local political cultures still determined by Soviet-generation leaders" (Wimbush, 2011, p. 260).

Instead, the point here is to explain how other external actors have been able to extend their foreign policy objectives in a region that still is considered Moscow's "near abroad."[15] Consequently, as it will be discussed in the concluding chapter of this book, the analytical engagement with the roles enacted by normative powers such as the EU, China, and India in Central Asia demonstrates that the practices of security governance that prevail in a particular area are relative to the historically specific legitimation of promoted rules and standards of behavior, the contextual recognition of the normative foreign policy actor, and its ability to maintain resilient and credible commitments.

Note on methodology

At its core, this book is an exercise in interpretation; the interpretation that it undertakes attempts to render legible the intent and content of a particular phenomenon from contemporary global affairs—the rising normative foreign policy agency of the EU, China, and India by focusing on their security governance practices in Central Asia. Methodologically, therefore, this volume should be perceived as an effort to conceptualize an aspect of the current dynamics of global life. The reference to "conceptualization" here indicates "the articulation of thoughts, ideas, or hunches and the representation of these in some objective, internally coherent and consistent form" (Gariup, 2009, p. 20). At the same time, this investigation sees itself as part of the ongoing "search for a vocabulary. . . by means of which we can start to ask systemic questions about the possibility of fundamental international transformations today" (Ruggie, 1993, p. 144).

Reflective of such aims, this investigation follows an eclectic approach[16] resting on recent developments in European International Relations (EIR) theory and the research program of "narrative splicing."[17] On the one hand, such an idiosyncratic combination of approaches is informed by the understanding that different disciplinary paradigms of the study of world politics *are* commensurate and their research agendas *can* be mediated (Makinda, 2000, p. 400). On the other hand, the demand for eclecticism arises from the application of analytical strategies to the study of "unobservable wholes"—such as the normative foreign policy agency of the EU, China, and India in Central Asia (in fact the region itself, as Chapter 1 will suggest, might be conceived as an "unobservable whole")—which reveal "considerable uncertainty about whether the parts observed are actually elements of the wholes inferred" (Puchala, 2003, pp. 21–2).

It needs to be stated from the outset that a distinguishing feature of this book's combination of EIR with "narrative splicing" is that it brings the analytical innovations from this eclecticism to bear on the emergent agency of not only the EU (as is usually the case), but also China and India. Thus, in teasing out the prospective climate in the relations between the EU, India, and China, this project does not analyze the bilateral interactions between these actors, but undertakes a comparative narrative assessment of their involvement in Central Asia. The contention is that Central Asia offers a relevant setting for the examination of the emergent global agency of Brussels, New Delhi, and Beijing. With this rationale in mind, the following sections briefly outline the analytical approaches guiding this investigation.

The discourse analysis of European International Relations theory

For all its alleged "eurocentrism," the study of world politics has only in the post-Cold War period begun to articulate the distinct outlines of a European International Relations (EIR) theory. Thus, while the key terms of the discipline—sovereign statehood, nationalism, balance of power, etc.—originate as descriptors of developments in European affairs, the analysis of world politics has long been designated as "an American social science" (Hoffmann, 1977). The "apple pie" (Gareau, 1981, p. 779) aftertaste of the discipline was greatly enhanced by the post-World War II superpower status of the United States and the concomitant preponderance (and consequent globalization) of the English language as the *lingua franca* of (not only American) diplomacy and academia. As Jörg Friedrichs (2004, p. 8) poignantly notes, the "Americanization" of the study of international politics has been an outcome of "unique convergence of research interests and political circumstances:"

> After the traumatic experience of the war, American scholars—to say nothing of European refugees such as Arnold Wolfers, Hans Morgenthau, and John Herz—were intrigued with the phenomenon of international power. At the same time, US decision-makers were in need of a theoretical underpinning of the strong focus on power and interest in Cold War politics.[18]

It can be argued that the consolidation of EIR in the 1990s has been facilitated by similar dynamics to those that assisted the "Americanization" of the field a few decades earlier. To start with, the "Europeanization" of the study of world affairs was prompted by the end of a war—the Cold War—which also produced a qualitative change in the patterns and practices of international relations. The proverbial fall of the Berlin Wall intensified the dormant dynamics of European integration, which were given a boost by the formation of the European Union (EU) in the wake of the 1993 Maastricht Treaty. Thus, just like in the case of post-World War II USA, the Brussels-based bloc demanded theoretical approaches that could provide an explanation and understanding of *its* trajectories, as well as analytical frameworks for *its* policy-making. At the same time, the "Europeanization" of continental politics was mirrored by a similar "Europeanization" of academia by way of making available new, EU-sponsored pools of research funds and exchange opportunities for scholars and students. In this process, an entirely new and distinctly European field of "European Union Studies" emerged (Cini and Bourne, 2006; Phinnemore and Warleigh-Lack, 2009), which developed its own concepts, methodologies, and tools. Consequently, as the scope, modes, and reach of the EU's international relations increased with the deepening and widening of the integration process, so did the distinctiveness of EIR.

However, the individualization of EIR as a distinct field of observation should not be understood as an indication of its homogeneity. On the contrary, just as the "American" study of international affairs has been distinguished by various schools and approaches, EIR has likewise branched off in numerous directions.[19] Yet, it could be argued that owing to the timing and context of its emergence, the majority of EIR-approaches are of a social-constructivist ilk.

It needs to be acknowledged that (pragmatically speaking) the adoption of EIR's methodology in this book is demanded by the use of two of the central concepts that it has advanced—"normative power" and "security governance." The emphasis on the intersubjective character of international politics (at least as the context of Europe seems to indicate) has suggested the value from the analytical engagement with foreign policy discourses.[20] EIR's discursive study of world affairs suggests that foreign policy is profoundly impacted by the strategic cultures of international actors. The inference is that national interests are not independent of the discursive context in which they emerge. Foreign policy articulations both "enable/constrain what is 'thinkable' in a given discursive context and they reward/punish institutions and practices that are contingent/deviant with the pre-set political boundaries of inclusion/exclusion" (Vucetic, 2011, p. 1300). Thus, foreign policy narratives suggest that "the meaning of an action" is constituted by "the storyteller not by the action" (Wæver, 2000, p. 284).

To paraphrase from a different context, foreign policy *is* a regime of a truth for the reproduction of a particular vision of international order (Dillon, 2004).

These assertions reflect a belief in the differential formation of conceptual meanings and the possibility of generating (narrative) explanations, while remaining skeptical about the existence of "stable (if arbitrary) relationships between signifier and signified" (Wæver, 2002, p. 23). This is the reason why this investigation relies on the notion of strategic culture for its parallel assessment of the security governance strategies of normative powers. The policy-effects of discourses are exposed not as *causal*, but rather as creating the *horizon of the possible* (Kavalski and Zolkos, 2007, pp. 377–80). On the other hand, the structure of discourse does not have an independent existence, but is *knowable* through practice. As Christopher Ford intimates, "habits of mind" provide the historical patterns and geopolitical causality within which decision-making functions. Thus, strategic culture offers an insight into the powerful effects of stock assumptions in shaping the policy perceptions backstopping the agency of international actors (Ford, 2010, p. 10).[21]

In this respect, as it will be demonstrated in Part II of this book, the different practices of security governance advanced by the EU, China, and India in Central Asia reveal distinct forms of storytelling about the nature of Brussels', Beijing's, and New Delhi's framing of the regional context. Such articulations reflect the "discursive grammars" (Gariup, 2009, p. 55) of their strategic cultures. This conviction presages the research approaches suggested by the methodology of "narrative splicing," to which we now turn our attention.

Narrative splicing

As the term suggests, narrative splicing is an approach that brings together the articulations of analysts and commentators on a specific issue. The result is a narrative produced by splicing together relevant statements that reveal the external stance of an actor by tapping into the discourses of and commentaries on its legitimation. Thus, narrative splicing engages in a textual process tracing which both uncovers "*the narratives within narratives*" context of external relations and exposes that what distinguishes the explanation of international phenomena are "the ingredients used in the narrative accounts" (Suganami, 2008, pp. 347–55).

To put it differently, the following account of the normative power of the EU, China, and India queries the character, patterns, and content of their agency by sifting through the norms, cognitive structures, legitimating frameworks, and practices of their security governance. Such discourses, to borrow from Daniel Nexon's eloquent assessment, emerge "as scripts that diffuse through networks and otherwise embed in the ongoing transactions" that constitute the basis of world affairs.[22] Thus, narrative splicing offers an opportunity for simultaneously experiencing and deducing *the ingredients* of the discursive formulations regarding the Central Asian agency of Brussels, Beijing, and New Delhi.[23]

Anticipating the discussion of strategic culture in Chapter 3, the suggestion here is that the reference to narratives offers "compelling storylines which can explain events convincingly and from which inferences can be drawn" (Freedman, 2006, p. 22).[24] As these instances of the EU, China, and India will reveal, narrative splicing demonstrates that narratives are "*constructs*" employed in the explanatory enterprise of EIR. In this regard, the following investigation relies extensively on citations and references. In such narrative splicing, "certain claims 'somehow' become related to one another" by weaving together in a meaningful storyline an "ensemble of ideas, concepts, and categorizations that are produced, reproduces, and transformed in a particular set of practices and through which meaning is given to physical and social realities" (Hajer, 1995, pp. 22–44).

Apart from the methodological rationale, the frequent recourse to direct citations reflects the particular kind of intervention that this book makes in the study both of Central Asian politics and world affairs. Unlike other books in the field, this one brings together the conceptual innovations of several distinct strands in the literature on international relations—to name only the most prominent of these strands: the analyses of (i) rising powers, (ii) the external relations of the EU, (iii) China's foreign policy, (iv) India's international outlook, (v) Central Asian affairs, (vi) normative power, and (vii) security governance—and puts them in an exclusive conversation with one another. Such an undertaking reveals novel explanations of the contemporary patterns of relations in Central Asia. Thus, the inclusion of extensive citations in the analysis is crucial for the construction of a unique narrative by weaving together the claims made by these different perspectives on international relations and then applying them to the *context* of Central Asia and the regional agency of normative powers.

Framed in this way, the narrative splicing approach offers a way for not only rendering, but also engaging the perceptions guiding the observation of normative foreign policy actors—such as the EU, China, and India—on "specific" issues regarding their international agency (especially, as they relate to their involvement in Central Asia). The claim here is that such an approach extends the following trumps to the study of normative powers. First, it allows the introduction to the discursive ingredients that go into the broth of foreign policy making without interfering in the actual voice of these articulations. Second, it does not impute, nor endow coherence on the story it tells. Instead, it facilitates a confrontation with the complexity underpinning seemingly akin propositions. Third, such an approach makes it explicit that the commentator *is* or *has consciously decided to take* the position of an external observer. Such an acknowledgment is especially pertinent to the study both of Central Asia and the positioning of China and India in world politics, where the role of an external/Western observer has been inherently problematic.

Thus, while not doing away with the controversies associated with "the eye of the Western beholder," the self-acknowledged subjective collation of the narrative splicing approach intimates that it neither attempts objectivity nor intends the promotion of grand narratives. Instead, it simply comes to suggest that no data provides "innocent" observations. Illustrations—regardless of whether they are the result of narrative splicing or parsimonious empirical testing—reflect observer bias. The difference is that the narrative splicing approach acknowledges that research is neither impartial nor a mechanical process, but an endeavor with an author. Thus, it is the author's "cognitive filter, frame, conceptual lens or paradigm" that identifies the existence of discursively enabled "set of ideas, often in the form of implicit and sedimented assumptions, upon which actors might draw in formulating strategy and, indeed, in legitimizing strategy pursued for quite distinct ends" (Christou et al., 2010, p. 346).

Therefore, narrative splicing offers flexible modes of explanation and understanding that render discursive contextualizations "fundamental" to the observation of international affairs "either because explanations are given in a narrative form or because they invariably contain narrative accounts within them" (Suganami, 2008, pp. 338–55). At the same time, narrative splicing recognizes that only *some*, not *any* explanation and understanding of the pattern of international affairs is possible. Thus, without fetishizing (any particular) method, narrative splicing helps uncover how the Central Asian context is being observed by politically and culturally diverse external-to-the-region commentators and international actors.

Structure and argument of the book

The proliferation of international agency in Central Asia is part of the ongoing layering of different regions into an interdependent and "globalized" network of complex interactions. Paradoxically, it was the ancient Silk Road that set this process into motion, by bringing into contact—and eventually merging—the geopolitical frameworks of Europe, Africa, and West Asia with the ones of East Asia via Central Asia (Cioffi-Revilla, 2006,p. 89). In this respect, the significance of Central Asia is only likely to increase in the context of the widening and deepening processes of globalization.

This dynamism underpins the considerations in Part I of this book. The three chapters included in this section illuminate the significance of the deliberate practices of socialization for the ability of normative foreign policy actors to initiate meaningful security governance mechanisms. As Chapters 2 and 3 indicate, it is by instigating nascent communities of practice that normative powers socialize target states into promoted models of behavior as scripted by the cognitive frameworks of their strategic culture. Thus, it is in the active process of repeated interaction that a normative power can effectively communicate its message to intended targets (Kroenig et al., 2010, p. 45). The point here is that rather than "we-feeling," practices foster "generative relationships" through "we-doing" (Adler, 2010, p. 68).

Yet, prior to developing these ideas, Chapter 1 outlines the history and contemporary positioning of Central Asia in the study of world affairs. Its assessment reveals the unease of mainstream frameworks for the explanation and understanding of international politics to render legible the complex and contradictory patterns of regional affairs. The chapter offers a brief outline of the historical positioning of Central Asia in the theories and practices of world affairs. Such an overview highlights the pervasive tendency to *other* the region, which has informed particular (oftentimes, colonizing) strategies for the involvement of external actors. Such contextual trajectories can elicit how and why Central Asia has been included in the patterns of world affairs.

In this respect, Chapter 1 reveals that the "major events" that have pockmarked the historical trajectories of Central Asia, in fact gain regional significance through their interpretation by external actors. Consequently, the contention is that the *regionness* of Central Asia is relative to the interaction between the influence of outsiders and the local practices of state-making. This claim should not be misunderstood as an indication of the irrelevance of political intentionality; instead, the proposition here is that practices—both those of security governance and of regional state-making—formulate and follow their own contingent patterns. The willingness to maintain the process of interaction, despite its endemic contingency, is intentional.

Chapter 1, therefore, indicates (what probably is) the most important feature of the Central Asian *context* from the point of view of external actors—the *awkwardness* of regional statehood.[25] The basic distinctive feature of awkward states is that they do not fit neatly into the Westphalian narrative of an international system made up of and for *integrated* states.[26] The prominence of awkward statehood in Central Asia points to "disjunctures and ambiguities in the notion of sovereignty" (Kavalski and McCullock, 2005, p. 111). Thus, the discussion of Chapter 1 suggests that based on the experience of Central Asia, awkward states are here to stay. They are neither a transitional stage toward a fully blown integrated statehood, nor on the way to outright collapse and disintegration. Instead, awkward states are entities underpinned by complex and contextual stability, which makes them a permanent feature of current global life—even though some might find them unpalatable.

It is this awkwardness of Central Asia that provides the *context* for the "new great game" in the region. The point here is that normative power is not exercised in a vacuum, but is simultaneously constrained and enabled by the context of its application. Thus, the regional agency of international actors reflects the (i) constraints imposed by the context on what is possible, which permits behaviors that are most appropriate within its pattern of relations; and (ii) enables governance models reflecting the external actor's perception of the region (Harrison, 2006, p. 35). Central Asia, thereby, provides an idiosyncratic environment that frames the range of possible behavior of the EU, China, and India in the region. By drawing attention to the interactivity between the agency of international actors and regional states, the actions and behaviors of normative powers may vary not only with time, but also with the context to which they are applied.

The proliferation of international agency in the post-Soviet period seems to confirm that even if local (and localized), Central Asian affairs have quickly become enmeshed in global networks of relations. At the same, the treatment of the region as a context for the normative foreign policy agency of the EU, China, and India distinguishes between the rules that frame the patterns of relations in the region and those that govern the interactions between the region and the international system. The argument developed in Chapter 2 is that the involvement of some actors in this "new great game" offers *practical* manifestation of the agency of normative powers. The reference to normative power reveals foreign policy agency that is "neither military, nor purely economic, but one that works through ideas and opinions" (Diez, 2005, p. 615). This description is contingent on an actor's agency in particular time and space.

Thus, the analysis of the normative foreign policy agency of the EU, China, and India in Central Asia focuses both on their *influence* in the region and on the distinct *strategic cultures* that frame their regional policies. The assessment draws attention to the notions of "actorness," "power of attraction," and the ability to project oneself as a "model." Such contextualization acknowledges that normative powers are not in the business of enforcing orders over other actors, but engaging them in the shared practices of security governance. At the same time, just because the Central Asian agency of the EU, China, and India is assumed to be normative, this does not mean that it is not strategic. On the contrary, the kind of relationships that they establish and the means through which they pursue their objectives are still motivated by strategic interests and intent.

Another important innovation on the literature of normative power is the interrogation of the strategic cultures of the EU, China, and India in Central Asia in Chapter 2. The claim is that while not necessarily aiding the predilection of specific policy choices, the awareness of an actor's strategic culture provides an insight into the broader context and beliefs within which policy-making occurs. In this respect, Huiyun Feng (2007, p. 5) posits that strategic culture is always the first port of call for decision-makers, especially when they are faced with limited information and knowledge that prevents them from "making objective optimal choices." The focus on strategic culture helps elicit security (and its governance) as a self-referential practice (Wæver, 1996, p. 107). Thus, strategic culture *makes* security governance a practice that reveals what an actor's identity and roles on the world stage are truly about.

Such engagement with the strategic culture of normative powers makes legible the specific cognitive structures that frame their experience (and the interpretation of that experience). The notion of strategic culture assumes a significant degree of congruence among those involved in the process of decision-making, which is consistent with the treatment of the EU, China, and India as unitary/corporate actors by this investigation. The analysis of strategic culture provides "a context for understanding" (Gray, 1999, p. 49) the agency of normative powers.

Paying attention to the implicit images framing the mental mapping, tacit knowledge, and operational beliefs of the EU, China, and India recognizes that the "cognitive unconscious" of their strategic culture shapes and structures their international agency by "radically determining their reading of and responses to the external world" (Coleman, 2004, p. 199). As Chapter 3 demonstrates, the exercise of normative power simultaneously rests upon and reveals an asymmetric relationship. What distinguishes the way(s) in which normative foreign policy actors manage such relations of asymmetry from the oppressive colonizing projects of imperial powers is the kind of *security governance* they practice. Thus, the main question for the security governance of Central Asia from the point of view of the analysis of normative power is whether different strategic cultures can coexist.

Strategically speaking, security governance describes the process through which norms and standards of appropriateness become prevalent in a particular region. This process depends on the practices of socialization extended by a normative foreign policy actor. Therefore, this study indicates that security governance is not merely a "rule-based governance," but also (and mainly) "relational governance" (Qin, 2011).[27] It is the interactive environment that allows for the ongoing reassessment of preferences and expectations between participating actors as well as the modification and tweaking of strategies. Socialization reveals its significance to the patterns of security governance not merely by perpetuating the strategic culture of a particular normative power, but mostly by assisting its propagation though "we-doing."[28]

As Chapter 3 reveals, such influence is not a one-way street. The context of Central Asia demonstrates that the security governance of awkward states by normative foreign policy actors is relative to their ability to create facilitating conditions for the internalization of their agency. In other words, it is not only the practices (and, occasionally, the identity) of socialized actors that (are expected to) change, but also the content and meaning of the external norm. Known as *localization*, this process draws attention to the complex dynamics underpinning the practices of security governance. The contention is that a normative power *security governs* a region as long as its message is received by local actors. Thus, the ability of a normative power to exert influence is contingent on its capacity to generate locally appropriate interactions. This is why security governance needs to be underwritten by a deliberate and contextual practice if it is to be effective.

Informed by the notion of *resilience*, the understanding of the security governance of the EU, China, and India in Central Asia reveals the sociality underpinning their normative foreign policy behavior. Julie Gilson (2005, p. 310) asserts that "as practices of interaction continue, ideas and understandings of self and other are constantly formed and reformed to the extent that, without the other, the self would be incomprehensible, since that other 'clothes us in comprehensibility'." The reference to the dynamics of localization, while cursory in this study, provides a relevant framework for the analysis of *when* and *how* norms actually do get internalized in the practice of security governance. The response offered in Chapter 3 is that norm-promotion depends on the *deliberate practice* of security governance. It provides a steering mechanism for the emergence of "generative relationships," which can "induce changes in the way participants see their world and act in it" (Lane and Maxfield, 1995, p. 4).

In the process of repeated interaction, normative powers have the ability to initiate communities of practice through the provision of credible commitments. Thus, rather than offering a one-off solution, the complex interactivity of security governance provides a steering mechanism for the continuous management of issues in the "intermediate zones of practice" (Klein, 2004, p. 4). It is actually in the context of these interactions that participants can reduce the anxiety about one another's intentions. At the same time, the focus on deliberate practice suggests that influence is not merely a one-way flow from a normative power toward the target of its socialization, but a two-way dynamic emerging in the process of interaction.

Following the analytical frameworks outlined in Part I, Part II of this book delves into the "unique mix" of experiences, perceptions, beliefs, and attitudes that inform the emergence of and contestation between the normative powers of the EU, China, and India in Central Asia. The studies included in this section of the book evidence that Brussels, Beijing, and New Delhi interact with the awkward states of Central Asia either from *the position of* or *the intention to* act like normative foreign policy actors. Yet, despite this similarity, the Central Asian agency of the EU, China, and India demonstrates diverse capacities to influence perceptible alterations in the behavior of regional states. As it will be explained, such capacities depend on the "orientation" of normative powers—that is, their inclination, disposition, and/or preferences to initiate communities of practice through deliberate interactions for the purposes of developing and maintaining a particular form of security order in Central Asia (Frazier and Stewart-Ingersoll, 2010, p. 744). In this respect, the analyses included in Part II indicate that the agency of normative powers reflects not only an ability to shape definitions of the "normal," but also of the "real"—and, thereby, structure attitudes according to the hierarchies of "what matters" and "what is not important," "what should be remembered," and "what should be forgotten" (Booth, 2007, p. 184).

As Chapter 4 reveals, the EU's practices of security governance rest on the securitization of the integration project in the wake of the 1999 Kosovo crisis. Consequently, the terms of "the post-1999 European order" have assisted the prioritization of the norms and values that allow the EU to be "what it is" (Kavalski, 2006c). Yet, the relations of the Brussels-based bloc with Central Asia suggest the entrapment of its normative agency by its strategic culture. It would seem that the EU's relations with the region have been befuddled by the incoherence of its approaches and, in particular, the "logic of appropriateness" underpinning its security governance strategy. While not wanting to deny the complexity of normative powers, their intricate makeup should not be used as an excuse for their incoherence.

Coherence emerges in the process of the deliberate practice of security governance. Ambivalence, on the other hand, scuppers the influence of normative powers. The association between the complexity and the ambivalence of security governance confuses both policy and observation. Yet, it is such confusion that underscores the engagement of Brussels in Central Asia. Thus, as Chapter 4 demonstrates, in Central Asia we have no other EU, but an ambivalent EU. This conclusion provides an important observation on its normative power. The EU's case reveals that normative power is not endogenous to an actor, but emerges in relation to the environment to which its agency is applied—that is, it is context-dependent. In particular, the prescriptive clarity underpinning the logic of appropriateness of the EU's security governance seems to be befuddled in Central Asia, where it is challenged by "a situation with unclear and conflicting norms" (Öberg et al., 2011, p. 351).

Thus, in the absence of available community norms and a deliberate practice of security governance, Brussels neither treats the awkward polities of Central Asia as targets for meaningful socialization, nor feels the "moral" compulsion to Europeanize them. Such attitudes have not yet provoked the EU to interpret its encounter with the strangeness/otherness of Central Asia as an opportunity to *reflect upon* its own normativity. Central Asia has, thereby, been subjected by the EU to a unique "*exclusionary* exclusion," which is an outcome of Brussels' "*yoking*" of the former communist states of Eastern Europe and the post-Soviet countries of the European Neighborhood Policy (ENP). Originating in the oeuvre of Andrew Abbott, the process of yoking denotes "connection of two or more proto-boundaries such that one side becomes defined as 'inside' the same entity." The purpose of such yoking is to overcome pre-existing divisions by providing a new external other through which the old inside and the new inside (which used to be an outside) can develop a shared identification. As Abbott proposes, "when a division of social space into entities is already established, the only ways to radically change arrangements. . . are to delegitimize old differences or to emphasize new ones. The former strategy yokes entities together, the latter divides them."[29]

It is suggested here that in order to overcome the divisions between old and new Member States (as well as those included in the ENP), the EU constructs new others—merely through the process of their exclusion from the enlargement (and the ENP) process—whose difference is intended to trounce former divisions and replace them with a new solidarity. Central Asia appears to be one of those new others that assist the processes of yoking new members and neighborhood partners. The region's "*exclusionary* exclusion" stands in sharp contrast with Brussels' approaches to other post-Communist areas. In fact, this has allowed several of the new Member States to engage in their first attempts at "playing like the EU"—that is, inhabiting their new postenlargement identity—in their relations with Central Asia (Kavalski, 2010d). In this way, even the new Member States have begun to treat the region as a context for their international agency. Furthermore, the cognitive lock-in triggered by the dense interactions within the EU and between Brussels and its neighborhood, has made it very difficult for the EU to notice (let alone meaningfully engage) with others beyond the pale of enlargement and enlargement-like (i.e. the ENP) initiatives. It is in this "beyond" the EU's communities of practice that Central Asia is situated.

China, on the other hand, seems to have put Central Asia at the heart of a regional community of practice. Thus, as Chapter 5 indicates, Central Asia has gradually been "Shanghaied" by China. However, instead of being hijacked by force or trickery, the region has slowly, but surely been socialized into Beijing's worldview through the promotion of various initiatives for regional cooperation. These have been ultimately consolidated through the establishment of the Shanghai Cooperation Organization (SCO) in 2001. The awkward Central Asian states are thus perceived to be increasingly susceptible to China's normative power. As suggested earlier in this introductory chapter, Russia's invasive policies in the post-Soviet spaces have contributed to Beijing's prominence in the region. Chapter 5 also suggests that while not the only actor contending to assert its authority in the region, China has nevertheless emerged as the measuring stick for the agency of other international actors in Central Asia—regardless of whether they are normative powers or not.

China's centrality in regional affairs is underpinned by a security governance approach that reveals an intriguing intersection between the discursive memory of the past and the contexts of the present, which then inform the normative construction of the anticipated tasks of the future. China has managed this by premising its agency on a "logic of relationships," which has permitted Beijing to construct a dialogical region by treating Central Asian states as "individuals in a group rather than individuals *per se*" (Qin, 2011, p. 134). Such contextualization of China's strategic culture has assisted the development of a deliberate practice of Central Asian socialization, exhibiting the ability to condition the conceptions of what is acceptable and what is unacceptable behavior. Thus, while many commentators would agree that, historically speaking, China has been (or has had) a normative power (in the sense that its foreign policy was devised to foster an environment consistent with Chinese interests), Chapter 5 posits that the normative foreign policy agency of China's security governance can be elicited from the idiosyncratic interactions between the key values of its external relations (Kavalski, 2010e).

Such normative foreign policy agency is underscored by China's desire to establish itself as a "strong cultural power" (Li, 2008, p. 303). As a result of this desire for the recognition of its international status, Chapter 5 reveals that Beijing's engagement in Central Asia has been greatly assisted by its ability to articulate self-reflective security governance policies, premised on China's deliberate efforts to practice the norms that animate its credible commitments in the region. Significantly, China has been unafraid to change itself (even if only subtly) in order to change others. Thus, the conceptualization of the international role of China as a shaper of norms intimates procedural socializing mechanisms through the deliberate practices of its security governance. It is this skillful management of asymmetric relationships that bolsters China's resilient security governance mechanisms. Thus, its relations in Central Asia confirm that in the post-Cold War period "there is no country that has made more friends than China, and this is by no means a natural fate for a rising power. China has much to learn and much adapting to do, but it also has lessons for the rest of us" (Womack, 2008, pp. 237–8).

India is one of those international actors that can learn much from China. New Delhi's security governance is far more hesitant and less persistent than that of Beijing, and so far seems to lack a strategic focus and determination (Wimbush, 2011, p. 266). As Chapter 6 explains, it is the perceptions of a competitive South Asian context that prevent India from extending a security governance approach to Central Asia that would match its normative foreign policy rhetoric. The "logic of consequences" underpinning its strategic culture has been further reinforced through the articulation of an assertive external stance following the 1998 nuclear tests. Aimed to project the newly found confidence of India's strategic culture by flaunting the prowess of its nuclear military capabilities, New Delhi has publicized its foreign policy independence. At the same time, such a context—perhaps, paradoxically—has provided a propitious environment for the uncritical acceptance of the convergence between "normative power India" and "brand India."

The confusion of divergent notions has reinforced the hiatus between the external and domestic perception of India's international agency. In particular, as Chapter 6 shows, it has led to an unusual style of security governance—one in which New Delhi does not attempt to establish relationships with other actors. As a result, India's security governance of Central Asia rests on the *passive* power of example, which suggests an expectation that others will follow New Delhi's lead. Thus, while Indian foreign policy makers seem to understand the relational nature of security governance, they nevertheless insist that New Delhi's ability to influence others resides in the preponderance of its military capacities. Thus, the analysis of Chapter 6 demonstrates not only that normative foreign policy actors—such as India—can be constrained by the narratives of their strategic culture, but also that they are just as likely to engage in competitive security scenarios as non-normative powers.

In this way, the discursive engagement with the normative foreign policy agency of the EU, China, and India in Central Asia provided in Part II assists the understanding of how their security governance represents "lived realities" (Raddon, 2007, pp. 61–5). The concluding chapter undertakes a parallel assessment of their approaches to the region. Such a comparative study uncovers that the security governance projects of the EU, China, and India in Central Asia are motivated by a desire to be recognized as actors that are not only capable, but should also be allowed to set the ramifications of the "normal" in global life. Thus, the reference to a "rise of normative powers" emerges as shorthand for their "struggle for recognition." The contention here is that contemporary world affairs are not merely about who gets what, when, and how, but about how normative powers engage other actors in the process of interaction. In this setting, recognition emerges as "the core constitutive moment" of international interactions and refers to "the communicative process in the international society of states through which states mutually acknowledge the status and social esteem of other states" (Nel, 2010, p. 963).

As the context of Central Asia reveals, the recognition of an actor as a normative power is relative to that actor's sense of obligation to those that it intends to socialize. Thus, the dependence of the recognition *by* others as a normative foreign policy actor on that actor's recognition *of* others appears to be an emerging property of contemporary global politics. The international identity of an actor is not so much about capabilities, but about recognition—which is both an outcome and a reassertion of an actor's normative power status. It is through the performance of normative power—that is, the establishment of interactions based on respect, obligation, and mutuality (all of which are maintained through communities of practice)—that actors engender relationships that can assist them to acquire the status they desire. Premised on the experience of the EU, China, and India in Central Asia, the concluding chapter outlines the demand for *adaptive normative power* and indicates what *acting politically* in a complex context might mean.

Conclusion

This book draws attention to the need to appreciate different perspectives and the adaptations undertaken by normative powers in Central Asia. As should be apparent by now, this study does not intend a detailed catalog of either the normative foreign policy agency of the EU, China, and India or their security governance strategies in Central Asia. Instead, it aims to uncover the dominant perceptions, cognitive structures, and practices that guide the regional agency of Brussels, Beijing, and New Delhi. Thus, Part I of the volume advances a number of analytical assumptions concerning the context of Central Asia, the agency of normative powers, and their practices of security governance. Part II offers analytical case studies of the normative foreign policy agency of the EU, China, and India in Central Asia. This mode of inquiry provides the facilitating environment for drawing broader inferences and also for assessing the trends in the international affairs of Brussels, Beijing, and New Delhi with the region, each other, and the world. The suggestion is that the meaning of normative power is context-dependent and emerges in the process of interaction.

At the same time, this book also endeavors to pull together the disjointed literature on the Central Asian agency of international actors and the regional involvement of the EU, China, and India. The contention is that the emphasis on analytical observation allows for eliciting policy patterns that tend to remain obscured by the intense focus on energy resources, clan politics, and the regional "great games" of different international actors. Such narrative analysis of foreign policy making allows for an innovative tracing of the genealogy, distinct grammars, and contradictions of the security governance approaches extended to Central Asia by the EU, India, and China.

The suggestion is that by making claims in social science we are also helping to make some social reality more or less real (Kavalski, 2007a, p. 446). In other words, this book provides an interpretive essay of topics and themes from the study of world affairs. At the same time it investigates what makes Central Asia a distinct context for the regional agency of external actors. Such an interpretive enterprise consciously zooms-in on the implications from a research focus on the practices of normative power to the ongoing dynamics of security governance. At the same time, this book indicates that the Central Asian region is an active transformative context for the normative foreign policy agency of the EU, India, and China.

The experience of Central Asia discussed in the following pages demonstrates that the appropriation of security governance principles without a deliberate practice of socialization undermines the effectiveness of normative foreign policy actors. Thus, the enactment of normative power by the EU, China, and India in Central Asia suggests that the practices of security governance that prevail in a particular region are relative to the historically specific legitimation of promoted norms, the contextual recognition of the normative foreign policy actor, and its ability to maintain resilient and credible commitments

PART ONE

Context and frameworks for the engagement with the rise of normative powers in Central Asia

1

Involving Central Asia in world politics

[T]he region appears as a sort of black hole in the middle of the world. . . it is hugely dark or darkly huge. . . Yet, Central Asia is perhaps both the most important and the most neglected part of the world. . . Therefore, the millennial centrality of Central Asia in inter- "national" relations goes virtually unnoticed.

Andre Gunder Frank (1992, pp. 43–5)

[T]here must be many people who would like to be given some account of this romantic part of the world, provided that it comes to them in palatable form.

Wilfrid Blunt (1973, p. 9)

Introduction

This chapter looks at the space(s) that Central Asia occupies in world politics. The contemporary positioning of Central Asia in the study of world politics reveals the unease of mainstream frameworks for explanation and understanding to render legible the complex and contradictory patterns of regional affairs. This seems to be particularly the case when grappling with the trajectories of Central Asian statehood molded by the simultaneous agency of discordant state-elites and contending international actors. The claim is that the region emerges as a *context* for the international agency of normative powers. In this respect, the ramifications of Central Asia on the mental maps of global life attest to distinct processes for its security governance.

This tendency has conjured up memories of the nineteenth-century "great game" played in the region by Britain and Russia. Bringing together a host of international organizations, states, multinational corporations, and nongovernmental actors, its contemporary re-enactment has rekindled the clichéd imagery of "land of discord," "pulpit of the world," "geographic pivot of history," "grand chessboard," "the disparate and anarchic theatre of global geopolitics," etc. The affective economy of these depictions befuddles the study of the historical and institutional legacies, cross-regional patterns, and socioeconomic structures impacting the shape, processes, and content of statehood across Central Asia.

The chapter proceeds with a brief overview of the engagement of Central Asia in world affairs. While cursory, it nevertheless prompts an understanding of the genealogy of the region's conceptualization as a *context* for external agency. The analysis then moves on to discuss the location of Central Asia on the mental maps of international politics. It suggests that because of the region's treatment as a context for the policies of international actors, the positioning of Central Asia on the spatial, temporal, and cognitive geographies of international politics has remained open to contestation. The chapter draws attention to the "awkwardness" of regional statehood and the dynamics of the "new great game" as key contributing factors for the complex overlay of security governance regimes spanning the region.

Brief history of the engagement of Central Asia in world affairs

The location of Central Asia on the stage of world politics seems to have been perennially informed by the discourses of its *orientalization*. Wilfrid Blunt's statement in the epigraph to this chapter confirms such strategy for the construction of a "palatable form" for the narrative of "the most romantic part of the world."[1] As a governing strategy, the orientalization of Central Asia echoes the disciplining approaches through "which European culture was able to manage—and even produce—the Orient politically, sociologically, militarily, ideologically, scientifically, and imaginatively during the post-Enlightenment period" (Said, 1978, p. 3). Unlike Said's narrative of othering, however, such orientalization of Central Asia was not only the property of the Western beholder. Instead, Central Asia has tended to be othered as the context for their external agency by different "outsiders, whether they be Muslim or Christian, European or Asian" (Rashid, 1994, p. 9).

While such perceptions present reductive moves that befuddle the engagement of Central Asia in international relations, they do not prevent an interrogation of the regional involvement in the history and patterns of world affairs (Heathershaw, 2010, p. 96). It would appear, therefore, that "rivalry" between different extraregional actors pockmarks the genealogical account of Central Asian affairs. Observers have, nevertheless, queried the objectivity of this contextualization and have suggested that such representations merely reflect the attitudes of their proponents which then get projected back onto the (account of the) past (Sengupta, 2009, p. 131). While bearing these nuances in mind, for the purposes of brevity and clarity, the contestations of external actors over Central Asia are surveyed in four main periods: pre-Islamic, Islamic, Russian/Soviet, and post-Soviet (Peimani, 1998, p. 23).

The pre-Islamic period saw the strong Persian influence in the region and its ultimate integration into the empire of the Achamenids around the sixth century BC (Peimani, 1998, p. 23). In this period, Central Asia came on the radar of world history in the process of Alexander's foray into the region. While the passage of Macedonian troops was not indicative of a major "turning point in the history of Central Asia" (Holt, 1988, p. 52),[2] it marked a defining moment in the history of its location in world affairs. Imagining the region became inflected by the myths of Alexander's exploits. In particular, such narrativization of the regional experience has provided the origins for the treatment of Central Asia as a *context* for the agency of external actors. At the same time, while temporally distant, the significance of this period lies in the initiation of the division of Central Asia between nomadic and settled populations. This distinction has had (and some would argue that it still does have) an important impact on regional developments. In fact, it is often claimed that the division between nomadic and sedentary populations is a contributing factor to Central Asia's hallmark "chronic affliction" with a conspicuous "reflexive resistance to, and distrust of, official authority" (Meyer, 2003, p. 168).

While acknowledging the developments in the pre-Islamic period, the historian Svat Soucek avers that 622AD is the crucial year for the meaningful engagement of Central Asia in the dynamics of world affairs. As he argues, "the birth of Islam" has produced a radical change in regional interactions by introducing "a new and uncompromising way of life, both spiritual and temporal" (Soucek, 2000, p. 49). It was during this period that the first Central Asian polities emerged. The Islamic period also saw the emergence of large-scale contestation over the region between Arab, Persian, Turkic, and Mongol armies. One of the long-term implications of Islam in Central Asia is its gradual emergence as a potent source for resistance and popular mobilization. For instance, Ahmed Rashid (1994, p. 42) uncovers instances of this dissident role of Islam both during Soviet times and in the post-Soviet period. Likewise, Laura Adams asserts that prior to the Soviet period, the people inhabiting the region "were united by a common identity as Muslims, which for many was as much a cultural as a religious identity" (Adams, 2008, p. 621).[3]

Russia's involvement in Central Asia was initially part of retaliatory activities against Mongol invasions. In time, such interest was motivated by Russia's protracted confrontation with the Ottoman Empire and its alleged Muslim affiliates in the region. It should not be overlooked that on a functional level, the Russian incursion into the region was instrumentally motivated both by the defeat in the Crimean War, which constrained Russia's colonial gaze toward the European territories of the Ottoman Empire, and by the distortion of cotton supplies as a result of the American Civil War, which turned Central Asia into a lucrative supplier of cheap cotton (Lloyd, 1997, p. 104).[4] At the same time, the conquest of Central Asia had become a critical part of Russia's civilizing Eurasian "manifest destiny" (Bassin, 1999).[5] Russian involvement in the region coincided with Chinese, Iranian, and British interests in Central Asia, which prompted the now hackneyed imagery of a "great game" among them.[6]

The gradual incorporation of Central Asia into the Russian Empire initiated one of the most comprehensive transformations of the polities, culture, and economy of the region. There has been some debate on how appropriate it is to attach the label of colonization to this experience. On the one hand, Edward Said has suggested that "[u]nlike Britain or France. . . Russia moved to swallow whatever land or peoples stood next to its borders." His claim, therefore, is that because of its focus on "adjacency," the Tsarist imperial project has to be set apart from the experience of other European colonial powers (Said, 1994, p. 10). On the other hand, however, Richard Pierce contends that on an ideational level, the Russian colonization of Central Asia was motivated by a very similar desire for security through the subjugation of the allegedly uncivilized and threatening (even though neighboring) others as that of any other colonial power. His claim, therefore, is that Russia advanced into the region "until [it] could establish secure frontiers" for itself (Pierce, 1960, p. 20).[7] These debates, notwithstanding, most commentators agree that Russia's incursion into Central Asia is a major juncture for the historical trajectories of the region.

The significance of Russia's imprint was further intensified as a result of the overthrow of the monarchy and the establishment of a Soviet state. As Adeeb Khalid (2006, p. 232) intimates, "the Soviet remaking of Central Asia makes sense only as the work of a different form of modern polity."[8] The distinguishing features of the Soviet polity were embedded in the Marxist-Leninist ideology underpinning its statehood, which also shaped the transformation of the region.[9] On the one hand, it was this experience that produced the current boundaries and states (and some would argue, the nations) of Central Asia. On the other hand, the incorporation of Central Asia into the Soviet Union "pushed" the region into a "diplomatic limbo where the outside world could only be viewed through Moscow's eyes" (Rashid, 1994, p. 208). Probably the most significant impact from the incorporation of the region into the USSR has been the dramatic overhaul of the traditional political, cultural, social, and economic relations in Central Asia. As a result, regional political developments were driven by an ideologically motivated reorganization. In this context, the observation of a contemporary rise of normative powers in the region can be interpreted as a comparable attempt to radically refocus the lenses of Central Asia's engagement in world politics (although in a less invasive and noncoercive manner).

The dissolution of the Soviet Union has set into motion the current fourth period in the regional engagement in the history of international interactions. For some, the Soviet breakup seems to have quite literally "tossed Central Asia back into the melting pot of history" (Hopkirk, 1992, p. xviii). For others, the significance of this event emerges from the opportunity for independent agency of regional actors. In particular, the claim has been that Central Asian states have finally taken "their rightful place in the world community and they have done so with a vengeance" (Soucek, 2000, p. 283). Yet, the paradox of such "return" of the region to world politics was not lost on Gregory Gleason. As he points out, "the greatest irony of independence in Central Asia [was that it arrived just] as has Soviet-style colonialism several decades before—it was imposed by Moscow" (Gleason, 1997, p. 15). Thus, while the comparison between Central Asia's position in 1917 and 1991 is an important one, other observers stress that both events have plunged the region into "the throes of an internal revolution, in which Islam, tribalism, nationalism, and socialism were fiercely competing for ideological dominance among the local elites and the masses" (Rashid, 1994, p. 25).[10] Moreover, developments in the post-Soviet period have suggested the need to "jettison the notion that Central Asia is a single strategic piece forged from the experience of being the object of Russia's foreign policy for several centuries" (Wimbush, 2011, p. 259).

While the discussion of the four main periods of Central Asia's engagement in the history of world affairs is necessarily cursory, its intention is to stress the punctuation of the regional developments by external agency. As Will Myer (2002, p. 28) poignantly observers, many of the major historical events in Central Asia have *gained* their regional significance because of their interpretation by outside actors. At the same time, even such a brief encounter with the international history of Central Asia uncovers some of the key trends that inform the social, cultural, economic, and political complexity defining the region today. Such a brief historical overview of Central Asia's location in the patterns of international politics intends to elucidate the futility of looking at security governance merely as part of the ruthless machinery of geopolitics. As the following sections will explain (and the analysis of Chapter 3 will demonstrate), territorially framed understandings of security governance miss the practical dimensions through which actors exert influence over the region (Krahman, 2003a, pp. 331–3).

Thus, by acknowledging the relational nature of external involvement in Central Asia, the suggestion is that the region's location on the stage of world affairs reflects "complex articulations of dislocations and rupturing breaks that are, in turn, always worked out through local and historical resources and institutions" (Pickles, 2008, p. 260). Consequently, since observers insist that the account of Central Asia's engagement in the process and practice of international politics is not tantamount to the individual experience of "the five Central Asian countries," but to that of "the region" (Peimani, 1998, p. 23), the following section undertakes a study of the meanings and content that the label of "Central Asia" has acquired in world affairs.

Locating Central Asia on the mental maps of international politics

Central Asia has become one of the emblematic features of the post-Cold War geography of international relations. During the 1990s, the region became an idiom symbolizing the pervasive uncertainty of the post-Cold War climate of global life. Thus, rather than a transitory stage, the persistence of the seemingly erratic character of Central Asian trends has challenged the dominant frameworks for the study of both global and regional patterns. Yet, despite the seeming coherence of the mental maps that Central Asia generates, the regional appellation remains one of those labels whose ramifications are still open to contestation. Some have even questioned the extent to which Central Asia exists as a region at all (Delcour, 2011, p. 107).

Thus, since thinking about Central Asia (i.e. defining and mapping its designations) has never been an easy enterprise, some commentators have simply suggested that "Central Asia is an old idea taking on a new life" (Rashid, 1994, p. 209). As Peter Ferdinand (1995, p. 1) admits, a significant part of the difficulty accompanying the ramifications of the Central Asian label emanates from its origins as a *contextual* designation for the agency of external actors:

> The epithet of "Central Asia" is not an indigenous term, but was imposed on the region by nineteenth-century Europeans in a vain attempt to establish at least a territorial identity for this protean, tantalizing stretch of land that had for so long survived uneasily in the interstices of great empires. It is indicative of the illusive nature of the region that "Central Asia" has remained a term without clear definition, used almost at random to refer to othe whole or any part of an area that extends from the Kipchak steppes of Central Russia to the Great Wall of China.[11]

Perhaps, one of the most appropriate designations that emerged at the turn of the twentieth century describes the region as a "debatable and debated ground" (Mahan, 1900, p. 20). Thus, the outline of its symbolic geography does not only follow the cartographic representation of Map 1, but also exposes the particular strategic connotations that the region acquires in the eyes of its beholders.

The claim here is that the analytical fickleness of the notion of Central Asia reflects the "fragmentedness" of designations—that is, such notions neither command what is spoken through them, nor can they simply be commanded. Instead,

Map 1 *Central Asia.* (*Source:* UN Department of Peacekeeping Operations, Cartographic Section)

> they slip and slide, evade our grasp and convey both more and less than we intended. They do this both because they have a history and because when we use them we set them off again on their historical way, in the unpredictable ways in which anything which lives in the way that it is received through time remains intractable to the designs that might be made upon it. Despite the art of the spin-doctor, then, you can never determine the outcome of that reception. . . To take a word, then, is to hold a fragment of life and its mystery in your hand. (Dillon, 1996, pp. 114–15)

In other words, the contested ramifications of Central Asia offer one of the clearest indications of the complexity that accompanies "what human beings do with space" (Parker, 2008, p. 4). Thus, if we are to generalize the dominant labels for the various mental maps of the region—Turkestan, Inner Asia, Middle Asia, Central Eurasia, etc.—all of them seem to share a fundamental perception of an *in-between* space. It then feeds imaginaries that draw on the region's alleged backwardness or exoticism (or both) as a legitimation for an outsider's intervention. The variable geography of such designations alleges an inability among local polities and populations to be "the masters of their own destiny." Such observations, in turn, provoke allegations for the *passivity* of Central Asian actors in international politics that presents them as mere recipients (if not victims) of external demands, interventions, and offers of tutelage (Myer, 2002, p. 243).

As Chapter 3 will demonstrate, the overlay of outside agency in Central Asia produces dependence on external security governance almost to the extent that "the local pattern of security relations virtually ceases to operate" (Webber, 2007, p. 49). Central Asia can thereby be seen as a "security constellation" that emerges in the process of security practices (Wæver, 1997a, p. 51). At the same time, the volatility of the Central Asian outlines has led to the suggestion that the region "essentially. . . is a cultural barrier that exists at the heart of man."[12] Such propositions infer both the relational and interactive quality behind geopolitical labels. Regions—such as Central Asia—emerge as a network of discourses and desires that arrange the patterns of world affairs within a geopolitical space. What distinguishes the web of interactions in the Central Asian space is the proliferation of *different kinds of polities*.

Thus, Central Asia is not merely a geographic or geostrategic locale "politically made" (Katzenstein, 2005, p. 9), "geopsychologically arranged" (Pempel, 2005, p. 3), or "spoken into existence" (Neumann, 2001, p. 60), but is also articulated and defined in the palimpsest of global affairs by the *awkwardness* of the states that populate it. The contention then is that the regionness of Central Asia—that is, its distinctiveness in global life—emerges in the practices of state-making. Such assertion confirms that the "individual states now constituting post-Soviet Central Asia are not an amalgam of shared strategic interests and objectives, despite having much in common with each other" (Wimbush, 2011, p. 259). The proposition here is that practices—especially the practices of statehood—formulate their own contingent patterns, which have turned Central Asia into a "zone of intense, complex interaction between local conditions and the larger world system" (Hall, 2006, p. 104).

In such a contingent analytical setting, the notion of a "new Central Asia" has been propagated in the post-Cold War period as the designation for a fresh perspective on regional patterns (Roy, 2000; Kavalski, 2009c). The *newness* of the region was initially associated with the novelty of independent national statehood.[13] The emergence of the sovereign post-Soviet "stans" was a development which—unlike the experience of other post-Communist countries—did not spell a return to or a revival of earlier forms and symbols of independent statehood (Anderson, 1997; Roy, 2000). It has been argued that Central Asians—both publics and state-elites—had less of a say in their independence than they had in their absorption into the realm of the Russian empire during the nineteenth century. As a result, independence appeared to be *thrust upon* the hesitant regional states with little warning. The tenuous experience as Soviet republics did not seem to offer the Central Asian countries the required "political, economic, and psychological" wherewithal for independent participation in and interactions with the global society of states (Lloyd, 1997, p. 97).

Thus, the notion of a "new Central Asia" was promulgated as an indication of the fluidity of regional politics, which has demanded more comprehensive conceptualizations of their dynamic frameworks. Rather than isolated in their landlocked location, the Central Asian "stans" have gradually become entangled in interactions stretching from Mongolia and China's Xinjiang Autonomous Region, through Kashmir, Pakistan's Northwestern Frontier Province, and Afghanistan, to Iran, Turkey, and the states of the Caucasus. The networked character of such relationships has urged some to announce "the collapse of the firm boundary between the northern and southern portions of Greater Central Asia" (Canfield, 1992, p. 882). Although the *regional* character of these communications more often than not is evidenced by different forms of criminal and illegal transnational networks (Ceccarelli, 2007), it has nevertheless shifted international perceptions of the region toward broader conceptualizations. In other words, the term "new Central Asia" reflects the shared socioeconomic, political, and environmental vulnerabilities which simultaneously animate and plague the practices of regional polities.

This proposition should not, however, be perceived as a suggestion that Central Asian populations do not constitute imagined communities, even if "the development of a pan-Central Asian regional identity will remain a chimera" (Bohr, 2004, p. 502). On the contrary, they do, but not necessarily ones that fit neatly the conventional Westphalian schemata of "nation states." Consequently, the established modes for analytical and policy adaptation aimed at grasping and addressing changing realities become obsolete and new ones are required (Kavalski, 2007a). This is probably one of the most important qualitative alterations of our perceptions inferred by the label of a "new Central Asia." Thus, external involvement—especially, external involvement intent on introducing a particular pattern of relations—shapes the social space and developmental possibilities for the awkward states of the region (Kavalski, 2010c, p. 9).

The framing of Central Asia's appellation in world politics once again draws attention to the dynamics of international involvement in the region. Simply referred to as "Great Game country" (Hopkirk, 1992, p. 167), Central Asia has long become shorthand for subordination to the whims of various external actors. Described as the "Heartland" by Sir Halford Mackinder, in the geopolitical imagination of Western agency, Central Asia has become inscribed as "the greatest natural fortress in the world, defended by polar ice-caps, deserts, arid tableland and mountain ranges" (Mackinder, 1904, p. 434). Paradoxically, it was this very landlocked nature of the area that subsequently "left Central Asia in the dark" (Frank, 1992, p. 86).

Yet, in the post-Soviet period, the designation of the region has provoked the suggestion of a "new great game" in Central Asia (Ehteshami, 1995). In this respect, what appears to be "new" about the current "great game" is the simultaneous proliferation of external (i.e. from outside the region) and internal (i.e. from within the region) agency. In other words, the "new great game" challenges entrenched perceptions of the passivity of Central Asian states and their lack of capability for independent agency in international life. As many commentators have noted, the proliferation of international agency in the region has provided a facilitating environment for Central Asian states to engage in "pick-and-choose" strategies and bandwagoning-for-profit policies (Kavalski, 2007b, p. 856). The space for such independent agency by Central Asian states reveals the qualitative distinction of the current "new great game" from its nineteenth-century variant. In other words, regional states might be compelled to indicate their preferred model of external agency, but they are not constrained to comply with its injunctions for long and oftentimes swing their preferences to another external pole of attraction.

This understanding has then provoked the drafting of extensive lists of actors with vested interests in Central Asia. Usually, such lists include (but are not limited to) China, the EU, India, Iran, Pakistan, Russia, Saudi Arabia, Turkey, the United States, etc. It has to be acknowledged that what distinguishes such involvement is that these international actors do not appear to be interested in an imperial expansion for the control of territory, but in gaining access to the strategic resources of Central Asia (Muni, 2003, pp. 97–8). Hence, the "new great game" is about the creation of "niches of influence" (Shams-ud-Din, 1997, p. 340). The construction of such influence does not rely on or derive from the territorial effects of external actors (as conventional geopolitics would suggest), but on their distinct *regimes of governance* (Goetze and Guzina, 2008, p. 334).

Central Asia, thereby, emerges as the contested site for competing "nodes of governance"—externally promoted strategies aimed at the transmission of rules, produced elsewhere (Bliesemann de Guevara, 2008, p. 348). In this setting, the "new great game" reveals the "strategic anarchy" of Central Asian politics—the emergence of flexible and opportunistic arrangements, whose interactive frameworks are driven by tactical expediency rather than by a shared strategic purpose between collaborating actors (Lo, 2008, p. 172). The dynamics of the "new great game" in Central Asia reveal an interaction between competing images of appropriateness that are being extended to the region simultaneously by external actors and the selection priorities and practices of the Central Asian states themselves. The onus, therefore, is not only on the external actors, but also (and mostly) on regional polities as they (have to) indicate whose image are they trying to fit. Thus, "what seems at first glance [to be] an artificial patchwork" of contingent post-Soviet entities both gains facticity and "makes new sense" through atunement to "the evolutive geostrategy of an area in the making" (Roy, 2000, p. 200).

Such agency then transforms regional interactions into a "'game' of cultural production [that] is played out on a set of geographically nested fields, each with its own prestige structure for cultural capital, but each of which is also subject to the prestige structure of the broader fields" (Adams, 2008, p. 618). These processes of cultural production reveal that even if local (and localized), Central Asian affairs are nevertheless enmeshed in global networks of relations. The proposition is that "'things' do occur locally but not necessarily solely as a result of local influences. Similarly, local changes can alter the nature of wider networks" (Gills and Thompson, 2006, p. 2). The ensuing increased awareness of vulnerability to distant causes conveys a sense of chaotic uncertainty prompted by the catalytic effects of small events, whose consequences are felt later, elsewhere, and by others (Kavalski, 2008b, p. 426). It is such dynamics that seem to foster an understanding of Central Asia as one of the most conspicuous instances of the nascent complexity of global life. As one commentator put it, the regional states

> are flanked to the east by a rising great power (China); to the north by their former hegemon (Russia); to the south by a country collapsed in a

> violent chaos (Afghanistan); a fundamentalist Islamic republic (Iran), and a fragile secular state in search of a greater regional role (Turkey). Along with these, a distant superpower seeks influence, if not dominance (America). (Minton-Beddoes, 1998)

The sense of unpredictability underlying this volatile context has provoked a nuanced engagement with the normative framework of the Central Asian agency of international actors. One of the most erudite accounts of the "multi-level hegemonic encounter" in the uncertain terrain of Central Asia has been provided by Ruth Deyermond (2009). Her analysis acknowledges that external actors bent on influencing Central Asian patterns can simultaneously coexist, cooperate, and compete at the different levels of their interactions in the region. Deyermond's reading of the "new great game" captures its dynamics through the "matrioshka model of hegemony"—that is, "in the same way that Russian matrioshka dolls, identical in appearance and function but varying in size, can be accommodated within one another, so hegemons—functionally similar but operating at global, regional, and sub-regional levels—appear to coexist." While accounting for the concurrence of competition and cooperation on the same issues, between the same set of actors, at the same time, and in the same region, Deyermond's suggestion of multilevel hegemony also indicates that "the global hegemon is not necessarily the hegemon in any given region" (Deyermond, 2009, pp. 151–73).

The significance of such hegemonic overlay to the rise of normative powers in Central Asia (as well as shifts in its dynamics) is further elaborated in Chapter 2. The suggestion is that the various international actors involved in the region are engaged in security governance practices that cannot merely be framed as "imperial policing" (Ignatieff, 2002, p. 31), but have to also demonstrate the capacity to provide socializing tutelage. It is this environment that provides the context for the confrontation with the *awkwardness* of Central Asian statehood.

The awkwardness of Central Asian polities

The notion of "awkward states" (Field, 2001; Kavalski, 2006a) is used here as a designation of the condition of international existence of Central Asian polities. It reflects the assertion that the countries of the region were "hardly prepared for an unexpected adventure in state building" (Lewis, 2008, p. 123). Thus, although the post-Soviet transition has marked a sharp (if uncertain) break with the past, the subsequent trajectories of Central Asian states exhibit "puzzling" ongoing dynamics "between the formal and the informal elements of politics, and a surprising re-emergence of informal organizations embedded in both the Soviet and the pre-Soviet political order of this region" (Collins, 2006, p. 5).

It would appear that the end of the Cold War has not provoked much engagement with the altering patterns and practices of statehood. The failure to interrogate the meaning of notions such as "state" and "stateness" as well as the practices of "state-making" identify one of the most "serious conceptual flaws in the transitological approach" (Cappelli, 2008, p. 334). Furthermore, while the transition of other post-Communist areas (such as Central Europe and the Balkans) and post-Soviet regions (such as the Baltic States, the Caucasus, and the so-called (Eastern) European Neighborhood—Belarus, Moldova, and Ukraine) has been integral to the reconsideration of the paradigms of different branches of political science, the focus on Central Asia has been largely episodic and detached from these trends.

Previous engagements with the Central Asian polities have uncovered that "the state tends to struggle against itself" (Jones Luong, 2004, p. 276). In fact, some go as far as to suggest that ever since its emergence in the region, the state "has represented only one source of power among many" (Karrar, 2009, p. 8). More often than not, commentators point to the history of state-making in the region as an important feature of these trends—that is, the Central Asian polities cannot be approached without acknowledging the foundational role played by the revolutionary state-formation project of the former Soviet Union. While the Marxist-Leninist ideology formed the backbone of this process, the dimensions of national identity were also enlisted in the project of socialist revolution. In this respect, the existence of various national groups was not only formally recognized, but for some of them it was also enshrined in the legal framework of Soviet statehood through the formation of constituent republics and autonomous regions (Gololobov, 2008, p. 148).

The "stateness"—that is, "the saliency of the state" (Nettle, 1968, p. 579)—of the Central Asian entities during this period evinced a simulation of the European style and form, while fostering content that expressed both local flavor and social ideals (Adams, 2008, p. 622). Soviet federalism, thereby, constructed federal units that assisted groups which "most likely would have been absorbed had Czarist Russia continued to develop along capitalist lines. . . to 'discover themselves' and also created state-structures for them" (Milanovic, 1994, pp. 63–4). Such an instrumental use of federalism for the objectives of an ideologically driven state-formation did not create a clear dividing line between the state and society in Central Asia. In fact, the "boundary between state and society was purposefully blurred, in accordance with the vision of creating a heroic-Leninist state" (Jones Luong, 2004, p. 24). Nettle (1968, p. 579) has in fact questioned the extent to which the Soviet Union ever existed as a "state"—in the Westphalian sense of this term—since its political organization was not autonomous from the "party." Thus, in terms of governing agency, state rule was handled "in the context of party and not state at all."

Ideology was, thereby, promoted as "a mechanism, set of ideas, and a locus of power for shaping social destiny by recruiting individuals into a certain imaginary unity" (Gololobov, 2008, p. 155). It would appear, therefore, that the institutional framing of Central Asian polities attests to the long shadow of history over the patterns of state-making in the region. Hence, the awkwardness of contemporary Central Asia is encoded by the "small events and chance circumstances" of the Soviet past (North, 1990, p. 94), which continue to constrain their current and future trajectories in different ways. For instance, some have traced the resilience and complexity of social networks in the region to the patterns of Soviet state-making in Central Asia. Thus,

> If Central Asians wanted to shake the rigidity in the occupying official network, they would have to look for flexibility in human personalities, not in the structure itself. . . Enforced frugality or modesty provided an opening to the region's political insiders for making outsiders in the hierarchy more amenable to Central Asian interests. Many political devices such as back-scratching and logrolling combined with outright influence peddling, payoffs, bribery, embezzlement, extortion, theft of government property, and the like *to effect an alliance.* They helped to draw the two hierarchies, the outsiders and insiders, together for mutual benefit. Not every official sinned so easily, but corruption became pervasive and institutionalized. . . This kind of unofficial "drawing together" between ethnic groups contrasted with the rapprochement envisaged between ethnic groups. (Allworth, 1994, pp. 555–6; emphasis in original)

In this process, Soviet institutions became (unwitting) "conduits for the globalization of culture in Central Asia" constructing a unique mixture of "culture production without a market economy, modernity without capitalism, and globalization without transnational corporations" (Adams, 2008, p. 615). As it will be discussed shortly, this legacy has impacted significantly on the dynamics of the international socialization of Central Asian states.

It is in this context that the "zone of indistinction" between state and society in Central Asia emerges. In particular, "the texture of contemporary stateness" in Central Asia has been defined as an embodiment of "the colonial/

imperial cloth from which the successor states were tailored" (Beissinger and Young, 2002, p. 7). Accordingly, the "Cold War structure has prohibited the colonizing powers and the ex-colonized from undertaking critical reflections; and such a prohibition has constantly reproduced the same problems that happened before in colonial histories" (Chen, 2002, p. 81). Thus, the post-Soviet phenomenon of fusion and fissure in Central Asian statehood offers an instance of the emerging topsyturvidum of world affairs where states are increasingly reinforcing their external appearance of stability while trying to contain, negotiate, and manage their domestic fragility (Kavalski, 2010c, p. 4).

According to Christopher Clapham (1998), this condition reflects a continuum of greater and lesser degrees of statehood. It also acknowledges that Central Asian states entered the process of state-making in what Joel Migdal calls "the most inhospitable environment of all." According to him, the Central Asian states typify the negative "double whammy" associated with the dynamics of state-making in the post-Cold War world:

> On the one side, rapid globalization. . . undercut[s] the "boundedness" of states, which is "at the very heart of the concepts of sovereignty and self-determination." And, on the other side, these states were thrust into a volatile, insecure environment in which their leaders desperately needed to mobilize their populations, based on none other then the very boundedness that now seem[s] so elusive. (Migdal, 2004, pp. 17–33)

In this respect, the dilution (if not outright disappearance) of the notion and practices of "guaranteed statehood" has further complicated the dynamics of the "triple transition" in Central Asia. Thus, achieving state viability in the post-Soviet space developed into a much more complex process than is usually construed. Acknowledging that "in many territories of the world today—especially in parts of the former Soviet Union—no adequately functioning state exists," Juan Linz and Alfred Stepan (1996, pp. 14–21) have long insisted on factoring the criterion of "stateteness" into the assessment of the content, quality, and direction of the transition of the post-Communist polities.

In more general terms, the fragility of post-Soviet statehood portends "an epoch of themeless juxtapositions, in which the classificatory grid of nation-states is going to be replaced by a jagged-glass pattern of city-states, shanty-states, nebulous and anarchic regionalisms" (Kaplan, 1994, p. 24). In this setting, the awkwardness of Central Asian statehood points to a different set of authority structures than those suggested by conventional models. Thus, unlike its treatment as another synonym for "weak," "failed," or "quasi" states, the use of the term "awkward states" here expands its meaning beyond a mere indication of the Weberian dysfunctionality of Central Asian statehood.

The notion of "awkwardness" problematizes simultaneously the concepts, images, and process of domestic rule and international behavior.

- On the one hand, awkward states are characterized not only by their volatility, but by a mode of government whose methods and practices contradict accepted norms and rules (Kavalski, 2008a, p. 74). In particular, *awkwardness* reflects a state's inability to maintain the standards of "responsible governance" vis-à-vis its citizens. As Helen Stacey asserts, the notion and practices of sovereignty are becoming increasingly *relational* in their explanation, understanding, and legitimation. As she argues, "relational sovereignty" infers a broader notion of the state's responsibilities towards its citizens and, at the same time, emphasizes "the multi-directional social contract" of the "dynamic interactions among sovereign states and among the citizens of those states—interactions that have been with us since the Silk Road but have become crucial with globalization" (Stacey, 2003, pp. 2030–6). Very often, the process of state-building, in this context implies a process of establishing authority over a given territory—i.e., "state-building in the literal sense of the word" (Krastev, 2003, p. 1).
- On the other hand, "awkward states" engage in occasionally erratic and oftentimes unpredictable international behavior (to the extent that they are willing to interact meaningfully with the outside world at all, as the instance of Turkmenistan's foreign policy of "positive neutrality" illustrates).[14] The relationality of sovereignty in this context points to the inability of awkward states to participate in the international realm both as "an object of scrutiny" and "a responsible member of the international system that is responsive to the needs of humankind beyond the boundaries of narrowly defined notions of sovereignty" (Deng, 1995, p. 273). At minimum, this aspect points to the ability of sovereign actors to perform the roles of "usable states" by (i) encouraging predictability; (ii) creating confidence; (iii) lending credibility; (iv) providing security; (v) displaying resolve; and (vi) controlling resources (Tsygankov, 2007, p. 426).
- At the same time, the awkwardness of Central Asian statehood stems from the lack of social cohesion in the region. As David Lewis has concluded, state-building in Central Asia has been seriously hampered by the absence of coherent nationalism that will be able to overcome the various forms of localism (Lewis, 2008, p. 161). In fact, Anna Matveeva asserts that nationalism "has never been a feature of Central Asia" and that the consolidation of patrimonial networks

> across the region has successfully stifled its likely emergence in the future (Matveeva, 2006, p. 29). In this context, the instance of Central Asian polities confirms the observation that "historically, the identification of state, territory, and nation is false" (Frank, 1992, p. 56). Thus, the awkwardness of Central Asian statehood comes to epitomize the distinctly modern dilemma of non-Western polities: "how to become modern and to return to sources; how to revive an old, dormant civilization and take part in universal civilization."[15]

Thus, the reference to the *awkwardness* of statehood intuits that the dividing line between "state" and "non-states" has become so blurred as to be virtually imperceptible (Clapham, 1998, p. 153). The issue here is *the kind of polities* that populate the stage of world politics. Ken Dark has presciently interpreted this dilemma as an assertion of the multiformality of the international system—the cohabitation of different forms of statehood. He insists that "even after new political forms emerged, older forms did not simply wither away, but remained coexisting (and competing) polities" (Dark, 2002, p. 62).

The issue in this respect has been further complicated by the confusion between "stateness" and "regime type." This mix-up has been made most conspicuous by the post-September 11, 2001 strategies for winning the "global war on terror," where the terms "state-building" and "regime-change" have been used interchangeably—as stylistic variations. The reference to awkwardness, therefore, often points to the muddling of these two concepts which demand different analytical and policy frameworks. For instance, one cannot regime-change if there is no state; just as it is impossible to state-build in the context of an already functioning state, if all that is needed is a change in the mode of governance. The example of post-2003 Iraq is a good case in point. It demonstrates that an actor (or a coalition-of-willing actors) can state-destroy—that is, dismantle the institutions of functioning statehood (regardless of what one might think about its system of governance)—in order to regime-change through the process of state-building. The consequent (and still ongoing) awkwardness of post-2003 Iraqi statehood reveals the problems of conflating the process and objectives of regime-change and state-(re) building (Kavalski and Zolkos, 2007).

In this respect, the label of "awkward statehood" offers a qualification both of the governance system of Central Asian polities and the character of their domestic and international sovereignty. At the same time, the emphasis on awkwardness intends to suggest that the type of statehood dominating the region will not be of short longevity, but is likely to remain a durable feature of international life. Owing to the privatization of policy making by regional rulers, the awkwardness of Central Asian statehood also reflects that international agency is oftentimes co-opted by Central Asian rulers to bolster the appearance of legitimacy—both domestically and internationally—for their authoritarian regimes (Lewis, 2008). It is these dynamics that indicate Central Asia's current engagement in the process and practice of world affairs and provide the context for the regional agency of the EU, China, and India.

Conclusion

The location of Central Asia in world politics is neither fixed nor stable. Instead, it is subject to ongoing changes and fluctuations. This discussion of the position of Central Asia on the mental maps of world affairs is not merely an academic fad. As we will see in Part II, it has important policy implications. For instance, as Chapter 4 will demonstrate, the EU's "regional perspective" on Central Asia leads it to assume a commonality of values and active processes of "change toward increased cooperation, integration, convergence, coherence, and identity," none of which has "been an obvious feature of security (or other) policy interactions in Central Asia" (Matveeva, 2006, pp. 105–6).

The proposition of this chapter is that the composite awkwardness of Central Asian statehood has become the distinctive feature of the regional *context* in global life. This inference is not intended to suggest that the Central Asian region is an anomaly in the patterns of international politics; on the contrary, the claim is that it offers (possibly) the most conspicuous indication of the nascent complexity of global life.[16] The suggestion then is that the effects of external agency are conditioned by the kind(s) of statehood in Central Asia. It is this awkwardness of regional polities that makes possible the security governance strategies of international actors. This chapter has, thereby, provided a valuable intellectual setting for engaging with the agency of normative foreign policy actors in Central Asia.

2

The shadows of normative powers

Introduction

Borrowing from the designation of the nineteenth-century Russian statesman Count Karl Nesselrode that Central Asia is a *context* for the "tournament of [the] shadows" of great powers,[1] the title of this chapter draws attention to the contestation that underpins the regional "rise of normative powers." The claim is that Central Asia provides the context for a "tournament of the shadows" between normative powers extending to the region rival images of preferred behavior sustained by distinct security governance strategies. This contestation is implicit in the normative foreign policy agency of the EU, China, and India in the region. Yet, as indicated in Chapter 1, it is in the shadows of the "new great game" between normative powers that Central Asian actors are able to assert their own agency by picking-and-choosing between (yet not necessarily sticking with) the various models that are promoted to the region.

This chapter revisits the notion and practices of normative power in order to provide an analytical background for asserting the individual agency of external actors in Central Asia. The analysis focuses both on their *influence* and on the distinct *strategic cultures* that frame their regional policies. The suggestion is that strategic culture provides the grammar of cognition within and through which normative power is being practiced. The significance of this inference will become apparent during the discussion of the patterns of security governance in Chapter 3. As it will be explained, security governance—like any other form of governance—involves both structure and process (Webber, 2007, p. 63). These, however, do not emerge in a vacuum, but through deliberate practice. The contention here is that such practices are guided by normative power. In other words, security governance is the *practical* manifestation of normative power, whose content is framed by the strategic culture of individual actors.

Hence, the answer to the question "why study normative powers?" should be pretty obvious by now—in order to uncover "the sources of values in the 'international culture'" (Holsti, 1991, p. 47). Thus, to paraphrase from a different context, it is the exploration of normative power which proffers an encounter with "the complexity of the process whereby human individuals and groups achieve desired results in their relations with each other" (Claude, 1965, p. 5). The chapter begins with framing the notion and practices of normative power. In particular, it brings together for the first time Ian Manners' definition of normative power from the early 2000s and Jay Jackon's original mid-1970s' conceptualization of the term. Such a framing provides the intellectual setting for an innovative engagement with normative foreign policy agency premised on an actor's ability to influence and the cognitive structure of its strategic culture. The contextualization of normative power makes possible the confrontation with the multiple currents of distinct (and often disparate) flows that characterize the vortex of agency not only in the context of Central Asia, but also in world politics.

Framing normative powers

The premise of this study is that in their external relations, the EU, China, and India are engaging Central Asia as normative powers. Such claim calls attention to the meaning of this term. Ian Manners' oft-quoted definition circumscribes the application of the notion of normative power to the study of world politics by accentuating an actor's ability to "shape what can be 'normal' in international life." As he insists, "the ability to define what passes for 'normal' in world politics is, ultimately, the greatest power of all" (Manners, 2002, p. 253). As it was indicated in the introductory chapter of this book, Manners' intervention was central to the emerging European International Relations (EIR) theory, and has corrected earlier assumptions about the international character of the EU as either a "civilian power" or a "soft power." Yet, in a much broader sense, it was Jay Jackson who in the mid-1970s offered the first definition of the "normative power" concept. According to him, normative power refers to "the potential for influencing activity. . . [through] the power of norms." Jackson argues that normative power is a "'dispositional' rather than 'episodic'" feature of actors and their identity, which outlines the "*domain* and *range*" of legitimate behavior (Jackson, 1975, pp. 237–9; emphasis in original).

In this respect, both Jackson and Manners intuit that the reference to normative power suggests that the international interactions of actors are conditioned by conceptions of what is acceptable and what is unacceptable behavior. This logic of appropriateness is instrumentalized through the rules and norms that underpin the strategic culture and international identity of actors. As Jackson asserts, "we cannot analyze the basic rules of everyday life (the interpretative procedure of reality construction) without regard to the rules of conduct (the normative expectation of role behavior)" (Jackson, 1975, p. 260). At the same time, however, such perceptions accentuate the expectations that these actors might hold about the pattern of global politics. The acknowledgment of distinct normative powers reinforces the sensitivity to the complexity of global politics marked by contending (if not necessarily conflictual) understandings of what the "proper" framework of international politics both *is* and *should be*. Such complexity arises from the "particular means" through which actors exercise their normative power (Diez and Manners, 2007, p. 175).

Therefore, in terms of the international agency of the EU, China, and India, the notion of normative power suggests that their international behavior is not only preconditioned by a particular kind of self, but also that their engagement with the world suggests an understanding that other actors *should* behave according to these principles (Kavalski, 2007b). The contention is that when applied to the international interactions of Brussels, Beijing, and New Delhi, the concept of normative power denotes: (i) a particular kind of actor, (ii) a framework for its external relations, and (iii) means for involving and interacting with others.[2] In this context, Thomas Diez insists that normative powers are actors whose "conception of [their] foreign policy role and behavior is bound to particular aims, values, principles as well as forms of influence and instruments of power in the name of a *civilization of international relations*" (Diez, 2005, p. 617; emphasis added).[3]

Such an assertion is reminiscent of Adda B. Bozeman's intimation that "each society is moved by the circumstances of its existence to develop its own approach to foreign relations. . . [and] bound to incorporate the traditions and values peculiar to the civilization in which it is practiced" (Bozeman, 1960, p. 324). It is this understanding which allows for the innovative application of the concept of normative power outside of its traditional European purview. The suggestion is that the conceptualization of normative power allows for overcoming the limitations of traditional analysis by problematizing the underlying ideational motivations of the EU, China, and India informed by the cognitive grammars scripted by their distinct strategic cultures.

At the same time, the reference to normative power has to suggest that on a pragmatic (if not purely functional) level, neither the EU, nor China, nor India champion a military solution to the posers of Central Asia. In effect, all the three have indicated that the stability of the region is vital to their own security and that any conflicts should be resolved through peaceful means. In this respect, the genealogists of normative power trace its origins to the notion of "civilian power" (Telò, 2006, p. 45). As normative agents, therefore, the engagement of the EU, India, and China in Central Asia reflects their predilection to economic, political, and legal instruments and means for the projection of their foreign policies rather than military capabilities. However, just because their positions can be defined as normative does not mean that they are not also strategic. On the contrary, the reference to normative power helps elicit the ways and means through which actors influence the behavior of others—an aspect framed by the specific practices of security governance (which are discussed in Chapter 3).

Yet, despite the seeming similarity between the normative underpinnings of Brussels', Beijing's, and New Delhi's foreign policies, this has not necessarily brought the three closer together in their Central Asian interactions (Golden, 2006). The EU, China, and India proffer themselves as exemplars of distinct patterns of international agency. The models they project to the region are framed by their idiosyncratic strategic cultures which inform not only the frameworks of their international identity, but as we will see the way(s) in which they practice policy-making. For the purposes of brevity, the following outline offers only a truncated snapshot of these distinctions, which are to be further elaborated in the concluding chapter of this book.

For instance, most commentators note Brussels' pride in its interdependent politicoeconomic framework, flaunting the benefits of liberal democracy. Such context informs the EU's perception of China's and India's rise to international prominence in terms of its implications on domestic transitions that can consolidate civil society and transparent forms of governance (Shambaugh, 2005, p. 14). At the same time, Beijing asserts the benefits of a government-controlled centralized command economy and stresses the inviolability of sovereignty and territorial integrity. New Delhi's approach to Central Asia seems to share some of the democratic underpinnings of the external policies of Brussels, but at the same time it seems to endorse Beijing's affirmation of government centralization and noninterference in the domestic affairs of states. These dissimilar points of departure inform not only distinct attitudes toward foreign policy, but also idiosyncratic strategic cultures that shape the EU's, China's, and India's security governance of Central Asia. In this respect, the argument here is that the exercise of normative power is premised on an actor's *influence*, which is framed by that actor's *strategic culture*. The following sections outline the two aspects of this proposition.

Engaging the influence *of normative powers*

Analyses of normative powers are quick to point out that the impact of their international agency is difficult to gauge through a simple analysis of the "sum of its parts" (Manners and Whitman, 1998, p. 246). Instead, the study of the effectiveness of normative power requires a contextual assessment of its practice (i.e. the content and process, of its application). The contention here is that regardless of the differences underlying its practice, normative power (just like any kind of power) rests on the *power to influence others*. Influence is revealed by the ability of an actor to make some policy-choices more attractive than others (but without recourse to force or the threat of force). In other words, influence refers to perceptible alterations in behavior and beliefs in order to suit the model/example set by someone else. In this respect, the influence of normative powers can have effects "even if unintentionally" (i.e. it has the ability to produce results) because it is an attribute that an actor possesses and it becomes apparent through social interactions (Barnett and Duvall, 2005, p. 45). In understanding the *influence* of normative powers, this section analyzes their *actorness*. Such a consideration draws attention to the particular *power of attraction* that normative powers seem to share.

Actorness defines the capacity of a normative power to speak, influence, and act cohesively in different international environments. It encompasses an actor's ability both to achieve its goals and to transmit institutions, practices, and norms that would construct an environment congruent with and conducive to its agency. Actorness, thereby, identifies an "ability to behave in ways that have consequences in international politics," which is conditioned by the special, temporal, and issue context (Caporaso and Jupille, 1998, p. 244). The assessment of the Central Asian actorness of the EU, China, and India offers insights mainly into their regional policies and not their (grand) foreign policy strategies, per se (although an extrapolation can be made). Thus, while the two are related, the (particular) Central Asian and the (general) international relations of normative powers reflect distinct conceptualizations of identity, interests, utility, and effort that are contingent both on contextual and ideational interpretations. For instance, the Central Asian agency of the EU, India, and China suggests the ways in which each of them conceives their agency in the region, not in global life (although the two aspects are not independent of each other, the point here is that while mutually reinforcing, they are also distinct). Actorness thereby is "conditioned by circumstances as well as by formal grants of authority" (Laffan et al., 1999, p. 169).

The framework of *actorness* provides a useful access point for the analytical engagement with the *influence* of normative powers. It points to the functional interdependence between actors and their environments. As we will see in the concluding chapter of this book, the relational character of security governance draws attention to the dynamics through which the demand for recognition affects the construction (and consideration) of an actor as a normative power. The contention here is that such influence reflects the *power of attraction* of normative powers. For instance, an actor A has a power of attraction over actor B, because actor B *wants* to *follow the example of, emulate*, and, thereby, *be socialized by* actor A. This is done *not by force*, but *by attraction*—actor B *likes* actor A's behavior, norms, and values as expressed both on the international and the domestic stage and wants to be associated with them. The hackneyed example is the EU, whose power of attraction became a magnet for the post-Communist countries of Eastern Europe. As a result they were charmed enough to demand membership. Arguably, it was this nonmilitary influence of the EU, which pulled the former communist states to willingly initiate a transformation of their institutions of governance through closely monitored stages of accession-driven socialization. Other instances of this power of attraction include the US-sponsored project of Euro-Atlantic security community building after World War II and, more recently, China through the dynamics of its—allegedly, conditionality free—"charm offensive" (Kurlantzick, 2007).

The issue of influence suggests an actor's ability to establish itself as a *model* in global politics. As already suggested, influence is closely related to the notion of power, which (in itself) is one of the central and, yet, most elusive concepts in the study of global politics. The focus on influence here uncovers the more traditional meaning of power which centered "on the idea of ability" (Carroll, 1972, p. 589).[4] Thence, the reference to influence (i.e. *power as ability*) indicates the socializing capacity of normative powers to shape the policy-preferences of target countries (such as the Central Asian states). In other words, the impact of normative powers rests on their influence (which is tied to their *power of attraction*)—reflected in their ability to stimulate learning (i.e. policy change).[5] In this respect, the power of attraction of normative powers should not be assumed to be altruistic, but strategic—that is, it is underwritten by perceptions of strategic benefits for both sides of the interaction.

One of the fullest accounts of influence is provided by Rudolph Rummel (1976) in his analysis of the notion of power as the *ability* and *capacity* to produce effects. He infers the impact of normative power through both its intended and unintended results. Thus, while the former indicates primarily the material capabilities to produce outcomes, the latter reflects the "quality of being" of those exercising it. The unintended consequences of power reveal influence as an effect of the "power to draw attention"—that is, the willingness to identify through association/partnership rather than confrontation—which has the "capacities-to-produce-effects." In global life, the desire to identify through association with other international actors can be for various reasons, but it provides the ones aspired to with the "capability to alter the perception and opportunities" of the aspirants (Rummel, 1976, pp. 163–8).[6]

As it will become apparent in Chapter 3, the designation of an actor as a normative power reflects a security governance practice, which is underpinned by the *ability* of an actor to maintain the compliance of state-elites and the *capacity* to ensure that their decision-making follows prescribed patterns of behavior. Consequently, the issue of influence suggests an actor's ability to establish itself as a *model* in global politics—the perception of an actor as a model engenders a desire in others to *recognize* the leadership position of that actor (usually, by willingly following its lead). Thus, it is through the complex dynamics of influence that normative powers practice their actorness in global politics—that is, through their power of attraction, they are capable of defining what is normal in international life. In this respect, the chapters in Part II of the volume discuss the influence of the EU, China, and India in Central Asia as an indication of the impact of their distinct normative powers.

Grasping the strategic culture *of normative powers*

The particular understanding of normative power developed in this chapter derives not only from the application of its framework to "out-of-Europe" areas, but also from the engagement with the distinct strategic cultures that animate the normative foreign policy agency of the actors that practice it. Thus, the analysis of the EU, China, and India as normative powers draws attention to the particular strategic cultures of their international actorness. The claim is that strategic cultures provide the grammar of cognition within and through which normative power is practiced. Strategic culture reveals the "discerning tendencies" (as opposed to the "rigid determinants")[7] of normative power. In this respect, normative power emerges as a *power in context*—it is not entirely an intrinsic property of an actor, but depends on the kind of interactions it has in specific contexts.

The concept of strategic culture was introduced to the study of world affairs in the late 1970s by Jack L. Snyder in his inquiry into the perceptions of and approaches to the use of nuclear weapons by the USA and the USSR. Indeed, what was striking at the time was that both Washington and Moscow had *different* positions about the use and utility of nuclear armaments. The acknowledgment of such difference revealed the strategic predicament of mirror-imaging—that is, American commentators tended to predicate their analyses on the assumption that the Soviets were working from within similar considerations of deterrence and mutually assured destruction. Instead, as Snyder's study has demonstrated, such assumptions were flawed. Snyder suggested that such difference in policy visions was an outcome of the distinct *strategic cultures* within which American and Soviet decision-makers functioned. He, therefore, defined strategic culture as

> a sociological whole that can provide a context to aid in the interpretation of [a] strategic doctrine [and consists of] the sum total of ideas, conditioned emotional responses, and patterns of habitual behavior that members of a national security community have acquired through instruction or imitation and share with each other with regard to. . . strategy. (Snyder, 1977, pp. 7–8)

Snyder's designation, however, did not emerge in a vacuum. Some trace its lineage to the engagement with the "political" and "organizational" culture of foreign policy.[8] Others root strategic culture in the 1930s' suggestion of "national 'ways of war'" promulgated by the former British army officer Basil H. Liddel Hart (Zaman, 2009, pp. 71). Related to this tradition is the contention that the origins of the idea of strategic culture can be traced back to the 1940s' and 1950s' engagement with "national character studies" (Lantis, 2005, p. 1).

What all these genealogies seem to share is the assertion that at the heart of the concept-expansion that led to the emergence of the notion of strategic culture is the preoccupation with "the art of war." In this respect, Yitzhak Klein's definition of strategic culture is indicative of this trend. According to him, it refers merely to "the set of attitudes and beliefs held within a military establishment concerning the political objectives of war and the most effective strategy and operational method of achieving it" (Klein, 1989, pp. 3–23). Yet, such interpretation curtails the conceptual span of strategic culture and reduces it only to a stylistic variation of "military culture."[9] As David G. Haglund (2004, p. 482) explains, such a limited demarcation of the meaning of strategic culture emerges from its correlation to the concept of strategy, which then leads to the assumption that strategic culture is purely about "things material" (i.e. the use of force and military capabilities). Thus, the translation of strategic culture as military culture is often taken as an indication of the continuing "cultural hegemony of organized state violence" (Klein, 1988, p. 36).

In contrast, the purview of strategic culture outlined here is both broader and much more comprehensive than a focus on military doctrine would allow. In other words, one should not be "too dogmatic about the boundaries of what might be discussed in order to understand the behavior and attitudes within a particular state and society" (Macmillan et al., 1999, p. 12). The claim is that the term "strategic culture" derives its provenance from the notion of "cognitive structure," which infers the simultaneity of "openness to the outside world, but also the overriding of many, if not most, outside signals by internally generated messages from one's own memories" (Alker, 2001, p. 362). Such descent is already hinted by Snyder, who has insisted that strategic culture "is largely cognitive behavior"—that is, "the body of attitudes and beliefs that guides and circumscribes thought on strategic questions, influences the way strategic issues are formulated, and sets the vocabulary and conceptual parameters of strategic debate" (Snyder, 1977, pp. 8–9). Attesting to the cognitive underpinnings of the concept, Colin S. Gray avers that strategic culture "*is the plot*" (Gray, 2006, p. 7; emphasis in original), which offers a cognitive blueprint for behavior based on acquired beliefs and attitudes that it reinforces (usually, uncritically). In fact, owing to the significance of cognitive assumptions, some commentators have introduced the much broader concept of "international relations culture" (Stuart-Fox, 2003, p. 5) as a substitute for the term "strategic culture".[10]

The concept of cognitive structure was introduced to the study of international relations in the late 1950s by William Scott, who defined it as "a matrix of attitudes toward external events" (Scott, 1958, p. 9). A decade later, Robert Jervis argued that the insertion of the term into the study of world politics cannot be limited by the "psycho-logic" of its origins. He, thereby, defined it as a "relation" between "incoming information" and the "receiver's already established images" (Jervis, 1968, p. 456). In the early 1970s, Michael Shapiro and Mathew Bonham referred to "cognitive structures" as "maps" of decision-making beliefs (Shapiro and Bonham, 1973, p. 147). Nearly 30 years later, Richard Herrmann and his collaborators interpreted the term simultaneously as a "representation" and a "mental model" of knowledge about a concept which influences the selection, interpretation, and memory of reality (Herrmann et al., 1997, p. 406); while Emanuel Adler and Michael Barnett (1996, p. 83) referred to it as "the shared system of intersubjective meanings." One of the more recent additions to this definitional genealogy of "cognitive structure" has been made by Ken Booth who referred to it as "the politics behind a conceptualization" (Booth, 2007, p. 109). In fact, Booth is among the first to stress the significance of the link between strategic culture and cognitive structure by pointing out that "the reality of our strategic world is inextricably interconnected with our manner of conceiving it" (Booth, 1979, p. 9). He later framed this relationship much more succinctly in his insistence that "we see things not as they are, but as we are" (Booth, 2005, p. 5).[11]

In this respect, strategic culture impacts the way international actors both conceive of and practice their normative power. It provides the "conceptual architecture" to think when taking decisions (Mitleton-Kelly, 2003, p. 67). In fact, Keith Krause and Andrew Latham reveal that

> While cultural forces do not directly determine policy responses, they exercise a powerful influence on the shaping of what might be called "policy reflexes." In other words, they can help shape an understanding of what constitutes "normal," "appropriate," or "desirable" practices and responses. (Krause and Latham, 1998, p. 26)

Strategic culture is, therefore, central to comprehending the patterns of normative powers—both in principle and of the EU, India, and China in Central Asia in particular. It provides heuristic devices for understanding the "historically-imposed inertia on choice" (Johnston, 1998b, p. 2) underpinning the agency of international actors.[12] Thus, while it does not necessarily assist in the predilection of specific policy choices, an awareness of an actor's strategic culture offers an understanding of the broader context of beliefs and attitudes within which policy-making occurs. This assertion should not be misunderstood as an indication that individual choice does not matter. Instead, the suggestion here is that such choice is contingent on the cultural milieu of the international actor and the context to which its agency is applied. Therefore, strategic culture is "unlikely to be of much help in explaining why alternative A was chosen over alternative B, but it may be of great help in understanding why A and B were considered, while no thought was given to C, D, or E" (Elkins and Simeon, 1979, p. 142). Having similar considerations in mind, Snyder asserts that strategic culture provides a framework of "shared images," which conditions an actor's thought and behavior. As he demonstrates in the case of the former Soviet Union, its "unique historical experiences, distinctive political and institutional relationships, and a preoccupation with strategic dilemmas different from these that have preoccupied the United States have combined to provide a unique mix of strategic beliefs and a unique pattern of strategic behavior based on those beliefs" (Snyder, 1977, pp. 34–8).[13]

Part II of this book demonstrates that a similar "unique mix" of experience, perceptions, beliefs, and attitudes informs the emergence of distinct patterns of normative power in Central Asia as indicated by the regional security governance of the EU, China, and India. Chapter 3 outlines the dynamics through which strategic cultures construct intersubjective understandings of security and its governance through the deliberate practice of socialization. Equally significantly, however, the recognition of cognitive structure as the constitutive interiority of normative power assists in responding to the query, where the sources of normative power lie?

> The answer, of course, is that it comes from what we call culture, strategic culture in this case. It is from our culture that we find the vision of the good or better life for ourselves and our security community. And it is from this vision that policy draws what it is able, given real-world constraints. Truly, culture must reign, sometimes it rules, while it is ever present, so well integrated as to be unbelled in our thoughts or judgments, because we cannot prevent it being so. (Gray, 2006, p. 12)

In this respect, the concept of strategic culture acknowledges the multiple currents of distinctive (and often disparate) flows that characterize the vortex of agency in international politics. Furthermore, the interrogation of such cognitive reflexes makes possible the encounter with the nonlinearity of normative power. The attention to strategic culture generates an understanding of world affairs that makes "no assumptions about equilibrium" (Jackson, 1975, p. 243). Instead, following the suggestion of Stephen Krasner, the pattern of global life that emerges is characterized by "punctuated equilibrium." According to him, in a world characterized by punctuated equilibrium, "there is more uncertainty and chance," because changes do not occur gradually, but as instantaneous (and discontinuous) events (Krasner, 1984, pp. 240–3). Such an understanding confirms the suggestion that normative powers (unlike "great powers" or superpowers) are "a particular kind of entity characterized by change rather than conserving the status quo" (Manners, 2006, p. 182). It is the recognition of such dispositional change that calls attention to the frameworks of security governance extended by normative powers to regulate the punctuated equilibrium of world politics.

Conclusion

This chapter has demonstrated that the exercise of normative power (framed by the cognitive structures of a specific strategic culture) helps us develop a contextually attuned understanding of the processes through which understandings of security emerge, develop, and become formulated in policies, practices, and institutions. Before concluding the framing of normative power provided by the distinct strategic cultures of actors, it is necessary to acknowledge the often overlooked "dark side" of normative power. Because the notion was developed to explain the international behavior of the EU, it is often assumed that normative powers are "forces for good" in international life (Sjursen, 2006, p. 235). The suggestion is that their influence is benign (at best) and consensually hegemonic (at worst).[14] Yet, even when the norms diffused by international actors may very well be considered legitimate and valid, this need not occlude the realization that the ability to define what is "normal" in world affairs is only a contemporary avatar of the hoary "standard of civilization," demarcating the inclusion or exclusion of "peoples and nations" from the "acceptable" international society (Bowden, 2009, p. 103).

Thus, instead of the racially motivated standards of civilized and uncivilized behavior, the contemporary exercise of normative power can imply an equally patronizing distinction between appropriate and inappropriate conduct. The former is the property of the normative power actor and the latter is a feature of those it intends to influence. For instance, as Chapter 4 will show, the EU's assumption of democracy as a "normal" feature of international life which needs to be extended to Central Asia can be read as akin to the Western *mission civilisatrice* predicated on a particular understanding of domestic governance, promotion of human rights, and a free-market model of economic development.[15] In this respect, paraphrasing from a different context, the definition of normative powers implicates their civilizing propensities by transforming the field of security governance "into one where cultural and symbolic forms of capital become vital—and one in which these forms of capital [are] dominantly possessed by Western states, societies, and security organizations" (Williams, 2007, p. 40).

While aware of this "dark side" of the exercise of normative power—regardless of whether it is being practiced by a "Western" or a "non-Western" actor—this study asserts that such a *civilizing* turn in the practices of normative powers is inescapable. The reason is that normative powers act from an assumption (if not always a position) of superiority—civilizing, therefore, is their way of understanding and responding to difference (Smith, 2009, p. 610). For instance, as Chapter 4 will demonstrate, the EU's confrontation with the awkwardness of Central Asia provokes a civilizing demand for compliance with the standards that it promotes in lieu of a reflection on its own normativity. Likewise, Chapter 6 will evidence India's civilizing propensities through the expectation engrained in its strategic culture that other actors *should* follow its example because of its unique and hoary history and civilization. Thus, regardless of the differences in context, the normative foreign policy agency of the EU, China, and India reveals a peculiar contemporary modality of "neotrusteeship" (or patron-client) relations.[16]

What has to be remembered, however, is that normative powers are neither the "goodies," nor the "baddies" of global life—they are merely *powers*. Othering is an inherent quality of their agency. It has to be stressed that the distinction between a normative power and the target of its socialization "is not simply a measure of defectiveness" (Womack, 2008, p. 294). The interpretation of the influence of normative foreign policy actors—even if perceived as an act of imperial civilizing—is in the eye of the beholder subject to their practice. Consequently, the designation of an actor's influence as a normative power is merely a descriptor of that actor's agency in global life. This description is contingent on the interpretation of an actor's agency in a particular time and space.

How then can we disentangle the practices of normative powers from the civilizing patterns of behavior characterizing the orders established by conventional imperial powers? The answer is both simple and straightforward: by looking at the strategic culture of an actor. The examination of strategic culture suggests that the agency of normative powers is not only the outcome of subjective assessment. Instead, as Jackson reminds us, normative power can be a "structural property" and an "objective attribute" of actors (Jackson, 1975, pp. 239–43). In other words, it does not rest only on perceptions of behavior, but reflects actual features of an actor's international identity. Thus, according to Jackson, at the crux of the distinction between normative and imperial foreign policy is *tolerance*. As tolerant international actors, normative powers are characterized by "a willingness to suspend evaluation of others' activity," which then triggers a specific set of "expectations by others for [a normative] actor's conduct" (Jackson, 1975, pp. 240–4). In a similar vein, Nathalie Tocci distinguishes between normative and imperial powers premised on whether their agency is "other-empowering" or "self-empowering." She argues that normative powers are driven by respect for their domestic and international legal obligations with the aim of strengthening international law and institutions, while imperial powers are unlikely to find multilateral frameworks binding and are more likely to insist on dominating the regulation of international relations in a manner that serves mainly their own self-interest (Tocci, 2008, pp. 9–13).

Yet, unlike Tocci, Jackson asserts that the properties of normative powers are "analytically distinct from the motivations of actors to belong or conform" to the orders that their practices circumscribe. In other words, Jackson intuits that unlike imperial powers, the agency of normative powers is not premised on expectations of conformity, but is "embedded in definitions of commitment in terms of actor's internalization of norms in the socialization process" (Jackson, 1975, pp. 258–9). Thus, in an increasingly interdependent world where the transfer of international "goods" and "bads" is becoming ever swifter and the potential for "negative globalization" is very real, the rise of normative powers indicates the transmission of practices (imbued with ideas) whose interpretation depends on the strategic culture and perspective of the actor undertaking the observation (Matveeva, 2006, p. 8; Smith, 2009, p. 602).

The qualification to Jackson's proposition demanded here is that while normative power can be a property of an actor's identity, it nonetheless rests on the acknowledgment and the consent of the target state. E. H. Carr has observed this much when he noted that "power goes far to create the morality convenient to itself, and coercion is a fruitful source of consent. But when all these reserves have been made, it remains true that a new international order and a new international harmony can be built up only on the basis of an ascendancy which is generally accepted as tolerant and unoppressive" (Carr, 1964, p. 236). Such contextualization acknowledges that normative powers are not in the business of enforcing orders over other actors, but of engaging other actors in shared practices of security governance. Thus, the ability to treat others with respect (and esteem) allows normative powers to define and redefine the standards of the "normal" in international life.

As the concluding chapter will demonstrate, the instances of the Central Asian agency of the EU, India, and China suggest a nascent "struggle for recognition." Thus, being reflective about one's contextual interactions—that is, taking into account (i) how external agency affects a regional pattern of relations and (ii) how, in turn, such local interactions impinge upon the behavior of the international actor—can enhance the influence of a normative power. In this respect, it is the particular practices of security governance that can facilitate the *recognition* of the authority of individual normative powers. It is to these dynamics that we turn in the following chapter.

3

The deliberate practice of relational security governance

More people debated the Great Game than ever played it.

John Keay (1994 [1977], p. 140)

The contention of this study is that the rise of and contestation between normative powers in Central Asia is effectively a conflict over governance. The momentous events of 1989 and the apparent failure of commentators to anticipate them have heightened the awareness about the pervasive contingency of international patterns. Commentators were quick to note that a "new era of international relations" was inaugurated as a result of a profound shift to "a time which is fundamentally different from all past eras" (Roberts, 1991, p. 509; Webber, 2007, p. 27).[1] In particular, the end of the Cold War appears to have drawn attention not only to the changing patterns of global life, but also to the vulnerability of the analytical frameworks through which these alterations have been addressed and understood.

The dramatic transformations set off by the fall of the Berlin Wall reminded observers of the Coxian adage that *changes in practice* reveal the inherent arbitrariness of knowledge about "the ways in which human affairs are organized."[2] In this regard, the abrupt dissolution of the Soviet Union has led James Rosenau to bring out the inchoate nature of systems of thought in international relations. As he has asserted, they "may last seventy years, but they are nonetheless always on the edge of collapse. . . once people break from their conceptual jails and see alternative ways of thinking and acting—the whole edifice can swiftly collapse" (Rosenau, 1993, p. 122).[3] It is in the context of such considerations that the notion of security governance was initially promulgated and has gradually asserted itself within the intersections between security and globalization in the articulations of global governance.

By both capturing and imputing the directionality of the alterations in world affairs, the "*nebuleuse*" (Murphy, 2000, p. 792) of global governance has permeated scholarly, policy, and public debates as a heuristic device, a rhetorical "fad" (Karns, 2000, p. 40), and an agreeable notion because it is largely "without substance" (Weiss, 2000, p. 808). Finkelstein, thereby, asserts that "global governance appears to be virtually anything" (Finkelstein, 1995, p. 368). Hence, in an attempt to escape the predicaments of the "dysfunctionally mythological character" (Yunker, 2004, p. 507) of the global governance label (while retaining its promise), some have pushed forward the concept of *security governance*.[4] This chapter interrogates the cognitive structures underpinning this enterprise. At the same time, it engages security governance as a defining feature of the fledgling European International Relations (EIR) theory.

The appraisal of security governance requires several qualifications. First, in setting up the inquiry in this way, the intention is not to suggest yet another "grand narrative" of security and its governance, but to indicate that the transformations of global life have significantly altered the conditions of securing (Dunn, 2007, p. 87). Second, the interrogation of the cognitive structures which shape and influence our understanding of security and its governance in Central Asia, although informed by "reality", is not necessarily "empirical", as it consciously engages the abstractions informing the theoretical discussions on the current status of regional security governance.[5] As argued in Chapter 2, the security governance of normative powers should not be understood as a mere reflection of civilizing projects. Instead, the instances of the EU, China, and India in Part II indicate that the security governance of normative powers simultaneously rests upon and reveals an asymmetric relationship. As this chapter will demonstrate, security governance is about the ways in which (normative) actors manage such relations of asymmetry. Therefore, it is *interaction* itself—that is, how normative power is applied in a particular context—that determines the quality, context, and outcomes of security governance.

This chapter proceeds with an overview of the conceptual ramifications of the continuous transformations in the notion and practices of security governance. In particular, it emphasizes its complexity—a feature which rarely draws attention of observers and policy-makers. As the concluding chapter of this volume will indicate, the resilience competences of security governance have crucial implications for the ramifications of what *acting politically* in awkward contexts—such as the one of Central Asia—might mean. Pragmatically speaking, however, such a conceptual engagement makes conspicuous that the deliberate practices of security governance uncover the security grammars underpinning normative powers. Such grammars are provided by the cognitive structures of their strategic culture.

Thus, in terms of the socialization of target states, this chapter emphasizes the significance of the deliberate efforts of doing things together. It is by initiating communities of practice that normative foreign policy actors can begin broadcasting (as well as transmitting) their conceptualizations of the "normal." The focus on deliberate practice suggests that the explanation and understanding of normative powers cannot be decoupled from the context of their interactions. As the following analysis demonstrates, shared practices assist the dynamics of *localizing* by target states of promoted norms. The chapter then suggests that the effectiveness of security governance is relative to the contextual recognition of the agency of a normative foreign policy actor. Such recognition is contingent on the capacity of normative power to foster "generative relationships" premised on the deliberate practice of dialogical rather than objectifying interactions.

Security governance of complexity

Security governance was promoted as an analytical and policy framework to address the problem of contingency in international affairs. It was, therefore, intended as a framework of resilience in the face of world politics marred by uncertainty, cognitive challenges, complex risks, and vulnerability. The following sub-sections outline the dominant understandings of the notion of security and its governance.

Security, change, and resilience

Security has become one of the most contested concepts in the study of world affairs and it is often likened to oxygen—we become aware of it only when it is absent (Keohane, 2002, p. 17).[6] In fact, some commentators go as far as to claim that it is the preoccupation with security that distinguishes the field of international relations from other disciplines and gives it its unique intellectual identity (Wæver, 1997, p. 372). The setup of this inquiry traces the prevailing narratives of the need to seek safety and avoid harm, and the choices informed by such beliefs (Stern, 2006, p. 188). In an applied sense, the notion of security tends to be understood as "a low probability of damage to acquired values" (Baldwin, 1997, p. 13). Such interpretation suggests the intimate relationship between security and stability through the attempt "to contain and overcome disturbances to order" (Ikenberry, 2001, p. 45). The claim here is that discourses of security reflect reactions to the *reality of change* and are defined by the particular responses to the ongoing need to adapt to it—and, in fact, more often than not, attempt to contain or completely ignore its dynamics.

The study of how things have changed and in what way(s) they have stayed the same has always been at the heart of security studies. Yet, as John G. Ruggie (1975, pp. 129–36) had anticipated, it is the intensification (as well as the acknowledgment) of global interdependence that will make it impossible to overlook the effects of randomness and unintended consequences. For instance, the recognition that amplifying forces—such as those set off by the human impact on the environment—prompt qualitative changes in the very settings within which sociopolitical orders function compels the study of global life to rethink its paradigms "based on the dynamic of non-equilibria, with its emphasis on multiple futures, bifurcation, and choice, historical dependence, and. . . intrinsic and inherent uncertainty" (Wallerstein, 1996, pp. 61–3). Such awareness of the complexity of security concerns underscores the attempts at their governance. Security governance in this setting emerges both as a pattern of nascent dynamics and as a process of interaction through which participants can act and interpret this pattern.

The endemic nature of change underscoring the dynamic framework of international relations has questioned conventional understandings of *security as control*. Informed by a cognitive commitment to and "faith in a 'makeable world'" (Heinzen, 2004, p. 4), the narrative of *security as control* relates a story of "essentialist understandings about selfish and fearful humans" and "reductive theories about '*the* logic of anarchy'" (Booth, 2007, p. 327). In this respect, "the myth of 1648" (Teschke, 2003) has become the central "technology of control" (Duffield, 2001) in the ordering of our perceptions of security. Thus, masquerading as "real things," state-centric "concepts of control" befuddle the analysis of security studies (Bigo, 2001, p. 99). The discursive practices of *security as control* make possible the fixing of the constantly changing fluidity of life within entrenched abstractions of order and objectivity (Stern, 2006, p. 192). In this setting, security becomes equated with "the absence of insecurity" (Wolfers, 1962, p. 151). The alleged ability of security narratives to *control* the changing nature of reality underpins the *paradox of (in)security*—"in security we find insecurity," that is "when people attempt to protect themselves and to create a sense of security, they also produce danger, fear, and harm" (Der Derian, 1992, p.75; Stern, 2006, p. 187).[7] Thus, the repudiation of the widespread normative and empirical uncertainties that mark the multidirectional transformations in global life—as evidenced by those defining the awkward context of Central Asia—has led traditional security studies to adapt a mindset of continuities that makes it difficult to address randomness and its complex interactions.

In order to engage with the dynamic changes in Central Asian affairs, this book advances the understanding of *security as resilience*. This proposition identifies security through the ability (i) *to cope* successfully with challenging or threatening circumstances, (ii) *to defy* destructive pressures, and (iii) *to construct* new proficiency out of unfavorable conditions (Kavalski, 2008b). In this respect, *security as resilience* redefines the innermost principle of international politics, not merely as survival, but as *adaptive contingency*—that is, the "capacity to respond to the moment of contingent interaction" (Dillon, 2007, p. 11). Resilience, as Emanuel Adler (2005, p. 47) asserts, becomes an indicator for "the ability of the system to absorb change-driving variables and parameters and survive."

The normative claim here is that such engagement with the meaning and practices of security in a dynamic context—such as the one provided by Central Asia—allows not only for uncovering the formation of new subjectivities and analytical structures for understanding and explanation, but also for gauging the meaning of acting politically in global life. For the purposes of brevity, the assumption here is that *acting politically* under the conditions of constant change entails rejecting "security seeking" in the conventional sense of this term (i.e. *security as control*) and taking responsibility for leaving an impact, for forcing things in one direction rather than another—"since there is no way of guaranteeing in advance whether an act is good or bad. . . [thus] in a specific situation, one must run the risk that the effects of one's actions turn out bad" (Wæver, 2004, pp. 1–5).[8] In this respect, the conjecture of *security as resilience* helps bring to light the distinct security governance strategies that international actors such as the EU, China, and India extend to different global locales. In particular, it infers that the deliberate practices of security governance reveal that strategic culture furnishes the security grammar of normative power.

Relational security governance

Intent on accounting for the "crazy-quilt nature" of global life (Rosenau, 1995, p. 15), the conceptual origins of security governance rest on three assumptions: (i) states are no longer the single most important source of threat to international security, (ii) the nature of security threats both strains state-capacities and indicates the inadequacy of sovereignty-bound policy-making, and (iii) state legitimacy is no longer premised on the monopoly over the provision of security, but on the cost-efficient delivery of security (Krahman, 2005, p. 537). Consequently, security governance tends to be identified as a system of collective security backed by institutional interactions and coherent guidance in response to breaches in international security (Kirchner, 2007, p. 13). This system is said to be characterized by heterarchy (the existence of multiple centers of power and, thus, "a multiplicity of combined and coordinated actions" in response to the challenges of governing in a globalizing world), the interaction of a large number of state and nonstate actors, the formal and informal institutionalization of these relations, their ideational character as well as their collective purpose (Webber et al., 2004, pp. 5–9). The region of Central Asia seems to confirm the assumption of heterarchical context for security governance practices. In this respect, the frameworks of security governance emerge as a consequence of countervailing dynamics of geographical, functional, resources-distribution, interest-driven, and decision-making trends (Krahman, 2003, pp. 13–19).

Conventional understandings of security governance have been underpinned by the logic of *security as control*, which constrains its application to the analysis of the alterations in power and authority. For instance, Inis L. Claude's articulation of the "management of power in international relations" offers an early intuition about the dynamics of security governance (Claude, 1965, pp. 6–7). In contrast, commentators espousing the perspective of *security as resilience* tend to question considerations of security governance that reduce its meaning(s) to a greatly augmented form of multilateralism (Whitman, 2005, p. 42). Instead, the mode of governance discussed here emerges spontaneously and through self-organization, and is underpinned by the constant and deliberate practice of adaptation (Rhodes, 1996; Stoker, 1998; Kavalski, 2008b, 2009b). Thus, security governance emerges as a system of international rules distinguished by (i) structure—the extent to which institutionalized forms of behavior have occurred among the relevant actors in the steering, management, and regulations of security tasks; and (ii) process—the procedures that produce policy-outcomes reflecting the main motives behind the agent(s) of governance (Kirchner, 2006, p. 948).

According to Mark Webber (2007, pp. 62–3), this understanding discloses that governance in the realms of security becomes a complex regulatory mechanism of international relations, which is not a consequence of enforcement from above (as *security as control* suggests), but of voluntary adherence to collectively held norms (as *security as resilience* implies).[9] Thence, by emphasizing the regionness, compliance, and institutionalization, the attention to the adaptive patterns of security governance indicates a different mode of exercising power—one, that is characteristic of the practices of normative powers. Emerging from the active and dedicated act of convincing intended targets, security governance can be understood as a dynamic process for the diffusion of ideas, attitudes, and habits underpinning the strategic cultures of distinct normative powers. Thus, reflecting the "directedness" of security governance, normative powers alter the manner in which states from a particular region pursue their interests both by altering their policy-preferences and by leading them to re-evaluate the net benefits attached to the pursuit of "inappropriate" policy-paths (Adler et al., 1991, p. 14).

The willingness of targets to "re-evaluate" their behavior reflects not only the incentives provided by the normative power, but also the existence of dialogical forms of interaction in which recipients can participate in the interpretation of the sender's message. Such understanding challenges the conceptualization of security governance as a mere "international system of rule" (Kirchner and Sperling, 2007, pp. 3) and, instead, positions it as a particular process of interaction. Hence, following Qin Yaqing's suggestion, this study draws attention to the relational qualities of security governance. Thus, in contrast to conventional "rule-based governance," the understanding of security governance as "relational governance" draws attention not to the actor, but to the process of interaction as the key unit of analysis. Thus, as long as the dialogical aspect of security governance is maintained, "relations will at least not deteriorate to an irreversible point beyond redemption. It is important therefore to maintain the process, which means keeping up at least an on-going relationship, rather than achieve immediate and tangible results." In this respect, "actors not in relationships, are non-actors because they produce little significant social meaning" (Qin, 2011, pp. 136–8).

The perception, therefore, is that interactions come prior to the existence of individual actors; in fact, actors acquire their identity in the process of contextual interactions. In this setting, relational security governance infers that normative powers have agency only when they are engaged in dialogical interactions. The suggestion here is that normative power—just like any other power—is both social (i.e. relational) and contingent (i.e. contextual) (Barkin, 2010, p. 88). Paraphrasing from Mark Lynch, such emphasis on relationality contradicts the understanding of security governance as the socialization of a weaker state into the norms of a stronger one. Instead, it promulgates a practice for the establishment of mutually acceptable rules of behavior. Thus, by thoughtfully engaging others, normative powers initiate a deliberative dynamic which allows the targets of socialization to contribute to the formulation of rules and norms—which enhances the chances that these will be complied with as they are likely to be acceptable to both sides (Lynch, 2002, pp. 191–217).

It is in this way that dialogical relationships can impact on the behavior of states. To put it bluntly, it is in the practice of interaction that norms gain their causal power—through the meanings and interpretations that they acquire in the process (Wang, 2011, p. 12). Such relational security governance has three main elements: (i) rather than emphasizing "the logic of control," it draws attention to "negotiation" as the essence of governance; (ii) it stresses that governance is a dynamic process of steering and making arrangements, which is far from static; and (iii) what is governed are not actors, but the relations among them (Qin, 2011, p. 133). The socializing effects of relational security governance emerge from the ongoing repetition of the practice of interaction and the ability to establish a process that can maintain its deliberative dynamics. Security governance is, therefore, about change—change, which is informed by the relational agency of normative powers (according to the framing of their strategic culture) and emerges through a deliberate practice of socialization.[10] It is to these dynamics that we turn in the following section.

Coming to terms with the practices of international socialization

The end of the Cold War and the dissolution of the Soviet Union opened the former communist spaces to the socializing influences of external agents. This meant that attention was given to the norms and rules of their domestic and international relations. Usually, the meaning of socialization is considered as the "experience" and "exercise of political responsibility" that "operates to keep [decision-makers] in touch with the facts of life, to practice them in reading their meaning, and to make them responsible for giving effect to the lesson" (Curtis, 1922, pp. 168–76). Strategically speaking, socialization describes the process through which norms and standards of appropriateness become prevalent in a particular region. Socialization reveals its importance for the processes of security governance not merely by perpetuating the strategic culture of a normative power, but mostly by assisting its propagation. In other words, the civilizing aspect of security governance (discussed above) quickly emerges in the practices of strategic enculturation—implicit in the cognitive structure of strategic behavior.[11]

As Harold D. Lasswell has asserted, "clearly, insofar as politics is the management of symbols and practices related to the shape and composition of value patterns. . . politics can assume no static certainty; it can strive for dynamic techniques of navigating the tides of insecurity generated within the nature of man in culture" (Lasswell, 1935, p. 217). Thus, even from a more positivist stance, socialization provides an overlaying framework which "encourages states to do some things and refrain from doing others" (Waltz, 1997, p. 915). The following sections, thereby, discuss the frameworks through which normative powers socialize states and the way their security governance gets localized. The contention is that the rise of normative powers in Central Asia is not only about the security governance of regional states, but also about the content and meaning of external agency in a complex (and heterarchical) global life. Thus, it is the practice of socialization that allows for uncovering the strategic preferences of both intraregional and extraregional actors in the process of interaction.

The international socialization of states into communities of practice

In the nascent discourses of EIR, socialization is identified as a process (i) directed toward a state's "internalization of the constitutive beliefs and practices institutionalized in its international environment" (Schimmelfennig, 2000, p. 111), and (ii) "inducting actors into the norms and rules of a given community" (Checkel, 2007, p. 5). Socialization describes the practices through which institutions, behaviors, and norms are transmitted between international actors—that is, socialization intimates the dynamics through which states learn to obey, comply, and submit to international standards. Thus, the conventional understanding of international socialization emphasizes that "states follow specific rules, even when inconvenient, because they have a longer-term interest in the maintenance of law-impregnated international community" (Hurrell, 1993, p. 59). In fact, this is what Headley Bull (1977, pp. 28–33) had in mind when he ascertained that

> if states today form an international society. . . this is because, recognizing certain common interests and perhaps common values, they regard themselves as bound by certain rules in their dealings with one another [and] cooperate in the working of institutions such as the forms of procedures of international law, the machinery of diplomacy and general international organization, and the customs and conventions of war.

Being a complex and context-specific process, socialization (for the purposes of this study) is understood to comprise two complementary aspects: compliance (socialization *by* international actors) and learning to comply (socialization *in* international organizations). For instance, in most of Eastern Europe, the socialization dynamics were geared toward preparing the former communist countries for prospective membership of NATO and the EU; and involved two methods: one, (potentially) coercive—that is, direct conditioning or enforcement; and the other, instructive—that is, by the management of differences (Kavalski, 2008a). Both dynamics, however, define socialization as a process geared toward the replication of particular Western models in post-Communist settings. In this context, contemporary practices of security governance reflect specific understandings of appropriate state behavior extended by different normative powers through the dynamics of international socialization.

Socialization in this regard provides a vehicle for the aggregation and projection of normative power. It also offers means of propagating (through emulation) of specific models of order. Thus, in the context of Central Asia, the capacity for influence of external actors is contingent on their ability to enact regionally based communities of practice. It is through the practice of doing things together that ideas about prescribed and proscribed patterns of international relations gain their impact on actions and behavior. The term "community of practice" designates a group of actors who, over a period of time, share in some set of either formal or informal social practices geared toward some common purpose (Borrie, 2005, p. 15). It has to be remembered that communities of practice "are not international actors in any formal sense, but coexist and overlap with them" (Adler, 2005, p. 15). For instance, Chapter 5 discusses the Shanghai Cooperation Organization (SCO) as an instance of such a community of practice. It is in the processes of such interactions that rules, norms, and standards of appropriate behavior acquire their meaning through their usage in practice. In this way, the practice of doing things together gradually institutes a relationship in which actors "can no longer be secure from one another, but only with one another" (Adler, 1991, p. 136).

Such a process can be interpreted as the first step toward the development of trust. It rests not just on any kind of practice, but on *deliberate practice*—the conscious and repeated effort to improve interactions (Ericsson et al., 1993, p. 368). In fact, this is what the discussion of tolerance at the end of Chapter 2 had in mind. Relations of tolerance show respect for the esteem of the other and what is valuable about them. On an instrumental level, *normative power entails the deliberate practice of security governance, which reveals an actor's willingness to suspend evaluation of others' activities as long as they have committed to shared practices.* Consequently, it is the dialogical process of interaction that can be evaluated in terms of inclusion and exclusion—which is where the practice of security governance begins (Nel, 2010, p. 964). Translated to the language of world affairs, the notion of deliberate practice suggests that normative powers deliberately seek to construct learning situations through which they can socialize target states (Ericsson, 2004, p. S73).

Robert Jervis outlines several reasons why deliberate practice is crucial to the exercise of security governance. First, results cannot be predicted from looking only at separate actions—in particular, the tendency to engage only with the agency of normative powers. Instead, outcomes emerge in the context of interactions—especially, interactions that are dialogical rather than objectifying. Second, "strategies depend on the strategies of others." Thus, the deliberate practice of security governance indicates that "the success and failures of policy are determined interactively." Significantly, the process of interaction empowers local participants (as they are meaningfully contributing to the practices of security governance) and enhances the perception that they (and their inputs) are respected. Third, "behavior changes the environment"—that is, the exercise of security governance has its own evolutionary effect. Such reflexive propensity of deliberate practice confirms the ongoing dynamic nature of international life, where "each dispute, policy, or action affects others and re-shapes the political landscape, inhibiting some behaviors and enabling others" (Jervis, 1997, pp. 23–5).

Because normative power rests on "communal practice"—that is, it is apparent only in the interactions with other actors—it is rarely (if ever) spontaneous (Gruber et al., 2004, p. 224). Thus, the focus on communities of practice suggests that relations of compliance are an acquired characteristic of an imagined community both constructed by and emerging from extended deliberate practice. The proposition then is that the success of the security governance mechanisms initiated by normative powers—such as the EU, China, and India in Central Asia—will depend on their willingness to initiate and the ability to maintain for an extended period of time a deliberate practice of socialization. Such deliberate practices demand both strong motivation and determination from external actors. As it will be suggested in the concluding chapter of this book, it is this capacity to make credible commitments to shared practices that belies the *recognition* of normative powers in global life.

Thus, it is the very deliberate practices of security governance which bear the potential to change attitudes and patterns of behavior. Such active dialogical engagement enhances the chances for the effective interpretation of preferences, and the modification of those preferences toward the development of "greater cooperation and empathy towards the other" (Lynch, 2002, p. 222). Socialization, therefore, infers that processes of security governance are more complex than the focus on military capabilities will allow. The deliberate practices of socialization initiated by normative powers become a substitute for institutionally constrained behavior. It is important to note here that the repeated deliberate practice of interaction informs "a predilection to assume the best when interpreting another's motives and actions" (Qin, 2011, p. 139). Thus, while not spontaneous, deliberate practices are not necessarily formalized—that is, learning occurs by observation and repeated interaction (not that eventual formalization is impossible).

For instance, as Chapter 5 will demonstrate, China's confidence-building measures on border security and demarcation in Central Asia through the "Shanghai Five" reveal a structured activity deliberately practiced by Beijing. The credibility of its commitments and the repeated, ongoing nature of such efforts has ultimately allowed China to institutionalize this experience through the SCO and, consequently, to make it the centerpiece of its security governance of Central Asia. In this respect, the "lateness" of regional institution-building should not be misunderstood as "the absence of regional norms" (Acharya, 2009, p. 148).

Practices can then be regarded as the crucial quality of security governance.[12] Thus, regardless of however loose or amorphous they are, communities of practice fashion negotiated outcomes in the process of doing things together. In particular, the opportunities for local input into the dynamics of security governance enhance the validity and relevance of interactions. Consequently, the boundaries of regional orders—especially, regional orders such as the one in Central Asia which are marked and marred by *awkwardness*—are determined by the practices that constitute them (Adler and Greve, 2009, p. 59). Within such a dynamic interactive environment, socialization takes place in the context of dispositions constituted within a community of practice (Adler, 2008, p. 204).

This inference draws attention to the domestication of international standards by the Central Asian states. Defined by Amitav Acharya as *localization*, this aspect of socialization accounts for the endogenous dynamics "by which norm-takers build congruence between transnational norms (including norms previously institutionalized in a region) and local beliefs and practices. In this process, foreign norms, which may not initially cohere with the latter are incorporated into local norms" (Acharya, 2009, p. 24).

The focus on localization suggests that the effectiveness of socialization is dependent on the recognition accorded by regional stakeholders to the validity of the externally promoted norms. Thus, rather than socializing states into compatibility with "accepted" models of governance, the demand for recognition of promoted standards by Central Asian states reinforces the significance of the deliberate practice of security governance. Importantly, it alters accepted perceptions on local entrepreneurship by demonstrating the potency of regional actors to construct "a different form of legality" (Nelken, 2006, pp. 938–50). It is deliberate practices that provide the facilitating environment for such recognition to occur. Socialization, thereby, reveals the interpretive aspect of security governance, which is embedded in the deliberate practice of establishing and maintaining relationships by normative powers.[13]

Strategically speaking then (as it is not an altruistic project), the influence of normative power is reflected in the practices that become prevalent (i.e. recognized) in a particular region. The success of socialization tends to be premised on the effective delegitimation of normative priors. As some commentators have demonstrated, such delegitimation has not necessarily occurred in Central Asia precisely because of the rise of normative powers, whose contestation (and layered disconnect) makes it difficult to institute a prevailing model of appropriateness in the region (Kavalski, 2010b).

Moreover, as Alvarez (2005, p. 974) presciently points out, the mainstream analytical frameworks of security governance rely on and imply an "unthinking conformity" while neglecting the possibility of opposition or manipulation. Socialization, thereby, reflects the "moral production" of patterns of international relations through the dynamics of security governance—that is, the underlying desire of normative powers to reduce the complexity of global life by introducing and (if necessary) inducing manageable categories and images of Central Asian politics premised on selective interpretations of local society structures and of globalized ideas of sovereignty (Bliesemann de Guevara, 2008, p. 352; Sörensen, 2002, p. 2). In this respect, there is a demand for uncovering the processes through which international norms become salient domestically (Cortell and Davis, 2000, p. 72).

Conclusion

This chapter has argued that the insight gleaned from the conjoined study of strategic cultures and the dynamics of international socialization makes available a fresh analytical model for engaging with the frameworks of security governance (especially as they are practiced by normative powers). As it will soon become apparent, such engagement with the notion and practices of security governance permits tracing the underlying ideational motivations underpinning the Central Asian agency of the EU, China, and India in Central Asia. Thus, their distinct strategic cultures provide different narratives for the interaction with the awkward context of the region. The emphasis on the socializing practices of security governance draws attention to the significance of recurring patterns of interaction.

As Robert Maxfield suggests, it is in the process of such relationships that a normative power can "learn best about its world and the changes to it." Thus, the deliberate practice of security governance allows normative powers to foster "generative relationships" through which they can both "recognize and influence emergent opportunities" (Maxfield, 1997, p. 95). As we shall soon see (especially in the case of China), the deliberate practice of interactions based on respect can maximize the generative potential of relationships. In such a dialogical context, the possibility for constructing "new histories" emerges by altering the suspicion and bias from past interactions and by opening up opportunities for new avenues for interaction (Qin, 2011).

This chapter, thereby, has revealed that security governance is about the ways in which normative foreign policy actors manage relations of asymmetry. As indicated in the introductory chapter of this book, the effectiveness of normative power is framed by its ability to influence not only others, but also oneself. Such resilient competences underpinning the cognitive structures of normative powers suggest that security governance is relative to the practices that become prevalent in a particular region. Consequently, referring back to the words of John Keay in the epigraph of this chapter, the claim here is that more actors considered the security governance of Central Asia than those that actually developed a deliberate practice for its socialization. Bearing these inferences in mind, Part II of this book undertakes a parallel assessment of the practical atunement of the normative foreign policy agency of the EU, China, and India to the context of Central Asia.

PART TWO

Following the Central Asian agency of normative powers

For lust of knowing what should not be known
We take the Golden Road to Samarkand.

James Elroy Flecker (1922, p. 31)

To each worm which needs but a tiny space
Heaven and earth become the same place.

Mullah Alim Mahmud Hajji (*History of Turkistan*, 1915) cited in Allworth (1967, p. 404)

4

The European Union and Central Asia: In search of a "new" strategy?

So far, the analytical considerations in Part I of the volume have illuminated the significance of deliberate practices to the initiation of regional security governance mechanisms by normative powers. As outlined in Chapters 2 and 3, it is by instigating communities of practice that normative powers socialize target states into promoted models of behavior as scripted by the cognitive frameworks of their strategic cultures. The current chapter then assesses the relevance of such a model to the explanation and understanding of the security governance mechanisms extended by the European Union (EU) to Central Asia.

The assessment of the EU's involvement in the region calls attention to the effectiveness of its external agency—especially, it queries the extent to which Brussels has a global outreach. In particular, in terms of the security governance of Central Asia, the query is whether the EU's normative power has been *catalyzed* (i.e. given impetus and direction) or *constrained* (i.e. subject to a process of external or self-limitation).[1] The pertinence of such analytical enquiry derives from the apparent sense of inevitability about the normative power of the EU. Bearing in mind the experience of the "big bang" enlargement of 2004, the claim is that the post-Communist countries of Eastern Europe are adjusting to the rules and norms of a continent-wide "new political system."[2] Even in the context of the deepening Eurozone debt crisis in 2011, the accession of Croatia and the ongoing commitment to the project of membership by the countries from the Western Balkans appears to reaffirm the continuing appeal of the EU's lodestone (Bechev, 2011). Thus, it appears only natural to some that such a "missionary" project will be expanded to the countries on the other side of the *enlarged EU* border for the purposes of spreading the benefits of the allegedly universal values "enjoyed at home" (Donnelly, 1998, p. 15).[3]

Owing to the dominant focus on enlargement, the EU's external policy has been treated largely as coterminous with the transformative potential underwriting the dynamics of accession-driven conditionality. Thereby, it was only recently that the relevance of the EU's ability to alter the practices of states (outside of the purview and the prospect of membership) has been given serious consideration. It seems, however, that the bulk of popular and policy attention has been captured by the development of the European Neighborhood Policy (ENP).[4] Stretching from the former European provinces of the Soviet Union, through the Caucasus, the Middle East, and North Africa, the ENP tends to be hailed as a novel development in the field of EU external relations. In particular, the relationship with Belarus, Moldova, and Ukraine seem to attract the limelight of commentaries on the ENP development (Lavenex, 2004). Such fixation tends to neglect the examination of the EU's agency in Central Asia, which is excluded from the ENP process.

Thus, the EU's engagement in the region seems to confront Brussels with the need "to design a real foreign policy beyond the enlargement paradigm" (Matveeva, 2006, p. 110). Resting on the experience of security community building in the wake of World War II, the EU's strategic culture is believed to be framed by the experience of what Jean Monnet, the father of European integration, has aptly described as "mak[ing] a breach in the ramparts of national sovereignty which will be narrow enough to secure consent, but deep enough to open the way towards the unity that is essential to peace" (Monnet, 1978, p. 298). This seems to inform a perception of "the states system as a war system" (Holsti, 1991, p. 204).[5] The security governance policies of Brussels are, therefore, intent on propagating the EU's cooperative patterns of relations as a way to lock-in the natural proclivity of nation-states toward violence.

Normative power Europe: Entrapment by strategic culture?

Most commentators note Brussels' pride in its interdependent politicoeconomic framework flaunting the benefits of liberal democracy. Such a context informs the EU's intent to introduce transparent forms of governance, viable market mechanisms, and a strong civil society in Central Asia. These objectives reflect the strategic culture underpinning the EU's international roles. Moreover, this is the very reason why the Brussels-based bloc has been referred to as not just any kind of power, but as a normative power. Its actorness—despite the hardening (even if only in rhetoric) contained in the Lisbon Treaty and identification through the civilian instruments of its soft power capabilities (aid, preferential trade agreements, institutional twinning, etc.)—is still defined by the norms and values that belie the strategic interests of the EU in global life.

This understanding is implicit in the security governance practiced by the EU—it aims to "Europeanize" the behavior of other states (mostly, but not only, in the context of potential enlargement). Such a pattern of relations reveals the EU as "a civilizational *security community* of practice" (Adler, 2010, p. 72; emphasis in original). In this respect, Europeanization can also be seen as a particular "civilizing process" (Linklater, 2005) intent on the universalization of what-are-assumed-to-be the foundational norms of the strategic culture of the EU. As one commentator put it, in its external affairs, Brussels feels the need to emphasize that the "Europeans have values as well as goods and services that they would like to export" (Tsoukalis, 2003, p. 193). As indicated in Chapter 2, the socialization processes embedded in the exercise of normative power reveal clear assumptions of superiority—that is, "it is the non-EU Europe that needs to learn to adapt," not the EU (Webber, 2007, p. 161). Consequently, the narrative of normative power presents the international identity of the EU in ways which allow Brussels to disregard its shortcomings (Diez, 2005, p. 626). Confirming this observation, the then EU Trade Commissioner, Pascal Lamy, asserted that

> It is no longer only economic interests that are in question, but also values, the concept of society, of what is desirable and of what is risky. Health, environment, the quality of life, culture are henceforth stakes that must be reconciled with open and competitive markets. Regarding development, human rights, social and environmental standards, the EU brings with it values that have the aim of becoming universal.[6]

Such proclamations reflect the kind of normalization of international affairs embedded in the assumed privileged position of the EU's normative power. In short, others are expected to conform to the projected "European model." Such conformity is not necessarily compelled by force, but as in the case of the post-Communist countries from Eastern Europe, it was introduced through a gradual process of socialization aimed at assisting them to begin *acting like the EU*. Corroborating the normative power of the EU, such socialization is not merely a dynamic for institutional transformation, but a "psychological process, a process of framing" (Vermeersch, 2005, p. 76) that alters the mindset and the ways of thinking of candidate countries. In fact, the context of Central Asia has allowed some of the new Member States to "play the EU"—that is, they have been actively positioning their national foreign policy stance in the region *as* that of the EU (Kavalski, 2010d).

The claim here is that to all intents and purposes, Europeanization has become shorthand for the model of security governance developed by the EU. Many commentators have noted that the "concept of Europeanization remains poorly and confusingly defined" (Mair, 2004, p. 338) and, therefore, it persists primarily as a "fashionable term" without much analytical utility (Olsen, 2003, p. 334). More often than not, the reference to Europeanization provides a moniker for the "EU-ization" (Radaelli, 2003, p. 27) of candidate countries through their conditioning into a "distinctly European political system" (Mair, 2004, p. 340). It is generally agreed that it was the status of "outsiders" and the "threat of exclusion" that allowed the EU to initiate the socialization of prospective members through the transmission of the *acquis communautaire* in order to propagate and ensure compliance with its system of governance (Grabbe, 2002).

Developed for the purposes of the "Eastern Enlargement" of the EU, the security governance prescribed by the dynamics of Europeanization reflects "an ongoing and mutually constitutive process of change linking national and European levels, and capturing the growing interdependence of both" through the complementary dimensions of (i) "uploading"—the projection of national preferences to the EU level, (ii) "downloading"—the domestic adaptation to/integration of EU-level initiatives, and (iii) "cross-loading"—the exchange of "ways of doing things" (i.e. best practices) so that "change takes place not only 'because of' but also within Europe" (Pomorska, 2007, p. 27).[7] It is this experience that has convinced the EU of the validity of the "logic of appropriateness" as a guide for its security governance strategies. Hence, it was the internalization of "European" identities, values, and norms by post-Communist countries that made possible the normative power of the EU (Schimmelfennig and Sedelmeier, 2005, p. 9).

It is in this setting that not only the EU has become "the most important external context for the foreign policy-making of [post-communist] states" (Wivel, 2004), but also the post-Communist states themselves have become the enabling environment for the EU's external agency. Consequently, the model of security governance implicit in the processes of Europeanization frames the EU accession as "the single most powerful policy instrument for peace and security in the world" (Moravcsik, 2004, p. 191).[8] Hence, the EU's promotion of its own model is intimately connected to the attempts to validate its own international identity by emphasizing the value rationality of making policy choices based on EU norms (Söderbaum and van Langenhove, 2006, pp. 120–9). It needs to be reminded, however, that the conceptualization of Europeanization as embedded in such "logic of appropriateness" reflects the terms of the so-called *post-1999 European order* (Kavalski, 2008a).[9]

The significance of 1999 is procedurally indicated by the EU's response to the Kosovo crisis. It was then that the EU collectively managed to offer both a discourse and a platform for rising to the challenge of relevance that appeared to plague its post-Cold War developments. Brussels did this by clearly articulating its responsibility for maintaining European security through the enlargement project. As Ole Wæver had anticipated, the issue of integration gradually became tantamount to the survival of the EU—"Europe now stands at a crossroads, where only by uniting may it still parry its decline. If it cannot accomplish this, the twenty-first century may well take shape without it" (Wæver, 1996, p. 123). In the wake of the Kosovo conflict, the EU launched its European Security and Defence Policy (ESDP), appointed its first High Representative of its Common Foreign and Security Policy (CFSP), and delineated the extent of its outreach leavened by its decision to open enlargement negotiations with all candidate-countries, initiate accession procedures with the states of the Western Balkans (Kavalski, 2006b), recognize Turkey's prospective status as a candidate country and, thereby, consign the rest of the continent to the outskirts of "Wider Europe"[10] (thus indicating Brussels' intentions for proactive engagement in regions that are not included in the accession process, but are proximate to the EU).

Writing in the wake of the Kosovo crisis, Ian Manners' emphasis on "normative power Europe," precisely captures the ideational impact of the post-1999 European order embedded in the external roles and international identity of the EU. As he argues,

> The concept of normative power is an attempt to suggest that not only is the EU constructed on normative basis, but importantly that this predisposes it to act in a normative way in world politics. It is built on the crucial and usually overlooked observation that the most important factor shaping the international role of the EU is know what it does or what it says, but what it is. Thus. . . the EU can be *conceptualized* as a changer of norms in the international system. . . that the EU *acts* to change norms in the international system; and. . . that the EU *should* act to extend its norms in the international system. (Manners, 2002, pp. 238–52; emphasis in original)

Such articulation of "normative power Europe" makes explicit the securitization of the integration process by and within the strategic culture of the EU. Integration (by way of Europeanization) gains urgency and immediacy because its alternative—disintegration—seems certain to unleash a self-organizing and unpredictable dynamic that portends to crush the project of "Europe" (Wæver, 1996, p. 123). Thus, the terms of the post-1999 European order maintain the viability of the EU as a normative power through the securitization of the integration project.[11] This then leads to the prioritization of the norms and values that allow the EU to *be* a normative power, because it is these standards of behavior that frame the outlines of the "normal." The strategic culture of the EU is, thus, understood:

> as comprising the socially-transmitted, identity-derived norms, ideas, and patterns of behavior that are shared among a broad majority of actors and social groups within a given security community, which helps to shape a ranked set of options for a community's pursuit of security and defence goals. (Meyer, 2005, pp. 524–9)

As suggested in Chapter 2, it is the stability of strategic cultures (i.e. they are rarely subject to unexpected and unpredictable changes) that underpins their strength and also their weakness. The norms that set the parameters of appropriate behavior can oftentimes *entrap* policy-making. Colin Gray intimates this possibility by suggesting that foreign policy decisions are subject to "cultural instincts"—the evaluation of strategic options according to the assumptions and rules with which state-elites are most familiar and within which they are encultured (Gray, 1999, p. 63). The ontology of policy-making as a knee-jerk reaction to entrenched cultural predispositions makes it very difficult to alter foreign policy behavior, especially, when such a change is promptly needed. This does not mean that the tone, tools, and mechanisms of policy cannot and do not change, only that their underlying cognitive frameworks remain largely unaltered.

Strategic culture can then become a "conceptual jailhouse" (Rosenau, 1979) that frames the exercise of normative power. This remains valid even for a diverse and heterogeneous actor such as the EU. Its emphasis on democracy, the rule of law, human rights, social solidarity, sustainable development, good governance, and antidiscrimination reveals the "normative foundations" of the strategic culture of the EU (Manners, 2002, p. 242). These ideals have come to resonate with the national strategic cultures of Member States and have gained enhanced significance in the integration of Europe. As indicated, such normative foundations of the EU's strategic culture have played (and continue to play) an important role in the Europeanization of prospective candidates.

Such normative framing of the EU's actorness appears to have increased the effectiveness of its European security governance—especially, after the Kosovo crisis. The claim here is that the strategic culture of the EU entraps its agency in Central Asia and has made it difficult for Brussels to develop contextual approaches to the region. In this context, the terms of the post-1999 European order have become critical to the notion and practices of the EU's security governance—both globally and in Central Asia.

In terms of Brussels' global outreach, the development of a sophisticated security governance mechanism through the Europeanization of candidate states appears to undercut the operational effectiveness of EU's normative power in "out-of-Europe" areas. This is not least, because the EU has had very little reasons (as well as time) to develop such capacities while the East European enlargement was still ongoing and, consequently, because of the preoccupation with the harmonization of the interactions among 27 Member States in the context of a protracted ratification of the Lisbon Treaty. The Eurozone debt crisis seems to offer another such "distraction" from the projection of effective normative power to "out-of-Europe" areas. As Michael Smith has eloquently argued,

> The status of the EU as a continental model of economic and social organization might be seen as giving a strong basis for the development of European foreign policy, but in many ways the strengths that give the EU a major role in the European order do not export easily; they are less immediately appropriate to a fluid and often chaotic world, and this means that the attempt to project "Europe" into the global arena brings with it new risks and potential costs. (Smith, 2009, p. 603)

More specifically, in terms of Central Asia, the post-1999 European order has clearly indicated that regional states are not proximate enough to be included in the category of prospective members, nor do they fall within the purview of the newly constituted "European Neighborhood." As the *European Security Strategy* (*ESS*) makes it (bluntly) explicit, "even in an era of globalization, geography is still important. It is in the European interest that countries on our borders are well governed." Thus, Central Asia falls outside the immediate enclosure of the explicitly defined *European* security governance and its broader (and, perhaps, fuzzier) surrounding neighborhood.[12]

The claim here is that these developments do not bode well for the EU's security governance of Central Asia. It seems that deprived of the lure of membership, the EU's normative power appears stunned and stunted. It cannot develop resonance in Central Asia because it lacks a deliberate practice that demonstrates a credible commitment to construct a meaningful relationship with the region. Keeping in line with the foundational logic of its strategic culture, the EU insists that its relations with "third countries" be assessed according to its ability to promote human rights and democratization (Warkotsch, 2006, p. 509). In fact, the European Commission has explicitly stated that the EU is engaged in Central Asia in order to support the establishment of "democratic principles and human rights in the transition towards market economy."[13] Likewise, in its *Strategy for New Partnership* with the region, Brussels stresses emphatically that "good governance, the rule of law, human rights, democratization, education and training are key areas where the EU *is willing to share experience and expertise*."[14]

Such statements are indicative of the EU's entrapment *by* and *within* the cognitive frameworks of its strategic culture. Brussels does not seem capable of formulating relations with countries beyond the realms of membership and privileged partnership that would sustain the ideational underpinnings of its normative power, which still remains attuned to the specificities of the project of Europeanizing integration. In this respect, the "cultural instincts" behind the security governance mechanisms developed for the prospective candidates and the current neighbors of the EU appear ill-suited to the dynamic political environment of Central Asia. It would seem that the Brussels-based club is constrained both by its lack of attention to the region and by the very strategic culture underpinning its normative power. While these issues are to be discussed in greater detail in the following section, it needs to be emphasized, however, that Central Asia is perhaps one of the few global locales where it is the EU that needs to learn to adapt rather than the regional partners of the EU.

In particular, the assumptions of superiority that have assisted Brussels in Europeanizing Eastern Europe (and the Western Balkans) do not have the same traction in Central Asia. Moreover, in Central Asia, the EU confronts itself with the reality where it not only is not a magnet for regional states, but also is in a situation where Brussels has to vie for the attention of awkward states that appear spoilt for choice by the many suitors participating in the "new great game." Thus, used to the security governance of post-Communist countries compliant with its normative power, the EU appears confused and uncertain by the lack of appeal of its values (Efegil, 2009, pp. 75–6). This is a qualitatively new condition for Brussels and its normative power—a situation, which appears to baffle the EU and one, which it still has not addressed convincingly.

The EU's relations with Central Asia: A strategic culture without normative power?

The EU's relations with Central Asia are part of the complex architecture of relations that Brussels is constructing in Asia. At the same time, the region has been involved in Brussels' interactions with the post-Soviet and post-Communist space. In this respect, the EU's engagement in the region cannot be divorced from the development and practice of its foreign policy in the post-Cold War period. In particular, it seems to conform to the general understanding that the ability of the EU's external relations to affect others is dependent upon its own awareness of a particular kind of self (Diez, 2005, p. 614). Thus, the socializing actorness of the EU depends not so much on its capabilities, but on the way it constructs the application of its normative power in particular global locales. As Henrik Larsen insists, focusing on the ways in which the EU perceives itself and its external roles is necessary for understanding "the dynamics of the EU's international relations" (Larsen, 2002, p. 286).

It appears that the current Central Asian engagements of the EU are intent on indicating its awareness of the diversity of Asia. As the then EU External Relations Commissioner, Chris Patten, has acknowledged, "Given the sprawling variety of Asia, it is absurd to think of a monolithic EU-Asia relationship."[15] For the EU, therefore, Central Asia is a piece of the puzzle that is Asia. Thus, its relations with the region aim to attest to Brussels' ongoing quest for appropriate roles and identities on the world stage.

Yet, in the jigsaw of the EU's Asian interactions, Central Asia does not seem to fit neatly with the other projects of Brussels. On the one hand, as already indicated, Central Asia has been gradually excluded from the EU's approaches to the other post-Soviet states—the region is neither part of the ENP initiatives, nor is it a partner to Brussels' relations with Russia. On the other hand, Central Asia is not included in the explicitly "Asian" initiatives of the EU—regional states are again involved neither in the Asia-Europe Meeting (ASEM), nor in Brussels' interactions with South Asia, Southeast Asia, and the Middle East. It would appear that Central Asia emerges as a ghost in the vacuum left between the network of these relationships.

Brussels insists that the positioning of Central Asia on the fringes of its other initiatives reflects the region's unique role as a *bridge*, with a "centuries-old tradition of bringing Europe and Asia together [because] it lies at a strategically important intersection between the two continents."[16] Central Asia, therefore, plays an important role in the articulation of the "Europeanness" of the EU's normative power as distinct from the Islamic world and, yet, maintaining a "special relationship" with it—a stance, which requires "a highly complex geopolitical as well as geo-cultural balancing act" (Smith, 2009, pp. 608–9).

However, the nuances of this balancing act appear lost and instead a more cynical view emerges—one which suggests that Central Asia is merely a bridge (if not—quite literally—a mere refueling station) between the EU's other and strategically more important commitments. Some commentators have noted that Central Asia emerges as either a "non-existent region, or as a merely forgotten one" (Delcour, 2011, p. 9). As Chapter 5 will demonstrate, such lack of attention from Brussels is a crucial contributing factor for the closer relationship of Central Asian states with China.[17]

In this respect, Central Asia appears to be excluded from the main EU initiatives for socialization. This seems to indicate that just as the EU perceives European regions with different intensity, similar logic informs its agency in Asia (Kavalski 2005a). As discussed in Chapter 3, the interactions between the dynamics of inclusion and exclusion outline regulatory mechanisms that are constitutive of a pattern of security governance. Mark Webber demonstrates that such exclusionary articulations have been a central feature of the "otherness" against which not only the European identity, but also the European security identity have been constructed (Webber, 2007, pp. 16). To put it differently, it is the notions of difference, fear, and danger implicit in the characterization of those excluded that project the EU's international identity as "not (only) threatened by the others, but also possible because of them" (Wæver, 1996, p. 127). Thus, in the case of Central Asia, exclusion clearly indicates that the region is not part of the same "community of fate" or "community of destiny" as that of the EU—that is, the two do not partake in a shared "we-ness" (a relationship of thick, interstate friendship characterized by shared values and trust).[18]

While similar patterns of exclusion are experienced by other international actors, what is unique about Central Asia is that it seems to be subject to an explicit *exclusionary* exclusion. In other words, while the EU practices exclusionary forms of security governance both as punishment and as setting examples (i.e. in both cases indicating the differentiation between those that comply with its standards and those that do not), these can be perceived as forms of *inclusive* exclusion—that is, those excluded are still subject to a form of socialization by the EU. For instance, to use the extreme case of Serbia during the Kosovo crisis, the choice put in front of Milosevic (to put it bluntly) was either "do as the West tells you" (and the concomitant rewards from inclusion in various programs as a result of such choice) or "we bomb you if you do not follow" (and the continued exclusion from international initiatives).[19] Thus, while excluded from the dynamics of Europeanization spanning the rest of the East European region, Serbia was still nevertheless subject to socialization by enforcement, which quite literally and explicitly set the norms of expected state behavior (and the desire for incorporating the country into the European "zone of peace").[20]

In contrast, while not pariahs like Serbia under Milosevic, the states of Central Asia are not subject to such inclusive forms of exclusion that recognizes the potential of the excluded to become part of the inside of the EU through (albeit) coercive modes of socialization into appropriate behavior. Instead, Brussels resorts to neither positive nor negative conditionality of the region (Warkotsch, 2006, p. 509). Some have even argued that owing to the violence accompanying the dissolution of former Yugoslavia, the relative stability of Central Asian states has turned the region into a *terra incognita* for the EU (Delcour, 2011, p. 92). And it is this lack of any form of (and seemingly desire for) socialization that defines the *exclusionary* exclusion through which the EU engages Central Asia. This puts the region in a peculiar situation vis-à-vis the other initiatives of Brussels in the post-Soviet space. It not only is situated as the "other" of the EU (by the sheer fact of its exclusion from the dynamics of socialization), but it is the "other" that is bound to remain the "other," because it cannot be included in the EU's zone of peace.[21]

It has long been suggested that both the "self-transforming" and "other-transforming" capabilities of the EU's security governance rest on the realization that "Europe's Other is Europe's own past which should not be allowed to become its future" (Wæver, 1996, p. 122). Thus, despite (if not because of) the territorial limitations on the project of European integration, Sergei Prozorov suggests that this logic of "temporal othering" intends the suspension of "the logic of sovereign territoriality by reconstructing the figure of the other, logically necessary for self-identification, in a reflexive manner that converts the antagonistic process of othering into a drive for self-transcendence." Yet, Prozorov notes that despite the temporal differentiation underpinning this logic of self-transcendence, the EU's security governance is not immune from the "ontopology of spatial othering." Hence, the position that difference is located temporally (internally) does not mean that it is not simultaneously located spatially (externally). For example, "by constructing Europe's past to be Others' present state. . . the past/present dichotomy maintains the distinction between inside versus outside." Hence, the dynamic of inclusion/exclusion of the EU's security governance "others spatially what it has othered temporally" by negating "the present existence of the spatial other" as something that "already 'belongs' to the past" (Prozorov, 2010, pp. 1274–85).[22]

Central Asia presents an idiosyncratic case of the temporal-spatial othering implicit in the EU's exercise of normative power. The region can be read as a version of Europe's past, whose future the EU does not seem interested in transforming and, therefore, does not mind leaving to the self-organizing forces and contexts of Central Asian politics. In a more radical attitude, Will Myer reads such distancing of the EU from the region as an evidence for its abdication of the "moral obligation" to make the Central Asian states behave in a "'European' manner" (Myer, 2002, pp. 224–7). The implication is that the EU's regional policies are clearly "not aimed at transforming [the Central Asian] others into like-minded liberal actors who deserve inclusion into the liberal democratic security community" (Gheciu, 2008, p. 59).

From the point of view of Brussels, therefore, the awkwardness of Central Asian countries is a sufficient condition to disqualify them (at least for the time being) from inclusion in the European society of states. That is, they are the kind of polities that the EU will neither consider as targets for meaningful and, more importantly, deliberate socialization, nor feel the "moral" compulsion to Europeanize. Hence, the encounter with the strangeness/otherness of Central Asia has not urged the EU to reflect upon (let alone question) its own normativity.

Perhaps, not surprisingly, such *exclusionary* exclusion appears to have simplified the EU's relations with the region. Usually, as indicated in Figure 1, the interactions of Brussels with other actors are subject to a double tension: first, whether it is going to resort to its enlargement or foreign policy approaches; and, second, whether it is going to engage countries individually (through bilateral relations) or as part of a regional grouping with neighboring states. Depending on the way in which the EU structures its relations with other countries, several possible options have been thrown up to it, each of which impacts on the prospective trajectories of the Europeanization project.

As Figure 1 indicates, in terms of introducing compliance with the EU's norms and standards—and, thereby, ensuring effective security governance—it is the bilateral relationship of accession-driven conditionality that seems to deliver the desired outcomes. This observation reflects that the effectiveness of the EU's security governance is based on explicit contractual conditionality rather than regionality. Thus, it is the bilateral relations of accession that put decision-makers of target states in a position in which they are "forced to choose" between the advantages of membership and the disadvantages of noncompliance (i.e. exclusion).[23] In this context, "we-ness" with the EU takes precedence over "we-ness" among applicants (although a sense of shared fate is, nevertheless, constructed).

	ENLARGEMENT	FOREIGN POLICY
BILATERAL	High degree of Europeanization Example: The preaccession conditionality for the new East European Member States; and the ongoing socialization of the Western Balkan states under the Stabilization and Association Process	Weak to moderate degree of Europeanization Example: Russia
REGIONAL	Moderate to weak degree of Europeanization Example: The Western Balkan states under the Stability Pact for South Eastern Europe; *(enlargement-like)* ENP Black Sea Synergy/Eastern Partnership countries	Weak degree of Europeanization Example: The Central Asian states; ENP Mediterranean Dialogue countries.

Figure 1 *The double tension of EU's external affairs.*

On the opposite end of available options are the EU's regional strategies developed under the purview of its external affairs. Such approaches seem to offer the least promising scenarios for effective Europeanization, because they are underpinned by little (if any) of the EU's normative power. For instance, the countries of the Western Balkans were subject to this kind of relationship for the better part of the 1990s. Therefore, their falling behind their East European neighbors in the process of accession is not least an outcome of the way they were engaged by Brussels. However, as the case of the Western Balkan states indicates, it is not impossible for post-Communist states to catch up with the Europeanization process by moving from a regional foreign policy approach to a relationship structured by the contractual bilateralism of enlargement.

It needs to be reminded here that Figure 1 depicts ideal types, rather than the complexities and nuances of each instance. For instance, the case of the ENP countries offers a good indication of the fuzziness of the borders established by the double tension of the EU's foreign policy formulation. On the one hand, the countries participating in the Black Sea Synergy/Eastern Partnership programs are part of a nearly *enlargement-like* socialization dynamic, which clearly sets them apart from the other participants of the ENP.[24] This opens the potential for the further differentiation among the Black Sea Synergy/Eastern Partnership participants (according to their compliance with EU norms), which might eventually see some of them develop contractual bilateral relations of accession with Brussels. On the other hand, the interactions of the ENP's Mediterranean Dialogue reflect much weaker forms of Europeanization. Yet, in terms of security governance, the EU is clearly engaging them in the deliberate practice of interaction, which with time (and depending on circumstances), might evolve into a fully fledged community of practice.[25]

Yet, as indicated, owing to the kind of *exclusionary* exclusion practiced by the EU in Central Asia, the region seems to have been spared the experience of Brussels' double tension outlined in Figure 1. Instead, the EU's approach appears to switch between the bilateral and regional points of the foreign policy pendulum. Enlargement (or an enlargement-like project) is clearly not on the cards for the region. That is why the claim here is that this situation simplifies the EU's foreign policy formulation in Central Asia. Some commentators have argued that this context makes it "easier" for Brussels to engage Central Asia as it is "free from having to think where the borders of Europe lie, with all of the constraints this question imposes on EU thinking and action" (Matveeva, 2006, p. 8). Others insist that the clear positioning of Central Asia outside the purview of enlargement (i.e. outside of the borders of an even extended or wider Europe) has meant that Brussels is not perceived as a serious threat by both external and regional actors (Efegil, 2009, p. 83).

Nevertheless, while easier in terms of formulation and despite encountering low threat perceptions, the absence of the enlargement option (and the resultant *exclusionary* exclusion) has handicapped the EU's security governance of the post-Soviet states of Central Asia. In practice, this has left the EU with the option to insist on the internalization of certain norms of appropriateness by regional states (as demanded by its strategic culture), however, without the support of its normative power (as exemplified by its various instruments for socialization). Thus, the EU's engagement in Central Asia has been spotty at best. Brussels seems to approach the region from the point of view of its geographic distance and as such, its policies have remained largely reactive. The following sections outline the two broad periods of the EU's foreign policy engagements in the region.

Post-Cold War reticence of the 1990s

There is an almost universal unanimity among observers that Central Asia barely registered on the radar of the external relations of the EU during the

1990s. The region did not seem to have its champion among the Member States. Some have even maintained that the EU has been unsure from the very beginning of how to apply its normative power in the region (ICG, 2006). Central Asia was merely bundled within the moral imperative guiding "the alliance of industrial democracies. . . to solidify basic change in the principles of international order" (Russett, 1993, p. 138).

The reticence that marks the EU's engagement in Central Asia during the 1990s is probably one of the clearest indications of the difficulty for both sides of the Cold War divide to alter their cognitive patterns and conceptual vocabulary carefully groomed during the decades of antagonism and confrontation. In this respect, the inability of Brussels to develop closer relations with Central Asia is not that distinct from its relations with other post-Soviet spaces owing to its unwillingness to dabble into the "Russian sphere of influence."[26] In other words, the EU anticipated that a potentially more active engagement in Central Asia might be perceived as threatening by Russia (and thus invite unwanted attention to issues of hard security). Hence, its assistance to Central Asia (and the rest of the post-Soviet space) has been couched under Technical Assistance to the Commonwealth of Independent States (TACIS) program.[27]

The claim here is that the unwillingness of Brussels to extend a more assertive approach to Central Asia reflects the uncertainty and confusion about the post-Cold War character of its roles and identity. This has been largely underwritten by its own uncertainty of how to develop its agency in the region. Almost from the beginning of their post-Soviet transitions, the EU has insisted that it is the OSCE—rather than Brussels—that will have to function as the primary institution for the security governance of Central Asian states (Warkotsch, 2006, p. 515). Moreover, a significant part of the programs that it developed under the TACIS programming was implemented together not only with the OSCE, but also with the United Nations Development Program (UNDP), the International Organization for Migration (IOM), and other international actors. These developments provided a clear indication of a "weak commitment" and hinted that the region is "off the EU radar screen" (Delcour, 2011, p. 94).

Thus, perhaps not unsurprisingly, the EU's engagement in Central Asia during the 1990s is in many respects reminiscent of the foreign policy strategies of Brussels toward the Western Balkans (prior to the articulation of the terms of the post-1999 European order). In its relations with the two post-Communist regions during the 1990s, the EU adopted a reactive (mostly *ad hoc*) approach of providing humanitarian assistance and demanding peaceful interstate relations without the application of a socialization project. Consequently, one of the most conspicuous legacies of this period is the construction of Central Asia as *outside the EU area of responsibility*. Such an exclusionary approach has led Simon Duke to label the EU's reluctance to develop more proactive and flexible external affairs roles as "a *reverse-realist* paradigm," where instead of competition for power and influence, there is an attempt to *avoid* positions of leadership and responsibility (Duke, 1994, p. 94).

These attitudes are reflected in the TACIS programming, which emerged during this period as the EU's main initiative for the post-Soviet space. The self-proclaimed objective of TACIS has been to "encourage democratization, the strengthening of the rule of law and the transition to a market economy in the New Independent States (NIS), created as a result of the break-up of the Soviet Union."[28] In line with the terms of the post-1999 European order, the EU reinforced these aims by developing Partnership and Cooperation Agreements (PCAs) that were intent to enhance its visibility in Central Asia. However, the PCAs seem to provide annual fora for interaction between the EU and Central Asian states, which do not seem to be accompanied by any project or process of deliberate practice of socialization. Thence, the EU has not managed to initiate even a nascent community of practice in the region. These developments reassert the pervasive ambivalence of Brussels' agency in Central Asia during the 1990s, which has remained a hallmark of its involvement in the region.

Post-2001 assertive stance

The terrorist attacks of 11 September 2001 (hereafter, 9/11) in the United States did not seem to undermine the validity of the terms of the post-1999 European order. On the contrary, they appear to have reinforced the EU's resolve and commitment to the project of European integration (Kavalski, 2005b). Nevertheless, the events of 9/11 have intensified the discussions of Brussels' engagement in "out-of-Europe" areas. There has been greater attention to the EU's interactions with regions that are not subject to enlargement initiatives (and enlargement-like projects such as the ENP). It is in this context that the EU has articulated its first ever *European Security Strategy* (*ESS*) and has initiated a comprehensive constitutionalizing process, which concluded with the ratification of the Lisbon Treaty in 2009. According to Gheciu, these transformations indicate a qualitative change of outlook—the EU's security governance has become increasingly preoccupied with "controlling the processes by which vulnerable societies slide towards the wrong camp." At the same time, the practices of socialization extended by Brussels have intended the "redefinition" of target states "as protectors of the EU and of modern civilization" (Gheciu, 2008, p. 53).

In this respect, 9/11—at least discursively—has also marked a "new beginning" for the EU's relations with Central Asia. It needs to be pointed out that such a shift in attention to the region (as well as approach to external affairs) mirrors a conspicuous "disaster mentality" that frames the decision-making purview of Brussels. For instance, it was the potential threat from a "second Srebrenica"—that is, the likelihood of another round of ethnic cleansing, this time in Kosovo—rather than the fact that it occurred in the first place, which led the EU to articulate the terms of the post-1999 European order. The inference is that the EU is unlikely to react to a gradual decline into authoritarianism, but to seemingly unexpected and egregious violations of human rights and democratic principles (Warkotsch, 2006, p. 518; Youngs, 2002, p. 22). Likewise, its engagement in Central Asia was prodded by an attempt to prevent a "second 9/11" from occurring.

While not unique to the EU, such a reactive "disaster mentality" in foreign policy reveals the influence of failure (as opposed to success) in changing the international behavior of actors. Thus,

> Outcomes that are consistent with expectations and achieve one's goals generate few incentives for a change in beliefs, whereas unexpected results and those that fall short of one's goals are more likely to trigger a change in beliefs and policy. Thus, the most likely outcomes to trigger learning are failures that were either unexpected at the time or unpredictable in retrospect. (Levy, 1994, p. 305)

In this respect, both the 1999 Kosovo crisis and 9/11 can be viewed as "failures" that demanded from the EU a change in its external roles, so that its normative power can maintain its relevance. However, there has been very little—if any—inquiry into the strategic culture that frames the EU's normative power. In this respect, while crises are very effective at provoking change, by definition, "the wake up call comes too late" (Johnson and Madin, 2008, p. 221). In a similar way, the EU's Central Asian agency had to confront itself with the need to initiate a much belated change of its external relations. Regardless of the alterations (already undertaken and projected), Brussels still remains disconnected from the region. The reason for this is that the changes in the Central Asian agency of the EU are still mainly in form, not in substance.

In practical terms, therefore, while not a "formative event," 9/11 has reinforced Brussels' perception that the most imminent threats to the security of an increasingly globalizing and complex world are not traditional military threats but rather "threats emanating from under or above the state, and enhanced by the web of interdependence among states today" (Press-Barnathan, 2005, p. 296). Nevertheless, 9/11 has provoked a soul-searching debate whether "a 'civilized' Europe [can] survive in a largely 'uncivilized' world" (Zielonka, 2004, p. 156). As Bertie Ahern, the then president of the European Council, insisted, "Terrorism is not just undemocratic. It is anti-democratic. *It is not just inhuman. It is an affront to humanity.* It runs counter to all the values on which the EU is founded."[29]

Thus, there have been different responses to the query into what are the appropriate ways for a *civilized* actor—such as the EU—to respond to terrorism (Smith, 2009, p. 605). In policy terms, it has provoked the "hardening" of the discourses on the EU's normative power. According to Robert Cooper, the Director-General for the EU's External and Politico-Military Affairs, such "hardening" is demanded by the imperative to compel conformity with EU norms among actors unable to respond to other incentives, but raw power: "Among ourselves we keep the law, but when we are operating in the jungle, we must also use the laws of the jungle" (Cooper, 2002). Thus, the post-9/11 invasions in Afghanistan and Iraq have backstopped the EU's re-engagement in the Central Asian "jungle." According to the *ESS*,

> The most recent wave of terrorism is linked to violent religious extremism. It arises out of complex causes. These include the pressures of modernization, cultural, social and political crisis, and the alienation of young people living in foreign societies. . . Thus neighbors who are engaged in violent conflict, weak states where organized crime flourishes, dysfunctional societies or exploding population growth all pose problems. . . Taking these different elements together. . .we could be confronted with a very radical threat indeed.[30]

Central Asia appears to straddle the root causes of such threats and the EU's attempt at the security governance of the region intends their containment. To that effect in 2002, the EU advanced the rudiments of a far-reaching and comprehensive policy tailored specifically to the five Central Asian states under the aegis of separate Regional Strategy Paper (RSP).[31] Furthermore, in terms of increasing its visibility, in 2005, the EU appointed its own Special Representative (EUSR) to Central Asia.[32] The appointment of the EUSR, while long time coming, coincided with the violent suppression of civilian protests in Andijan by Uzbek government troops. It, therefore, seemed to further reinforce the perception of a "disaster mentality" underpinning the decision-making of Brussels by yet again making important changes to its Central Asian policy seemingly in reaction to a specific crisis on the ground.

Some commentators have pointed out that the appointment of the EUSR indicated the activation of the ESDP in Central Asia (Matveeva, 2006, p. 92). The EUSR's prerogatives are quite extensive:

> To *follow* political developments in Central Asia by developing and maintaining close contacts with governments, parliaments, judiciary, civil society, and mass media; *encourage* the countries to cooperate on regional issues of common interest; *develop* contacts and cooperation with the main interested actors in the region; *contribute*, in close cooperation with the OSCE, to conflict prevention and resolution by developing contacts with the authorities and other local actors; *promote* overall political coordination of the Union in Central Asia and *ensure* consistency of the external actions of the Union without prejudice to Community competence; *assist* the Council in further developing a comprehensive policy towards Central Asia.[33]

The EUSR activities have been framed by the ongoing evolution of the RSP initiative—the first RSP (2002–06) and the second RSP (2007–13). The latter is administered by the new Development Cooperation and Economic Cooperation Instrument (DCECI), which came to substitute the TACIS program.[34] The RSP initiative has to indicate that the EU is recognizing the idiosyncrasies of the five Central Asian states as well as the need to project distinct and contextual policies in the region. Intent on reinforcing its commitment to Central Asia, during the German presidency of the European Council, the EU launched its *Strategy for a New Partnership* with the region. This new strategy reiterates the EU's "strong interest in a peaceful, democratic, and economically prosperous Central Asia." Yet, as already indicated, it perpetuates the unquestioning promotion of the norms of the EU's strategic culture. Hence, Brussels is explicit that

> The development of a stable political framework and functioning economic structures are dependent on respect for the rule of law, human rights, good governance, and the development of transparent, democratic political structures. . . [Such a] task calls for the active involvement of civil society. A developed and active civil society and independent media are vital for the development of a pluralistic civil society. The EU will cooperate with Central Asian states to this end and promote enhanced exchanges in civil society.[35]

Such articulations suggest that even though the EU does not intend the same level of integration with Central Asia as it did in other post-Communist areas, Brussels still anticipates that its regional outreach will provide sufficient leverage to push for democratic reforms that would lead to political pluralism and social modernization (Efegil, 2009, p. 84). To that effect, the EU has explicitly indicated that 70% of its regional assistance will be directed at programs for bilateral assistance.[36] In fact, the EU itself has stressed the "special importance" of establishing bilateral relations with Central Asian states.[37] This appears to resolve the perennial tension of the EU's initiatives in Central Asia—whether to develop a regional approach or to engage the five Central Asian states individually through bilateral contractual relations. The preference for the latter promises the emergence of tangible forms of socialization that might assist the internalization of EU standards.

However, the majority of commentators have noted that the EU has taken "a sound, but belated step to boost its political role in Central Asia" (Matveeva, 2006, p. 95). Thus, confirming the seemingly unreflective nature of its actorness, Brussels' post-9/11 involvement in the region seems to have ignored the "systemic reality" of Central Asia, which belies its lack of "instinctive understanding of its political system" (Lewis, 2008, pp. 25–6). For instance, the prioritization of stability by Central Asian state-elites appears to clash with the EU's demand for democratization. As Stephen Blank maintains, regional elites resist European pressures to reform because they fear a "deconcentralization" of their power. He even brands the EU's talk of democratization as a "triumph of hope over experience. . . [which] amounts to a call for a revolutionary transformation" (Blank, 2004, p. 133–40). A trend that appeared to be confirmed by the results from the October 2010 election in Kyrgyzstan.

In fact, the alleged shift in the EU's attention to the region in the wake of 9/11 does not seem to have altered the "reverse-realist paradigm" of its Central Asian approach during the 1990s. As the High Representative for the CFSP, Javier Solana insisted at the time, the EU's "main priority is the Balkans and how to bring them closer to the EU. . . [At the same time] we have to start rethinking our policy towards the 'Stans'. This means cooperating with other *international organizations* to tackle the huge problems facing them."[38] Confirming this detached attitude, the EUSR for Central Asia, Pierre Morel, has gone on record to state that "We think that it is better to act together [through] coordination among international structures, which we consider to be the most efficient method" (Morel, 2010).

At the same time, confirming the perception that Brussels' preoccupation with internal processes prevents the EU from playing a global role, the office of the EUSR to the region is notoriously understaffed and underfunded (ICG, 2005, p. 18). To complicate matters further, on 25 September 2008, Pierre Morel was given the additional portfolio of EUSR for the crisis in Georgia.[39] Such developments provide support for the allegations of a convivial tension (if not clash) between the EU's "normative values" and its "interests," which stalls Brussels' overall agency in Central Asia (Myer, 2002, p. 230). The tension is an outcome of the pervasive absence of a deliberate practice for the security governance of the region.

Thus, despite the alterations in perception, just like with its 1990s' engagement, the EU's involvement in Central Asia is primarily through resolutions that criticize what-Brussels-deems-to-be inappropriate developments (Matveeva, 2006, p. 91). Such a trend has urged some to suggest that the EU's normatively underpinned foreign policy strategies are merely a distraction from the confrontation with "the reality of Europe's provincialization in world politics [that] constitutes a bordered international site" (Postel-Vinay, 2008, p. 47). The very conspicuous failure to link the EU's demands for reform in Central Asian states to any meaningful dynamic of socialization indicates that the EU is far short of conceptualizing (let alone validating) the role of its normative power in the region.

Conclusion

The overview of the cognitive frameworks of the EU's relations with Central Asia provided in this chapter indicates Brussels' struggle to articulate not merely a "new" strategy for its relations with the region, but more generally an effective external affairs strategy which will be able to extend its normative power outside the framework of enlargement (or enlargement-like) initiatives. In particular, what appears striking about the EU's agency in Central Asia is the consistent lack of deliberate practice of security governance. The absence of initiatives that engage regional states in the deliberate practice of regular interactions with Brussels undercuts the EU's ability to make an impact on Central Asian affairs.

As indicated in Part I, the transformation of awkward states is a complex endeavor, which does not occur without the deliberate practice of interaction. Thus, rather than building relationships in Central Asia through security governance mechanisms (such as ASEM for instance), Brussels appears content to demand compliance with the norms and values of its strategic culture, but without offering any credible commitments for building meaningful relationships with regional actors. This suggests a lack of purpose, deliberate effort, and motivation. It also demonstrates the conscious exclusion of Central Asia from the post-Cold War socializing project whose narrative is premised on the conviction that all post-Communist entities "could and should aspire towards a liberal democratic identity" (Gheciu, 2008, p. 13). The EU, therefore, emerges as both unable and unwilling to extend a meaningful practice of socialization to the region. This, in turn, prevents it from becoming a fully fledged normative power in Central Asia.

Instead, the EU emerges as a "bit player"—an actor with a very limited impact and leverage on Central Asian affairs (increasingly even in trade issues).[40] The concluding chapter of this book returns to this point and explains that the EU is prevented to play a more significant role in the region because its position of authority is not *recognized* by Central Asian actors. In particular, the restrictions on the exercise of the EU's normative power that emerge in its regional security governance appear to be tied to the "logic of appropriateness" of its strategic culture. As a result, the EU's security governance is constrained by assumptions about what the process of socialization *should* look like rather than the specific environment for and practices of its application. Thus, while in the context of post-Cold War Europe, such an approach to security governance has worked (because of a unique confluence between ontopology and contingency), its relevance to "out-of-Europe" areas—such as Central Asia—is still underdeveloped.

Brussels' relations with Central Asia demonstrate that owing to the interactive pattern of world affairs, normative powers are not identified merely by the rules and norms underpinning their agency, but are also "dependent upon the practices of mutual recognition" (Murray, 2008, p. 250). The magnetism of the EU's agency in Central Asia is dependent upon regional understandings of "what is awe-inspiring, what is morally compelling, and what is attractive" (Bially-Mattern, 2005, p. 23). Of course, the EU is not a passive recipient of such recognition by others—that is, recognition is socially constructed in the process of intersubjective interactions. Thence, the prospective roles of Brussels in the region depend on the "translatability" of the EU's security governance to the experience and context of the Central Asian states—which demand not a mere change of institutions and policies (i.e. changes in form), but an alteration in the discursive and cognitive structures that frame them (i.e. changes in substance).[41] In other words, if the EU wants to be taken seriously in the region, it needs to develop a deliberate practice for its security governance and be prepared to maintain it in the long run.

The claim—and also the response to the question with which this chapter began—is that the EU's normative power in Central Asia is *constrained* rather than *catalyzed* by its strategic culture. A policy change that would allow Brussels a more visible presence in the region—for instance, by either accepting to work with (rather than reform) the awkwardness of Central Asian states or partnering with China (rather than the OSCE)—will be a serious test for the cognitive frameworks of its normative power. In this respect, the EU's search for a "new" strategy not only in Central Asia, but also in its external affairs (beyond enlargement and enlargement-like initiatives) demands a serious reflection upon the impact of its own normativity. Without such questioning, the EU is unlikely to emerge as a viable normative power beyond the geographical confines of Europe and its immediate neighborhood.[42] Thus, paraphrasing Brussels' own language, it will not be sufficient that the EU "works actively" in Central Asia for its security governance strategy to have regional effects, but that it actively engages Central Asian states in the deliberate practice of socialization.

5

Shanghaied into cooperation? Framing the Central Asian agency of China

After the Cold War, commentators began pondering how far Western ideas can/would spread in a geopolitical environment characterized by "the end of history." Today, the debate seems to be how far Chinese ideas will spread. Such a shift in observation has been significantly impacted by the nascent practices of China's security governance. It would appear, therefore, that Beijing's agency offers a meaningful alternative to Western models of international relations—"the first promising formula for state-led, third-world development" (Puchala, 2003, p. 71). The susceptibility of Central Asian states to Beijing's agency seems to be credibly confirmed by the establishment of the Shanghai Cooperation Organization (SCO) in 2001. In fact, such capacity to engage the region has urged some Western commentators to declare China as "the [Central Asian] hegemon in waiting" (Blank, 2005), while Chinese observers have suggested that Beijing enjoys "structural power" in the region (Song, 2011, p. 52).[1]

This chapter engages in a contextual analysis of China's international interactions with Central Asia. The focus on Beijing's fledgling normative power indicates that regions do not exist merely as material objects indicated by their behavioral dimension, but also as constructs that are imagined and can bend to the efforts of political entrepreneurs (Katzenstein and Sil, 2004, p. 24). China's security governance of Central Asia acknowledges that the international relations of the region need to be understood as fractures into spaces whose ramifications are delineated not only by territorial boundaries, but also by social relations and their sociological, cultural, and (eco-)historical nexus of reference (Alagappa, 1998). The intention of this chapter is to demonstrate that China's emergence as the major economic partner of Central Asia is not merely because of its alleged counterpoise simultaneously to Russia, the West, and the Islamic world (Rashid, 1994, p. 223),[2] but its normative power. In fact, it is this normative power that has made possible Beijing's influence in the region. China's engagements in Central Asia demonstrate an understanding that material incentives without deliberate relationships do not produce socializing effects.

Thus, by synthesizing the literature on Asian international relations and, in particular, by contextualizing its insights to recent trends in Central Asia, this chapter identifies the main elements of China's involvement in the region—Beijing's "normative power" and its "socializing" propensities. As the analysis of China's strategic culture in the following section demonstrates, Beijing's international agency is not (exclusively) about *balancing against* the power or the threats posed by others, but about building partnerships (Feng, 2007, p. 4). The discussion of SCO will reveal the flair, skill, and adaptability of China's regional diplomacy. In fact, SCO's multilateral framework has already suggested "an embryonic form of a community of practice that embodies China's new security concept" (Paltiel, 2009, p. 51). This proposition intimates the interpretive modes of China's security governance of Central Asia through SCO. The following analysis, therefore, not only brings into focus the norms and values of China's foreign policy, but also reconsiders their import to the cognitive structures of the field of international relations.

The strategic culture of Beijing's normative power

China's expanding outreach and diversifying roles have provided a novel context for the ongoing reconsiderations of world politics. Beijing's international engagements draw attention because of its agency, rather than the specificities of its particular policies. Such setting, therefore, beckons the discussion of the "socializing" propensities and the "normative power" underwriting China's emergent security governance practices. As already indicated in the introductory chapter, the engagement with China's agency in Central Asia calls attention to the issue of the capacity for parallel assessment of what is still an essentially "western" international relations theory.[3] The challenge, thereby, is not only to the epistemological foundations of the discipline, but also, as Jeremy Paltiel has cogently observed, to the very ontological assumptions of world politics. As he indicates, while the western field of observation assumes order to be the opposite of chaos, the Chinese strategic outlook contrasts chaos with harmony. According to Paltiel, this distinction reflects the centrality of *immanence* rather than *transcendence* in Chinese political thought. In other words, chaos and harmony are not in a dualistic opposition to each other (in the sense that chaos and order are in EIR), but reveal a complex rhizomatic relationship of "differential association" (Paltiel, 2009, pp. 57–8).

This distinct point of departure complicates the confrontation with the patterns of China's security governance (not only in Central Asia) by proliferating differing opinions on the normative practices that underpin it. Not surprisingly, at the heart of this debate is the interpretation of the content and intention of Chinese strategic culture. As hinted by Akira Iriye in the wake of the 1970s' Sino-American "ping pong diplomacy," one of the difficulties for grasping China's international outlook has been the traditional overlap between the notions of "power" and "culture," and their treatment as "virtually synonymous and interchangeable. . . Since culture was power, one had to transform the former in order to eliminate the latter" (Iriye, 1979, p. 118).

It has to be acknowledged that current attempts to come to terms with the cognitive structure of China's international agency are further complicated by Beijing's own attempt to "rethink China" and its global role(s) (Zhang, 2009, p. 31).[4] This reconsideration has been closely intertwined with the re-articulation of China's *guoqing* (national peculiarities) (Barmé, 1999, p. 18).[5] Xiaoyuan Liu stresses that an important idiosyncracy of China's strategic culture is its vacillating "historical temperament:" on the one hand, the legalist tradition decrees "befriend the remote and attack the near," while, on the other hand, Confucius teaches "delight the near and attack the remote." Commenting on the contradictory messages of these strategic instructions, Liu concludes that "in modern times, such a complex and long historical experience can be either a treasure or a burden to Chinese leaders" (Liu, 2009, p. 295). Consequently, such a dynamic analytical environment has prompted (at least) three distinct readings of China's strategic culture: offensive, pacifist, and defensive.

The offensive view is mostly associated with the work of Alistair Iain Johnston, who insists on the hard *realpolitik* tendencies of Chinese strategic behavior (Johnston, 1995, p. 55). He, thereby, propounds that Beijing's external agency cannot be divorced from the historical predilection toward a "*parabellum* strategic culture," whose cognitive frameworks have been successfully internalized by Chinese decision-makers and reveal a "preference for offensive uses of force, mediated by a keen sensitivity to relative capabilities" (Johnston, 1996, p. 217). This interpretation of Chinese strategic culture has buttressed the "China-threat" narrative, whose discourses portend that Beijing's growing stature in international trade is going to backstop the political and military emergence of an increasingly aggressive and hegemonic attitude (Mearsheimer, 2001, p. 402).[6]

The pacifist view is located on the opposite end of the continuum of perspectives on Chinese strategic culture. While this point of view does not have a principal spokesperson, its proponents are in agreement on two issues. First, the offensive perception of Chinese strategic culture is an outcome of the tendency to overemphasize Chinese proclivity to use force. Such a trend has produced an obviation of the historical reluctance to engage in military action in preference for the cultivation of "cultural appeal" and "social capital" through persuasion and negotiations (Feng, 2007, p. 25). Second, despite assertions to the contrary, China has acted (and continues to do so) as a *status quo* actor engaged in maintaining (rather than revising) the international system (Loke, 2009, p. 201). In this context, China has not only tended to comply with the rules of the international society, but also that it has been a meaningful participant in "the organic process of change, evolution, and decay in the international system" (Kent, 2007, p. 3).[7]

Finally, the defensive perspective on Chinese strategic culture argues that the bellicose and the pacific strands are operational features that influence its cognitive frameworks and contribute to the dialectic "Chinese Cult of Defence" (Scobell, 2001, 2002). Hiuyun Feng argues that this dualism between "*wen* (civilization or culture) and *wu* (war, force, or military)"—underpinning the pacifist and offensive views on Chinese strategic culture—has produced "a unique strategic culture, which is more peaceful and non-violent than the realpolitik Western one." In this respect, Feng asserts that the defensive perspective, while distinct, has intellectual affiliation with the pacifist rather than the offensive proposition (Feng, 2007, pp. 23–5).

It has to be stressed that despite their differences, all the three perspectives on Chinese strategic culture derive their provenance and legitimacy from a shared intellectual pool—Chinese philosophical traditions (especially, Confucianism). It is for this reason that an increasing number of Chinese commentators and policy-makers have heeded President Hu Jintao's recommendation for enhancing the cultural soft power of China.[8] As Hu put it, culture is becoming a "more and more important source of national cohesion and creativity, and a factor of growing significance in the competition in overall national strength. . . We must enhance culture as part of the soft power of our country to better guarantee the people's basic cultural rights and interests."[9]

Thus, regardless of whether they subscribe to an offensive, pacific, or defensive stance, the proponents of all the three perspectives assert that Chinese strategic culture is informed by the legacy of traditional worldviews (and in particular Confucian principles). According to Jiawen Ai, this is the gist of the monograph *Cultural Power* (*Wen Hua Li*) written by Gao Zhanxian, a former official in the Ministry of Culture. Gao's contention is that the recovery of traditional values is "more fundamental and essential than political values and foreign policies" (cited in Ai, 2011, pp. 103–5). This is an important observation as it demonstrates the significance of the Confucian cognitive framing to the ongoing re-articulation of China's perceptions of international order, self-identity, and global role(s) (Loke, 2009, p. 201). In fact, paraphrasing Confucius himself, some commentators ascertain that Chinese policy-makers can be perceived as "co-worker[s] with antiquity" (Ford, 2010, p. 17.[10] Such contextualization has urged even Beijing to begin reflecting upon the implication of its enhanced international actorness. There have been two key aspects to such explorations.

On the one hand, as Nicola Spakowski demonstrates, China has been keen to learn from the experience of previous "great powers." Using the example of the popular TV-documentary series on *The Rise of Great Powers*, which was commissioned by the Chinese Communist Party and focused on the nine "world powers since the fifteenth century" (Portugal, Spain, Holland, Great Britain, France, Germany, Japan, Russia/the USSR, and the USA), Spakowski uncovers the plurality of norms and views in China on both "the criteria for historical 'greatness'" and "the major ingredients of a rise to a great power status." He interprets the popularity of the documentary and the extensive public debate which it has provoked as part of a broader fascination with the lessons that China can learn as the "potential tenth 'great power'" (Spakowski, 2009, pp. 485–9).

On the other hand, the reflexivity animating China's international agency has been much more introspective and has tended to focus on China's own historical recollection. In this respect, the lessons that are gleaned are not only from the experience of other international actors, but also from the legacy of China's past glory (Zhang, 2009, p. 31). In this respect, the patterns of China's security governance present an intriguing intersection of the discursive memory of the past with the contexts of the present and the anticipated tasks of the future. It is the dynamics of such a complex introspection that underpin the emergence of the so-called Beijing Consensus. Positioned in contrast to the "widely-discredited Washington Consensus,"

> China's new development approach is. . . flexible enough that it is barely classifiable as a doctrine. It does not believe in uniform solutions for every situation. It is defined by a ruthless willingness to innovate and experiment, by a lively defense of national borders and interests, and by the increasingly thoughtful accumulation of tools of asymmetric power projection. . . Change, newness, and innovation are the essential words of power in this consensus. (Ramo, 2004, pp. 3–6)

In this setting, China's introspective look recollects a security governance approach premised on the practices of interaction rather than explicit norms of appropriateness. That is why the influential public intellectual and commentator Hu Angang has argued for the substitution of the label "Beijing Consensus" with the "Beijing Proposal." According to him, the latter term offers a better illustration of the relational character of China's security governance. As Hu suggests, the significance of such renaming is that

> The expression *Beijing Consensus* implies that China is imposing its way on others. If anything, it should be known as the *Beijing Proposal*. Other countries can choose whether or not they would like to accept it. In addition, they may accept it wholesale or accept it only in part. (Hu, 2011, p. 7)

The dialogical nature of such governance strategy has had significant implications for the exercise of China's normative power. As evidenced by its relations with Central Asia, China places a particular emphasis on its experience of modernization as an important feature of the discourses and practices of its security governance. The conviction is that as a successful late-developing country, Beijing might become a model for others to follow (Spakowski, 2009, p. 489). This inference has also been impacted by the introspective query into the legacy of its former glory. In particular, it has projected an understanding that China's unique experience should not be inflicted upon others by force, but by making Beijing attractive to them. Hiuyun Feng argues that this attitude is an outcome of current re-engagements with Confucian philosophy in China, according to which "to seek domination by force will simply turn the world against you. . . [only] the benevolent one has no enemy" (Feng, 2007, p. 21).

Jeremy Paltiel (2009), therefore, insists that the reflexive engagement with China's global agency has led to an examination of the "prescriptive obligations of power-holders." He argues that unlike Western preoccupations with legal and material constraints on power, the Chinese normative framework "has no stronger sanction than 'shame' and the prudential constraint of reputational costs that may involve the potential loss of leadership and the promotion of resistance to those in power." For instance, China's attempt to suppress a UN report on the use of Chinese bullets against UN personnel in Darfur can be read in this context.[11] Paltiel, thereby, illuminates the complex pattern of Chinese security governance as a forum for reassuring others about Beijing's intentions and in the process building up social capital through the shared practices of interaction (Paltiel, 2009, p. 54).

Thus, by reflecting upon the cognitive frameworks of its strategic behavior, Beijing has been gradually developing its distinct practice of security governance. In this context, Brantly Womack argues that the exercise of

China's normative power reflects the legacy of a "tremendous self-discipline" (Womack, 2008, p. 268). His analysis offers probably the most convincing study of the socializing propensities of China's strategic culture. Womack singles out "respect for the other" as the "cardinal virtue" of Beijing's security governance. Thus, by lavishing attention to countries "that normally do not get much respect," China sets itself as a different kind of actor (if not necessarily as an alternative model). Taking his cue from the realization that "all actors, international or individual, are located actors," Womack suggests that "they move within a framework of possible actions that is given meaning by their history, their resources, and their judgment of those with whom they are interacting." In this respect, Beijing's insistence on "respect for the other" becomes an important boon for its normative power:

> In a world of equals, each is in a similar situation, and each can respond in kind to the actions of others. With symmetry, respect for others can be reduced to the Golden Rule, because in fact others can do to you what you do to them. In a world of asymmetric relationships, respect—appreciation for the situation and autonomy of the other—requires special attention. Respect for the weaker side is not simply noblesse oblige or an act of generosity of the stronger. The weaker can only afford to be deferential to the strong when they feel that their identity and boundaries will be respected. (Womack, 2008, pp. 294–7)

The emphasis on *respect for the other* draws attention to China's social roles in global life. Actorness in this respect is necessarily contextual—Chinese (especially Confucian) traditions assert that definitions of the "normal" are particularistic (and, thus contingent) and depend on "who we are interacting with, and when" (Rosemont, 2006, p. 14).[12] Beverley Loke intuits this relationship by accentuating the interaction between "national interest" and "national responsibility" evidenced by the practices of Beijing's security governance. As she insists, the construction of international agency around respect for the other prompts the realization that "both to interpret others' behavior and to design one's own behavior so that others will draw the desired conclusions from it, the actor must try to see the world the way the other sees it."[13] Loke, thereby, infers that the sense and practice of responsibility is not only "tied to one's position of power" (i.e. the actor's "rank within international society"), but also constituted by it (Loke, 2009, p. 203).

This inference brings us back to Brantly Womack, who proposes that unlike the normative power of the EU which is framed by the "logic of appropriateness" and of India, which is framed by the "logic of consequences," China's normative power is framed by the "logic of relationships." Such logic

> assumes that while the future is unknown, the partners in the future are the same as in the past and present. Therefore, the significance of any specific interaction lies in how it shapes a particular relationship. . . The bottom line in a relationship logic is that both sides feel that they are better off if the relationship continues—this is the minimum meaning of "mutual benefit." A normal relationship does not require symmetry of partners or equality of exchanges, but it does require reciprocity [i.e. respect for the other]. (Womack, 2008, pp. 295–7)[14]

What is crucial about the understanding of normative power through such logic of relationships is that the *norms* for the normal are no longer defined by the leading state in terms of "rights and obligations," but emerge as "behavioral standards" accepted by the majority of participating states in the process of interaction (Yan, 2011, p. 238).[15] The emphasis here is that Beijing's normative power engages other states in the practice of doing together—that is, *they do as China does*. This pattern is distinct from the security governance practiced by Western actors (especially, the EU), which is premised on the conditionality of "*do as I say, not as I do*."[16] Asserting that normative action is "effective in the example it provides to another," Jack Barbalet (2011) makes a prescient observation on China's normative power through the prism of the concept *wuwei* (effortless or noncoercive action). As Barbalet points out, *wuwei* is neither willful nor random behavior, but reflects an understanding of normative power framed by three key elements:

> First, the thing or event acted upon is never regarded as inert or without its own agentic capacity; second, no actor is independent of other actors and non-actors, but is interconnected with them in various ways; third, things are subordinate to the processes through which they have manifestation and these processes are dynamic and things in them are even becoming different. These background ideas inform the notion of *wuwei* as non interfering action which accommodates to social processes as non-willful action directed to realizing the potential events and others, and as action that animates others to act on their own behalf. (Barbalet, 2011, pp. 342–7)

Some commentators have noted that *wuwei*'s logic of relationships has emerged out of a contingent "policy of 'pre-emptive participation'" intended to maintain China's "status" while Beijing develops reassurance strategies to allay the fears of others (Paltiel, 2009, p. 49). Others point to the Confucian underpinnings of Chinese strategic culture as the progenitor of such relational security governance. In this setting, showing respect for the other intends to demonstrate Beijing's "self-discipline and self-restraint" in the process of developing "positive relationships among actors for the common good, including cooperation and coordination to create an extensive social network of win-win results" (Qin, 2011, p. 138). Such understanding of normative power demands of those who practice it that they be "more aware of the relationships that constitute the objects of their concern than they are of their own interests" (Barbalet, 2011, p. 346).

Regardless of the provenance of such "logic of relationships," China's respect has contributed to (what Philip Nel labels as) the struggle of awkward countries—regardless of whether they are in Central Asia, Africa, or Latin America—"against their own invisibility in terms of the reigning [Western] discourses of development, modernization, and global economic and cultural integration." Thus, the individuation implicit in the logic of relationships suggests the profound ontological implications of relational security governance—"the appreciation of what is important to you in terms of your own self-conception, in contrast to the general expectations that [the international] society may impose on you [provides] an increasing scope for self-realization" (Nel, 2010, pp. 970–1).

As the experience of Central Asia indicates, the logic of relationships has introduced a facilitating environment for the socialization of regional states within a community of practice that has been formalized under the auspices of the SCO. China's governance of regional interactions, therefore, aims not only at educating neighboring states about what Beijing perceives as appropriate behavior, but also at their adoption of the Chinese "perspectives toward themselves" (Shih, 1990, pp. 21–5). For instance, Beijing's enunciation of the "new security concept," "strategic partnerships," and other initiatives intimate a desire to construct different relationship-based fora for the management of diverse "security predicaments" (Zhang, 2001b, p. 242). It is these patterns of security governance that reflect the socializing capacities and the strategic culture of normative powers. The following section elaborates these tendencies in China's external agency.

Elements of China's nascent security governance

The socializing dynamics animating China's security governance posit that in its international relations it acts as a *normative power*. As discussed in Chapter 2, the application of this term to the study of world affairs accentuates an actor's ability to "shape what can be 'normal' in international life" (Manners,

2002, p. 253). In this respect when applied to Beijing's security governance practices, the concept of normative power denotes: a particular kind of actor, a framework for its external relations, and means for involving others (Kavalski, 2007b). The proposition, therefore, is that owing to the specificities of its historical trajectory, its idiosyncratic polity, and its power constellations, China advances a particular understanding of what is a preferable pattern of relations in international life that predisposes it to act in a normative way in its relations with Central Asia.

In this setting, a number of commentators have prompted assessments that portray Beijing's outreach on a continuum from a cuddly "panda" to a fire-breathing "dragon" (Peerenboom, 2006). The complexity of such characterizations conveys China's self-identification as an "excluded" or "isolated" state (Deng, 2005, p. 55). This perception reflects the structural dynamics in post-Cold War world politics, which have left China out as a "deviant" state representing one of "the last bastions of communism" challenging the practices and the propagation of liberal democratic values (Zhang, 2001b, p. 247).

In this respect, the preoccupation with "international status" motivates Beijing's nascent international agency and its willingness to rectify—not *revise*—what it perceives as "the corrupt world order" (Shih, 1993, p. 201). Its global "charm offensive" thus confirms China's attempt to construct itself as a responsible as well as a reliable international player that offers an alternative to Western actors and organizations. At the same time, Beijing has generally resisted engaging in direct subversion of established institutions and regimes, and has more often than not complied with their standards and/or sought inclusion through membership of their organizational clubs (Lanteigne, 2005). Therefore, some commentators have claimed that China's international relations are informed by an analytical two-step involving a "system of symbols" about what is acceptable in international life and an understanding of "the most efficacious policies" for pursuing and ensuring the maintenance of such acceptability (Johnston, 1996, p. 222).

Although some observers would argue that China has always been (or has always had) a normative power (in the sense that its socializing agency was devised to foster an environment consistent with Chinese interests), this study posits that the normative foreign policy agency of China's contemporary security governance can be elicited from the interaction between the key values of its external relations: (i) "peaceful rise" to international status, (ii) noninterference in the domestic affairs of states, and (iii) preservation of Chinese national values. The inference then is that from the point of view of Beijing, world politics is not about "the application of abstract norms to cases," but about "a set of particular international relationships, with concrete obligations defined within the context of each relationship" (Womack, 2008, p. 265).[17]

"Peaceful rise" to international status

China's ability to manage its own economic and social transformation as well as its increasing impact on regional and global interstate affairs tends to be historicized within the context of its peaceful ascendance to global prominence (Zheng, 2005). As Wenran Jiang has noted, the Beijing-promoted discourse of a peaceful rise is underwritten by the articulation of "the historically unprecedented scenario that China's rise to world power status would be fundamentally different from the rise of great powers in history: the world can avoid large-scale wars that rising powers fight with status quo powers" (Jiang, 2006, p. 340).

According to Shih, such historicization of China's socializing agency reiterates its normative intention "to organize world politics." Hence, the emphasis on its peaceful development has to indicate the correctness of the norms and rules of Chinese international relations. Such normative validation of Beijing's socializing authority reflects a conviction that peace and development have an "intimate mutual relationship: development can protect and strengthen peace while only peace can ensure development" (Shih, 1993, pp. 45–8). At the same time, the emphasis on the peacefulness of China's rise reiterates the prioritization of stability as a key social norm in Chinese international relations. In China, "the overriding need is for stability," Deng Xiaoping used to say, because "without a stable environment, we can accomplish nothing and may even lose what we have gained."[18] President Hu Jintao has also gone to stress the legacy of the country's strategic culture when he proclaimed that "China embarks on the road of peaceful development because of its historical and traditional culture."[19]

The accent on peaceful development offers rhetorical confirmation of the claim that China "will always be a source for world peace: it will never seek hegemony, and never seek any sphere of influence" (Zhou, 2004, p. 167). This stance has been reiterated during the 10th National People's Congress by the Chinese Prime Minister, Wen Jiabao, who insisted that China "would not stand in the way of any other country or pose a threat to any other country, or achieve [its interests] at the expense of any particular country."[20] While indicative of Beijing's normative outlook, the emphasis on peaceful rise is also strategic and is intent on assisting China to "develop higher-quality relations than the United States [by providing] leadership of humane authority [as opposed to American hegemony] which will help it win more international support" (Yan, 2011, p. 260).[21]

Thus, the narrative of China's peaceful rise endorses a vision of world order and an understanding of peace distinct from Western notions of security community (as practiced by the EU, for instance), which is underwritten by an emphasis on the sharing/pooling of sovereignty, mutual vulnerability, and liberal democracy (Kavalski, 2010e). Such comparison, however, is not intended as a value judgment, but only aims to acknowledge the different context(s) of China's normative power.

Noninterference in the domestic affairs of states

In December 2005, while on a visit in Myanmar, Chinese Prime Minister Wen Jiabao declared that China "vowed not to meddle in Myanmar's affairs in return for investment deals, a template for Chinese behavior elsewhere such as in Africa, the Middle East, and Central Asia" (Chen, 2007, p. 46). Such proclamations tend to add to the qualms of Western actors and organization about China's increased international agency through the promise and practice of enhanced trade relations. The socializing strategy that evidences China's growing confidence in its ability to fashion interstate relations has been described in the slogan: "participate actively, demonstrate restraint, offer reassurance, open markets, foster interdependence, create common interests, and reduce conflict" (Shambaugh, 2005, p. 54).

The insistence on noninterference in the domestic affairs of states underwrites the emphasis on "strategic sovereignty" (Zhou, 2004). Historically, this stance reflects a policy pattern that has seen decision-makers in Beijing "willing to behave in ways that *jeopardized* China's security in order to preserve China's autonomy and independence" (Johnston, 1998, pp. 66). Yongjin Zhang explains the firm institutional grounds of the notion and practice of sovereignty and its centrality to the cognitive frameworks of Chinese strategic culture through the contextual restraints that it is supposed to impose on the aggressive traits of human nature (Zhang, 2001a, pp. 48–50). In terms of policy practice, therefore, such a rhetorical stance intends to reinforce China's position as an international actor that can both be trusted and emulated. Already during the Cold War, Beijing criticized both the USSR and the USA for their disregard for and encroaching upon the principle and practice of state sovereignty (Kavalski, 2010e). The emphasis on sovereignty, thereby asserts the Chinese (at least, rhetorical) conviction that international legal and moral norms have supplanted the era of "might makes right" (Shi, 2007, p. 163).

Owing to the centrality of noninterference, Beijing defines the meaning of sovereignty through the assertion that "no country should interfere in the internal affairs of other countries under any pretext, let alone using its strength to invade, bully or overthrow [the government of] other countries. China never imposes its social system or ideology on others, and it will never allow others to impose their social systems or ideologies on itself" (Zhou, 2004, p. 53). The insistence on the rules and norms of sovereignty, therefore, reflects Beijing's subscription to the "five principles of peaceful coexistence"—mutual respect for territorial integrity, mutual nonaggression, mutual nonintervention, mutual benefit and equality, and peaceful coexistence (Shih, 1993, p. 43). This understanding of sovereignty underwrites China's objection to the practices of international intervention (regardless of whether it is military or through demands for democratization). The Chinese foreign policy belief, therefore, is that the erosion of sovereignty frustrates the development of the perceived "victim," undermines the stability of neighboring countries, and ultimately counteracts the objectives of the "perpetrator" (Shih, 1990, p. 41).

Overcoming the specters of the past

The projections of normative power constitute (and are constitutive of) specific identity politics. The conjecture is that the arena of world affairs is populated not by *agents* per se but by (embryonic) *international identities* (with their attitudes, attributes, and values) that are actualized by actors in the process of international interactions. Thus, the attempt to overcome the specters of history instills a critical reflexivity in the discursive identity-consciousness (Diez, 2005, p. 634). Such understanding infers that foreign policy is an identity issue which takes coherence in the context of (negotiating) national insecurities. In this respect, national identity is construed as a complex narrative, whose coherence is conveyed through the discursive articulations of foreign policy.

China is no exception to this trend. The patterns of external relations simultaneously reflect, reiterate, and reconstitute its self-image. The assertiveness of China's prescriptive stance on the significance of sovereignty in the context of its peaceful rise to global prominence implicates the identity politics of its normative power. In particular, it hints at China's "washing away the past shame" (Shih, 1990, p. 61), when Beijing was denied its legitimate status. Thus, while the function of foreign policy is to maintain the integrity of the national self, China's inferiority complex for the better part of the twentieth century dented its socializing propensities. The foreign policy predicament of this period is captured in the saying "weak nations have no diplomacy (*ruo guo wu waijiao*)" (Bin, 2005, p. 230).

In this respect, China's normative power has been preconditioned on the reflexive construction of the *past of national humiliation as other*. In his discerning process-tracing of the articulations, performances, and meanings of "National Humiliation Day," Callahan outlines the cognitive mapping of the legacy of "losing face" in post-Boxer Rebellion China. He points out that the discursive memory of national disgrace constructed a narrative that "the shame of history cannot be forgotten" (Callahan, 2006, p. 190). Chinese foreign policy can be read as an attempt to rectify this legacy by projecting a self-conscious international identity dispelling the specters of the past; yet, whose socializing rhetoric proclaims that others need not experience humiliation either.[22]

Since historical understandings are often (at best) ambiguous interpretations of past events, the dynamics of socialization underwriting China's emphasis on sovereignty and peaceful rise to international prominence are conceived as the most conspicuous form of its national self-actualization (Shih, 1993, p. 189). From this perspective, Beijing's confidence in and assertiveness of its normative power in regional and global affairs offers one of the most conspicuous indications of China's "completion of the painful search for a coherent national identity" (Shambaugh, 2005, p. 59).

The Shanghai cooperation organization and China's security governance of Central Asia

As the previous section has demonstrated, it is the interaction between the socializing propensities and the normative power of China's external agency that identify the dominant elements of its security governance. The rhetorical three-step of China's normative power—"peaceful rise" to international status, noninterference in the domestic affairs of states, and maintenance of Chinese national values—reflects the underpinnings of its strategic culture. Such conceptualization intimates the perplexing phenomenon of its security governance—the union of "subconscious rationality and conscious irrationality" that brings together "moral internationalism and selfish nationalism" within Beijing's socializing rhetoric.[23] Undoubtedly, the picture that emerges is more complex and perhaps less amenable to models of predictability required by policy-planners; yet, the contention is that such analysis makes possible the conceptual and contextual examination of China's security governance of Central Asia.

The region of Central Asia offers perhaps one of the most conspicuous instances of *why* and *how* the practices of interaction come to define China's nascent security governance strategies. Confirming the relevance of a continuous deliberate practice for the construction of generative relationships that underpin the influence of normative powers, Hasan Karrar draws attention to China's unique persistence in developing its interactions with the region. As he notes, "while these relations were gradual, they were also continuous. Therefore, while there were no momentous declarations, neither were there any periods during which some tangible progress was not made" (Karrar, 2009, p. 15). This pattern of relations reflects the logic of relationships underpinning China's strategic culture. It stresses a security governance approach steeped in the deliberate practice of "leading by following," which operates "progressively rather than radically" for the achievement of long-term change (Barbalet, 2011, p. 345).

The aim of actively contributing to the emergence of a "harmonious Central Asia" (Pan, 2009, p. 40) has been backstopped by the five dominant narratives of Beijing's involvement in the region: (i) diversifying and ensuring China's access to energy resources; (ii) cutting any international links between Muslim Uyghur separatists in the province of Xinjiang and their ethnic and religious kin across Central Asia; (iii) preventing Taipei's shopping for diplomatic allies in the region; (iv) encouraging economic and trade relations between China's western provinces and Central Asian states; and (v) indicating China's preparedness to become a global actor.[24] From these four discursive contexts, the stability of Xinjiang seems to have been of central concern to Beijing. For instance, China's ability during the 1990s to convince Central Asian states through different confidence and security-building measures to sign treaties demarcating their joint border has been specifically linked to the issue of Uyghur separatism.

Yet, Beijing's rapid movement from the difficult task of delineating and demilitarizing its borders with Kazakhstan, Kyrgyzstan, Russia, and Tajikistan to promoting a multilateral organization and establishing economic and security ties attest to more than just the conventional "power politics" of national self-interest (Sun, 2004). The complex provenance of China's strategic outlook toward Central Asia can be inferred from Xing Guangcheng's conjecture that

> Only when Central Asian states are politically and economically stable can Sino-Central Asian economic cooperation be conducted effectively and smoothly. Such economic cooperation can and will speed up economic development in the Northwest of China. It can therefore be argued that *to a large extent the stability and prosperity of Northwest China is closely bound up with the stability and prosperity of Central Asia*. It is, rightly, because of this consideration that China advocates and promotes active trade and economic cooperation between China and the Central Asian states for common economic prosperity. (Xing, 2001, p. 35; emphasis in original)

Bearing such proclamations in mind, Michael Clarke draws attention to the "circular logic" underpinning the development of SCO. Such circular logic reveals Beijing's perception that "security within Xinijang [is] predicated on delivering economic growth, while economic growth is assured by the reinforcement of the state's instruments of political and social control, which in turn is to be achieved by opening the region to Central Asia." Clarke, thereby, concludes that the consolidation of China's control over Xinjiang and the expansion of Chinese power in Central Asia ultimately contributes to "Beijing's quest for a 'peaceful rise' to great power status" (Clarke, 2009, pp. 121–3). In other words, "China's objective is through cooperation to strengthen its position in the international system."[25]

The creation of the "Shanghai Five" in the mid-1990s has been crucial for engendering a practice of regular interaction that alleviated Central Asian suspicions about China's intentions. Thus, the accession of Uzbekistan and the transformation of the "Shanghai Five" into SCO in 2001 seem to implicate regional susceptibility to Beijing's power of attraction. In particular, the emergence of the SCO attests to the appeal of a strategic behavior reluctant to use force for the solution of security threats, but reliant on diplomatic means and confidence-building measures (Feng, 2007, p. 25).

At the same time, others have interpreted Beijing's wooing of Central Asian states as a return to "the more 'natural' state affairs" in Asia that prevailed during the Chinese tributary system (Munro, 1994, p. 605).[26] While intellectually stimulating, such comparison (as will soon be explained) does not appear fruitful for the discussion of China's current normative foreign policy engagements in Central Asia. Not least, because the patterns of relations emerging in Central Asia represent "fundamental compromises that China has chosen to make in limiting its own sovereign interest for the sake of engagement in multilateral frameworks and pursuit of greater regional interdependence" (Shambaugh, 2004/2005, p. 76).

In fact, Beijing itself has indicated that it perceives SCO as a "major innovation in the history of China's diplomacy and in the international relations of the Central Asian region" (Shi, 2007, p. 167). The organization is presented as a qualitative departure from "the Cold War mentality (*lengzhan siwei*)" of creating hegemonic spheres of influence (Karrar, 2001, p. 6).[27] As SCO's first Secretary-General asserts, "it is not an ordinary organization of cooperation. On the one hand, the SCO cooperation on security is not carried out in the way of a traditional military bloc such as NATO; on the other hand, its economic cooperation is not aimed at closer integration as in the EU" (Zhang, 2006a). In this respect, through SCO's diplomatic rhetoric and policy-practice of peace-building, development, and economic integration, Beijing signals its willingness to share with Central Asian states the opportunities associated with China's "peaceful rise" within the context of open relationships in an international "harmonious society" (Zhang and Tang, 2005, p. 55).

Although its main goal is defined as the "strengthening of peace and ensuring the security and stability in the region," both the 2001 SCO Declaration and the 2002 SCO Charter emphasize the normative rather than military rationale of SCO's security governance (it has to be reiterated that the reference to *normative* is not an indication that it cannot be *strategic*). In this regard, the security predicaments posed by the prospect of "splittism"—a term describing a violent secession of Chinese territory—motivates Beijing to experiment with novel arrangements for ensuring the stability of governments and states in Central Asia (Lanteigne, 2005, pp. 121–5). Some commentators have, thereby, concluded that Beijing's reliance on its normative power as the exporter of goodwill and consumer goods rather than weapons and revolution provides a much more adept and nuanced mode of socializing its neighborhood (Shambaugh, 2005).

The two founding documents of SCO reiterate the central role of "good-neighborly friendship" to the promotion of "efficient regional cooperation" and "the steady increase of living standards and improvement of living conditions of the people of member states." Thus, by "preserving and safeguarding regional peace, security, and stability," SCO intends to assist in the creation of a "fair and rational political and economic order." These assertions compel the signatories to "adherence with the goals and principles of the Charter of the United Nations, other commonly acknowledged principles and rules of international law related to the maintenance of international peace, security and the development of good-neighborly and friendly relations, as well as the cooperation between states" (SCO Declaration, 2001; SCO Charter, 2002).

Promoted as an organization for Central Asian cooperation that seeks to maintain regional stability and advance economic relations, SCO not only reiterates Beijing's increasing clout in international life, but also boosts its credentials by emphasizing the peaceful foreign policy intentions and commitment to regional security (Ong, 2005, p. 436). Yet, attesting to the normative politics of Beijing's involvement in Central Asia, SCO reveals a security governance approach which "seeks commonalities while preserving differences" (Chung, 2004, p. 991). SCO, therefore, emerges as an "illuminating case" of China's strategy for influencing "the intersubjective social structures that constitute the normative and epistemic ground for action in Central Asia" (Aris, 2009, p. 155). Thus, Beijing's expectations about the behavior of Central Asian states become an essential part of its own intentionality; it is, therefore, in and through the pattern of interaction that the "horizons of the feasible" for China's security governance emerge (Womack, 2008, p. 294).

Reflecting the Chinese normative claim of peaceful rise to international prominence, the reference to the "Shanghai Spirit" has become shorthand for the observance of "mutual trust, mutual benefit, equality, consultation, respect for multi-civilizations, and striving for common development." The assertion is that adherence to these principles "strengthens the consultation and coordination [among SCO Member States] in regional and international affairs" and assists their "search for common positions on foreign policy issues" (SCO Declaration, 2001; SCO Charter, 2002). The expectation is that SCO emerges as a "mechanism through which social learning may occur, thus leading to interest redefinition and identity change" (Aris, 2009, p. 155).

To that effect, SCO has established a permanent Secretariat (inaugurated on 15 January 2004) headquartered in Beijing. The former Chinese Ambassador to Russia, Zhang Deguang, was selected as SCO's first Secretary-General (2004–06), the former Deputy Foreign Minister of Kazakhstan, Bolat Nurgaliev, was appointed as the second SCO Secretary-General (2007–09), and on 1 January 2010, Muratbek Imanliev, the first Foreign Minister of independent Kyrgyzstan (1991–92) and a long-time professor at the American University of Central Asia, became the third SCO Secretary-General. In order to further the "coordination of efforts for the maintenance of peace and enhancing security and confidence in the region" (SCO Charter, 2002), SCO has instituted a set of issue-specific dialogues under the so-called mechanism of meetings (see Figure 2). In 2007, Beijing established "a special fund to train within three years 1,500 management and professional talents in different fields for [SCO] member states."[28]

In this respect, China's evolving socialization of Central Asia has led Beijing to take the initiative in fostering a security environment that (while consistent with its interests also) engages its neighbors in cooperative initiatives. These dynamics are evidenced through the Regional Anti-Terrorist Structure (RATS). It builds upon the work of the 1999 Joint Control Group which verified compliance with the 1996 Agreement on Confidence Building in the Military Field along the Border Areas and the 1997 Agreement on the Mutual Reduction of Military Forces in the Border Areas signed by the members of the then 'Shanghai Five'. RATS is a multilateral security arrangement that establishes precise security commitments between SCO Member States (SCO Concept, 2005). It confirms their subscription to what China perceives to be the "three evil forces"—separatism, extremism, and terrorism (Chung, 2004, 991).

The 2001 SCO Convention on Combating Terrorism, Separatism, and Extremism has fixed the meanings of these terms in order to facilitate the establishment of a "framework. . . for the prevention, identification, and suppression of such acts" (SCO Convention, 2001). Such form of international socialization promotes rule conformity both as a rhetorical practice and as an

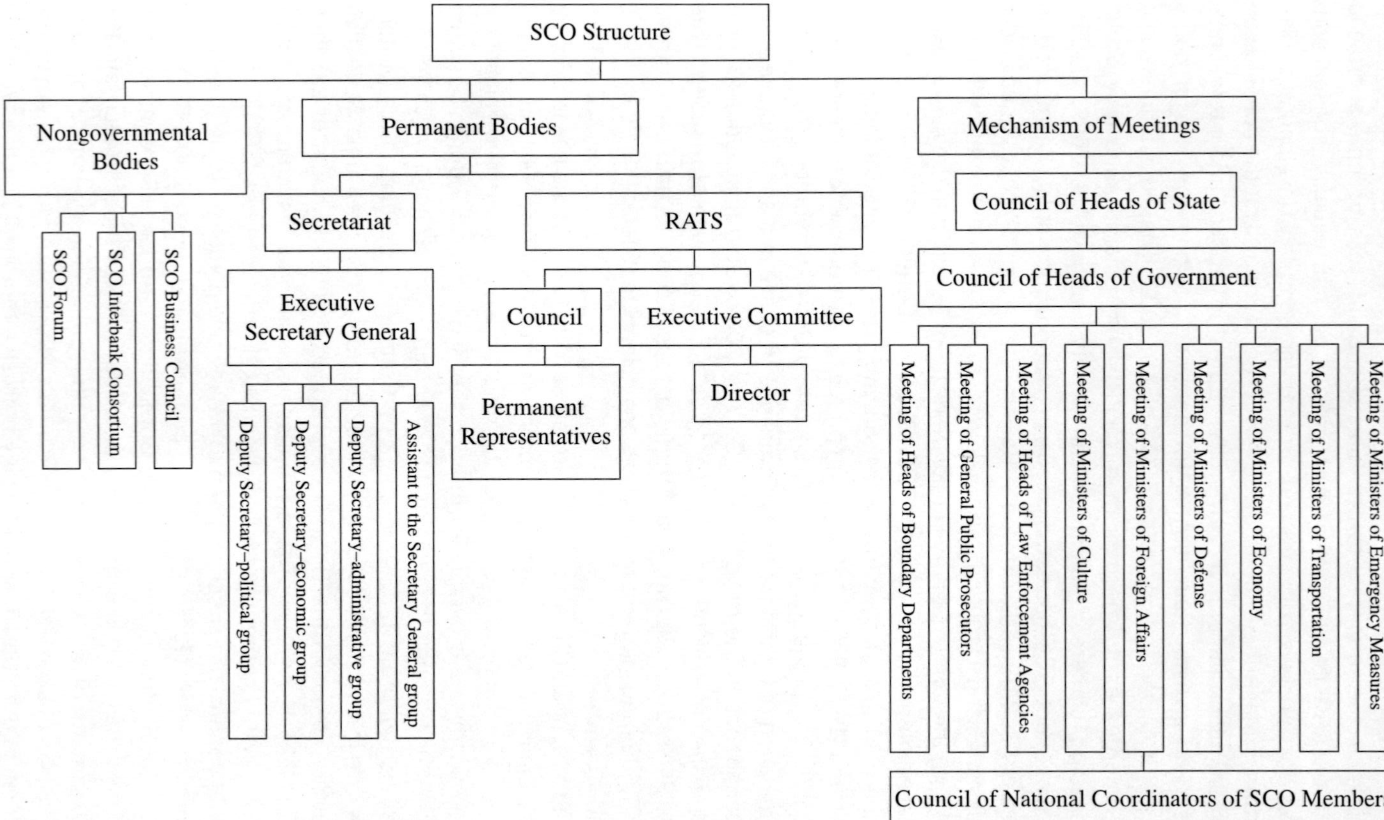

Figure 2 *The structure of the Shanghai Cooperation Organization.*

operational mechanism. The establishment of RATS has urged a number of commentators to declare that China is gradually becoming the key security provider in Central Asia (Zhao, 2003, p. 106). Confirming such claims, under the RATS aegis, there have been several cross-border military and counter-terrorism exercises attesting to "the highly unusual—even unprecedented—for China participation in organization whose primary purpose is security cooperation" (Shambaugh, 2005, p. 31). It is noteworthy that in the context of these joint war games, China has gone as far as to sponsor, for the first time ever, multilateral military exercises on its own territory.[29]

According to the Chinese Foreign Minister, Tang Jiaxuan, this development is an indication that the SCO is not "a club for empty discussion, but a viable institution capable of making an important contribution to the international war on terror."[30] Moreover, it confirms key aspects of China's strategic culture. As Yan Xuetong (2011, pp. 261–2) reminds us, Chinese philosophical traditions suggest that

> International support for a rising power springs from the security protection that it provides for weaker countries and from making itself a role model state, rather than from [only] giving economic aid. This means that China cannot win others' hearts if it is reluctant to provide security protection for its surrounding countries, and to shift its domestic priorities from economic development to establishing a harmonious society.

Thus, intent on strengthening its security relationship with the region, Beijing has (i) fostered military-to-military relations, (ii) initiated security assistance programs for border control and management, and (iii) begun a preferential sale of its weapons systems and technologies to Central Asian states (Blank, 2002). In this respect, China's participation in the security infrastructure of Central Asia reflects its more confident perception of its identity in regional and global politics.

At the same time, SCO's security governance pattern intimates the emergence of a particular institutional culture and identity promoted through a pattern of shared practices. SCO's first Secretary-General Zhang Deguang asserts that "the principle of consensus works [because] members show an extremely high solidarity." He also insists that it is the subscription to the principles of the "Shanghai Spirit" that has created "common interests and common positions on important issues" (Zhang, 2006b). Such claims reflect Beijing's foreign policy belief that institutional identities intimate socializing processes that affect the norms and behavior of participating countries (Shih, 1993, p. 16). In this respect, SCO's culture is presented as the consequence of interactions—that is, it "appeared as a result of a national evolution of the

Eurasian geopolitical process" (Zhang, 2006a). In fact, the language of both the SCO Declaration and the SCO Charter implicate that SCO Member States already see themselves as having internalized the principles written into those documents. Attesting to the normative slant of the organization, SCO's Secretary-General has proclaimed that SCO "represents not just the system of values, but the civilizational formula" of its members (Zhang, 2006a).

It can be argued that the explicit articulation of those principles "makes sense primarily as a means to exert influence on a set of others that do not stick to them" (Diez, 2005, p. 631). As the SCO Charter makes it clear, other states can be invited to join the organization only if they "undertake to respect the objectives and principles of this Charter"—the implication being that as nonmembers they do not comply with those standards. In further reiteration of such normative distinction between SCO members and nonmembers, in 2002, SCO adopted a "Scheme for Mutual Relations with Other International Organizations and States" (SCO Scheme, 2002; Al-Qahtanin, 2006, p. 145). The exclusive identity politics of such othering discourses are suggested by the designations of nonmembers as "guests," the provision that "guests may be given the floor only when representatives of all SCO Member States will have spoken," the requirement that "no more than two states and/or two international organizations may participate simultaneously in a meeting," etc.[31]

Although not exclusive to the SCO, such stipulations reflect the inside/outside distinctions that underwrite the normative power of international organizations and their socializing dynamics. And what is crucial to the argument here is that this is an identity practice created by China itself. Currently, the organization has four observer states: India, Iran, Pakistan, and Mongolia. India, Iran, and Pakistan have lodged formal applications to become full SCO members, but so far none of them has been able to obtain the required backing of all current member states. During the 2008 SCO Summit in Dushanbe (Tajikistan), the organization created the category of "dialogue partner." So far, only Belarus and Sri Lanka have been accorded with this status. In this context, some observers have interpreted the rejection of the US application to become a SCO observer country as a confirmation of SCO's anti-Western identity (Hussain, 2011).

There were also strong indications that at the November 2011 SCO Summit in St. Petersburg (Russia), Turkey would be invited to become a dialogue partner, while Afghanistan will be included as an observer state (Zaman, 2011). In terms of the latter, there has been a SCO-Afghanistan Contact Group since November 2005, whose purpose has been to develop "proposals and recommendations on the realization of cooperation between the SCO and Afghanistan on issues of mutual interest" (SCO Protocol, 2005). While no new members, observers, or dialogue partners were admitted to the SCO at the 2011 St. Petersburg Summit, such differentiation confirms the distinct thresholds of socialization into SCO's rules and norms. Promoting the identity of the "Shanghai Spirit," SCO has representation at and formal relations with the UN, ASEAN, the Russian-dominated Collective Security Treaty Organization (CSTO), etc. (Aris, 2011). At the same time, SCO has begun to act as "an alternative Asian OSCE" dispatching a number of election-monitoring missions (Korkmaz, 2010, p. 361). Perhaps, one of the most conspicuous confirmations of the distinct identity politics of the organization was the separate SCO Pavilion at the 2010 Shanghai Expo. The bumptious description of the pavilion proclaimed that it is a

> Western-style structure inlaid with Chinese antithetical couplet featuring the theme "World Harmony Begins in the Neighborhood." Its exterior design, full of dynamism and energy inspires imaginations of people cheerfully dancing and stepping forward to Shanghai hand-in-hand. Inside, the walls and dome [of the Pavilion] unfold a magnificent scene of sunrise and rosy glow, symbolizing the bright and promising future of SCO.[32]

It is the identity dynamics underpinning SCO's nascent community of practice which confirm the assumption that the dialogical framework provided by the organization outlines the normative patterns of China's security governance of Central Asia. The logic of relationships driving such interaction has been acknowledged by President Hu Jintao in his statement at the 2004 SCO Summit when he stressed that "all SCO members have their distinct human resources [offering] good potential for mutual understanding and friendship."[33] At the same time, SCO's consolidation of the web of contractual arrangements that China has woven in Central Asia in the post-Cold War period seems to confirm the re-enactment of the normative power of *Pax Sinica*. Thus, the distinct explanatory strategies of Beijing's "conditional multilateralism" (Jiang, 2006, p. 337) have associated the surge in China's socializing latitude with its unprecedented economic takeoff, which revives memories of China's "traditional tributary state system" (Aris, 2009; Zhang, 2009). *Pax Sinica*—the name usually used to describe the "Chinese world order" from around the year 300BCE to about the mid-1800CE—indicates a "normative order" that promoted (and maintained) the "Chinese worldview" through the institutional arrangement of a tribute system which translated the "moral authority" of the Chinese state into "normative pacification" in Chinese international relations (Zhang, 2001a, p. 53).

However, the emphasis on SCO as the lodestone of a new *Pax Sinica*—that is, an ambitious strategy for regional domination through the establishment of a Sinocentric order—seems like a major oversimplification. For instance, the images conjured up by such articulations depict a quasi-imperialist vision of regional security governance. Yet, such assertions tend to reflect Western strategies of narrativizing historical experience;[34] consequently, the reference to the notion of normative power aims "to capture the movement away from the Cold War (and neocolonial) approaches" to international agency (Manners, 2006, p. 184). China's security governance of Central Asia, thereby, intimates socializing discourses and practices through which Beijing engages in informational, procedural, and symbolic transference and diffusion of its norms.

The reference to SCO as a contemporary avatar of *Pax Sinica* asserts the practice of deliberate security governance which has allowed China to promote the policy of "win-win cooperation with Central Asia" (Zhang, 2006b). At the same time, such socializing strategy has assisted China to have an impact beyond the Central Asian states by engaging with an expanding group of SCO observers and dialogue partners (Wacker, 2011, p. 85). Beijing's security governance also emphasizes respect for the sovereignty of Central Asian states. For instance, Chinese policy-makers appear anxious by the nascent assertiveness of both Western actors in the field of human rights and Russia's growing disregard for the independence of the former Soviet republics. On the one hand, Beijing has been quite savvy to exploit, what Chinese commentators have called Central Asia's "high alert against the export of democracy" (Hao, 2010). On the other hand, as already discussed in the introductory chapter, Beijing understands that Central Asian states are keen to use China as a leverage against (the perceived and actual) Russian intrusion in the region.

The symbolic politics of sovereignty, therefore, seem attuned to the vicissitudes of Central Asian regimes. In this context, China's self-reflexive agency asserting the benefits of economic modernization without political liberalization becomes a substitute for the elevation of human rights and democratization as a global political practice (Ong, 2005, p. 432). As SCO's Secretary-General made it clear, "democracy is a product of internal development of the society in each state and it is impossible to introduce it from outside" (Zhang, 2005). The leverage of Beijing's normative rhetoric on sovereignty has been backstopped by "real initiatives," which reflect China's commitment to creating a code of conduct in Central Asia (Kurlantzick, 2006, p. 2).

In this respect, China's security governance of the region confirms Beijing's insistence on its peaceful rise to international prominence. SCO, therefore, provides both a confirmation of this claim and an institutional infrastructure for preempting the turbulence on China's periphery. As Zhang Deguang points out, "SCO does not bear a gene of confrontation. . . [It] emerged on the basis of generalization of the historical experience of the Cold War period and fits the demands of our time: aspiration towards peace and cooperation, anchoring stability and development in the region" (Zhang, 2006b). At the same time, Beijing's socialization of Central Asia suggests "China's fundamental interest in the establishment and maintenance of a new regional security order" (White Paper, 2000).

Thus, the key aspects of China's normative power—confident self-reflexive identity, emphasis on sovereignty, and sharing the economic benefits of its peaceful rise—have increased the effectiveness of its socialization of Central Asia. In a comment on China's role in the region, Bulat Nurgaliev, the second SCO Secretary-General, has acknowledged Beijing's socializing capacities by hinting that "only the tree which bears fruit attracts attention" (Nurgaliev, 2007). Likewise, the President of Turkmenistan, Gurbanguly Berdymukhamedov, has stressed that China's regional security governance is effective because it is "positive in context."[35] Such conditioning propensity, therefore, attests to Beijing's ability to project coherent (and contextualized) practices for the deliberate security governance of the region, which "attract attention" because of the tangible and appealing "fruits" that it bears.

Conclusion

By indicating the overlapping contexts of China's normative power, the analytical synthesis of this chapter has suggested that the institutionalization of SCO affords Beijing an opportunity to project itself as a blueprint for the future trajectories of Central Asian states. Consequently, China's involvement in the region has exhibited the socializing effects of Beijing's normative power. In this setting, China's influence in the region has been assisted by its ability to articulate self-reflexive security governance policies premised on the centrality of sovereignty and the economic benefits of its "peaceful rise." These, in turn, have assisted Beijing to "Shanghai" the region into its orbit of influence. However, instead of being hijacked by force or trickery, the region has slowly, but surely been socialized into Beijing's worldview through the promotion of various initiatives for regional cooperation. The claim here is that it is Chinese definitions of the "normal" that have provided the "sustainable nutrients" for this process (Song, 2011, p. 63).

Not surprisingly, focusing on the network of intertwining relations between regional states and China through different infrastructural, economic, and security projects, Pierre Morel, the EU Special Representative to Central Asia, has referred to the SCO both as a "mirror of new trends in an unstable world" and as a "barometer of a new relationship in the making" (Morel, 2008). Such statements indicate the recognition of China's emergence as a viable model for Central Asia by offering "practical means of changing rent-seeking incentives" (Bhatty and Auty, 2006, p. 255). The argument, therefore, is that the framework of normative power offers a relevant setting for evaluating China's capacity to engage other states. The participation of Central Asian states in Chinese-promoted initiatives (such as the SCO) exhibits their socializing effects on the region by generating meaningful community of practice. However, the effects of its normative power—described as an attempt to shape the attitude of other states—are felt beyond Central Asia. In fact, "the main characteristic of China's great peripheral diplomacy is to establish a foothold in Asia and look toward the world."[36] In this respect, some commentators have asserted that Beijing's security governance of Central Asia also instances its emergent *global* foreign policy strategy "to secure and shape a security, economic, and political environment that is conducive to China" (Zhang and Tang, 2005, p. 48).

Bearing in mind the unpredictability and disorder characterizing the external relations of "newly established states in a poorly defined region," the development of SCO emerges as "a major accomplishment" and "China's greatest success in regional multilateralism" (Womack, 2008, p. 274). The concluding chapter of this book will reveal that such agency is intimately intertwined with China's struggle for *recognition*. The assertion is that China's Central Asian policies are part and parcel of a strategy for the acquisition of "greater prestige" by advertising Beijing's "*presence gigantesque*" and emphasizing "its desire to be a participant in international discourse" (Lanteigne, 2005, p. 29; emphasis in original).

6

India and Central Asia: A strategic culture "looking north" for its normative power

Introduction

During a visit to Turkmenistan in September 1995, the then Prime Minister P. V. Narasimha Rao made it clear that "for India," Central Asia is an area "of high priority, where we aim to stay engaged far into the future. We are an independent partner with no selfish motives. We only desire honest and open friendship and to promote stability and cooperation without causing harm to any third country" (quoted in Muni, 2003, p. 110).[1] Rao's proclamation offers a glimpse at the discursive genesis of the "Look North" policy—the narrative framework of India's relations with Central Asia. As its appellation suggests, the "Look North" policy strives to emulate the logic and achievements of India's "Look East" approach to Southeast Asia, which seemed to indicate that India has a "strategic will," whose "footprint reaches well beyond South Asia" (Saran, 2003, p. 115). Thus, the discourses of the "Look North" policy have to demonstrate India's attempt to "break out of the claustrophobic confines" of the subcontinent (Gupta, 1997, p. 309).

In this respect, the evaluation of New Delhi's agency in Central Asia attests to the regionalization of India's foreign policy—that is, the development of distinct external policies toward different global regions. The discourses of India's external relations offer insights into the country's strategic culture and the modes of security governance that it fashions. For instance, the propositions of the "Look North" policy point to "secularism," "democracy," and "literacy" as "national strengths" that India and Central Asia share

(Sinha, 2004, p. 6). This chapter reveals that for the better part of the 1990s, India's foreign policy formulation has remained in the grips of conceptual tensions, strategic uncertainty, and geopolitical constraints. These diplomatic predicaments reflect New Delhi's difficulties with adjusting to the altered realities of the post-Cold War world order.

In particular, the dissolution of the Soviet Union provoked a profound crisis in India's international identity and sense of national security. Thus, it is only the nuclear tests of May 1998 that reveal a discursive overhaul of India's international relations premised on a much more assertive (if not aggressive) foreign policy stance. The security attitudes uncovered by those detonations expose the very bedrock of India's strategic culture—the conviction of the inevitability of India's rise to global prominence. The claim here is that if India is indeed to become a 'great power', it first needs to develop the deliberate practice of its normative power, despite—and not because of—its overt nuclear capabilities (Cohen, 2001, p. 197). This issue is given considerable attention in the following section. The chapter then proceeds with outlining the post-Cold War trajectories of India's foreign policy making, especially as indicated by its security governance of Central Asia.

Such an overview provides the background for contextualizing the narrative assessment of the "Look North" policy. The examination identifies the implications emanating from the narrative juncture provided by the 1998 nuclear tests on the formulation of the "Look North" policy. In this setting, the chapter details the idiosyncrasies of India's bilateral relations with Tajikistan. This context becomes a point of departure for an analysis of the lack of influence in New Delhi's interactions with Central Asia. The investigation concludes with an assertion that India's interactions with regional states evidence that its security governance fails to extend a coherent normative power in global affairs, owing to New Delhi's inability to engage its counterparts in an interactive (and self-organizing) community of practice.

Normative power and strategic culture in Indian foreign policy

Rather than a detailed analysis of India's normative power and strategic culture, this section only briefly outlines some qualifications in the application of those concepts to the study of New Delhi's external relations. As it will be explained (regardless of India's proclamations to the contrary), it is the perception of a competitive South Asian strategic environment that prevents New Delhi from developing a deliberate practice of Central Asian security governance.

To begin with, it has to be acknowledged that there appears to be an important confusion between the notions of "normative power India" and "Brand India." In particular, the latter is used to infer the former. "Brand India" (as the term suggests) refers to the brands that export India's image abroad—from the cultural products of Bollywood to the entrepreneurial endeavors of Bangalore. Too often, therefore, analysts take as their point of departure the assertion that India has "earned *international respect* and *influence*" through its booming economy, IT revolution, and nuclear weapons (Lak, 2008, p. 260; emphasis added). "Brand India," therefore, is taken not only as a shorthand for the "awakening of a slumbering elephant" (Rai and Simon, 2007, p. ix), but also as a label for a unique "unshackling of the imagination" (Menon and Nigam, 2007, p. 85) that ushers in an "India unbound" (Das, 2000) onto the global state.

The mashup of the notions of "normative power India" and "Brand India" has provenance in the post-Cold War trajectories of India's foreign policy formulation. It is important to note here that the lack of analytical distinction between these two concepts lays bare the failure to problematize the nature and dynamics within which these transformations have originated. In fact, the uncritical attempt to project normative power through "Brand India" appears to unwittingly contribute to the descent of India's image into "pejorative stereotyping" (Hymans, 2009, p. 259). Such tendencies confirm the palpable hiatus between India's self-aggrandizing perception of itself and the less flattering evaluations by others (Mitra, 2003, p. 404). Thus, very often Indian commentators allege that their country has significantly impacted international trends, while external observers barely take notice of New Delhi's agency (Mehta, 2009).[2]

The uncritical acceptance of the convergence between "normative power India" and "Brand India" has reinforced the hiatus between the external and domestic perception of India's international agency. Such a confusion of divergent notions points to a key aspect of its security governance—the palpable lack of an underpinning "big idea" (such as democratization for the EU or a government-led economic development for China). Pratap Bhanu Mehta (2009) traces the origins of this phenomenon to the 1919 Paris Peace Conference, at which some of the leading Indian intellectuals at the time argued for the independence of their country on the premise that if free, India would inevitably become a great power, but its power would not be projected outward (i.e. it would not be used to dominate others). Mehta interprets these arguments as an early indication of the absence of "a global objective" in Indian strategic culture. This attitude appears to have been suffused in the narratives of nonalignment that produced a peculiar sense of sovereignty and autarky in India, which was understood as independence *from* the rest of the world, rather than as a particular way of engaging others.

Owing to the want of vision in India's external relations, "commercial development and security seem to connect accidentally more often than purposefully" (Wimbush, 2011, p. 269). This absence of an overarching "big idea" in India's strategic culture leads to an unusual style of security governance—one in which New Delhi does not attempt to establish relationships with other actors by deliberately engaging them in shared practices. Instead, as Rodney W. Jones demonstrates, New Delhi seems determined "to wait the opponent out," rather than initiate interactions that might lead to a pragmatic compromise. Jones argues that such an approach to security governance is embedded in the profound sense of entitlement, superiority, and presumed deeper knowledge about the correlation of forces that distinguish India's strategic culture. In turn, these traits engender an outlook of inevitable success as "India cannot help but prevail in the long run" (Jones, 2006, pp. 10–14). This style of security governance reveals the pervasive "logic of consequences" underpinning the strategic culture of its security governance. Attesting to a policy-making based on self-interested cost-benefit calculation, the "logic of consequences" frames India as an instrumentally rational actor intent on maximizing its own power (Schimmelfennig and Sedelmeier, 2005, p. 9 and p. 181).

Not surprisingly, therefore, India's policy-making lacks a "culture of bargaining" (Mehta, 2009, p. 228). Thus, rather than engaging other actors in deliberate practices for the establishment of common understandings and shared expectations, India seems intent on hedging its bets it order to avoid the risks associated with commitment to relational security governance mechanisms. The implication then is not only that India might remain a "rising power" for longer than its pundits portend, but also that the analysis of the cognitive framework of its strategic culture puts it in "the class of countries that are always emerging but never quite arriving" (Kumar, 2008, p. 255; Jones, 2006, p. 21; Mitra, 2009, p. 402).

This suggestion refers us back to the analytical propositions of Chapter 2 and, in particular, to the issue of entrapment accompanying any strategic culture. Strategic entrapment—like a ghost chasing its victims down a preordained path—directs policy making into already scripted terrains. Therefore, as Naunihal Singh (2006) asserts, it should not be surprising that "despite foreign policy failures and much debate over tactics, the Indian elite holds fast to *a vision of national greatness*." The historical memory of great Indian civilizations has practical impact on the "logic of consequences" of the country's security governance. Indian officials believe that they are representing not just a state (or an emerging power) but a great civilization. In fact, few "state-civilizations" are perceived to be India's equal. Hence, believing that India should be accorded deference and respect because of its intrinsic (and superior) civilizational qualities, many Indian diplomats and strategists are wary of having to depend upon states that do not appreciate India's special and unique characteristics. In fact, Nehru can be credited as one of the initiators of this narrative of exceptionalism with his statement that India has "*special* rights and duties in the management of international society based on the status as one of the world's major civilizations."[3]

Furthermore, Indians are convinced that India as a *civilization* has "something unique to offer to the rest of the world" (Singh, 2006, pp. 48–9). Confirming this proposition, Shivshankar Menon, the Foreign Secretary of the Ministry of External Affairs, acknowledges that

> sadly the language of strategic discourse in India is not yet developed enough to describe what we empirically know and face as reality around us. We need to develop our own strategic concepts and vocabulary. I am repeatedly struck by the use of concepts, ideas, and methods of analysis that come from other situations and interests (such as deterrence, parity, or reciprocity) and bear little relationship to our unique circumstance. That is something which needs serious examination on its own. (Menon, 2007, p. 391)[4]

In this respect, (not unlike the EU) India's strategic adjustments in the post-Cold War period appear constrained (rather than enabled) by the cognitive frameworks of its strategic culture. As discussed in Chapter 3, while the language and practices of security governance emerge in order to overcome the restrictions imposed by strategic cultures, New Delhi's articulations and projection of normative power remain constrained by the ramifications of the very myths it intends to overcome. Commenting on this trend, Selig Harrison has suggested that India suffers from a "post-dated self-image"—that is, the palpable confidence among many in India that the country is destined for great power status and therefore they "want others to treat them as if they had in fact already arrived."[5] The following discussion of India's involvement in Central Asia suggests that it has not (yet) been able to project itself as an influential normative foreign policy actor. As a result, New Delhi's international image has few appealing attributes that regional states might be tempted to emulate.

Dominant patterns in India's post-Cold War foreign policy

The trajectories of India's post-Cold War foreign policy reflect the complex articulations of its strategic culture. Some observers have claimed that the "seesawing foreign policies" witnessed in this period attest to the "infinite malleability" of India's international identity as evidenced by the constant modification, manipulation, and adaptation of its "national security culture" (Latham, 1998, pp. 134–54). Others have interpreted the perceived affliction with "a general ambience of indiscipline and lack of national purpose" as an indication that in its international relations, India acts "like a lady who has powerful suitors but is determined not to marry [any of them], because it is not in her interest to do so. A lady in this position has to play the game with considerable skill because every suitor is likely to feel that she is too inclined to the other party" (Basu, 2007, p. 213).

Such statements offer a smattering of the cacophony of voices involved in the interpretation of India's diplomatic formulations. They also reveal the contradictions at the heart of India's strategic culture that turns its security governance into a complex (and usually noncommittal) mixture of *realpolitik* and idealism held together by a wobbly normative framework (Kumar, 2008, p. 255). This pattern reflects an understanding of strategic culture as a "prism of perception" that molds the "ideational inter-subjective realm" of the country (Das, 2009, p. 396). Thus, as the former minister of External Affairs, Jaswant Singh, has indicated: "to define India's strategic culture one has to examine the very nature of India's nationhood; the very characteristics of its society; and the evolution of its strategic thought over the ages. [Thus], above all else, India is Hindu and Hindus think differently from non-Hindus. . . It is [Hinduism] that has given birth to a culture from which we hope to extract the essence of [India's] strategic thought" (Singh, 1999, pp. 2–5).

As it will be explained below, Singh's statement reflects a particular post-1998 "prism of perception," which re-nationalizes India's external relations by establishing an essentialized connection between "the present, the future, and a re-created past" (Kinnvall, 2006, pp. 29–56). Embodied in "the Hindu nuclear bomb,"[6] such strategic responses reflect a particular cognitive framing of globalization through the foundational imaginary of Hindu myths; which—in this process—are gradually becoming cornerstones of a new Indian international (and security) identity (Kavalski, 2010a). For the purposes of clarity, the following sections sketch out the main developments in the post-Cold War narratives of India's strategic culture.

Post-Cold War Blues

India's external relations reflect the contingencies of its geopolitical climate. Unlike other international actors, however, India seemed not only unprepared for the changes triggered by the end of Cold War, but it also perceived them as an unwelcome turn of events. In a nutshell, for India, the crumbling of the Berlin Wall represented "the loss of an entire world," because of "the disappearance of the familiar contours of the post-war world" (Menon and Nigam, 2007, p. 166; Chiriyankandath, 2004, p. 202). Thus, while it lasted, the "Cold War [had] provided an ideally stable environment: it allowed India to play an *exaggerated role* on the international stage for many years, where it could moralize about the inequalities of bipolarity and the 'Cold War mentality' while still benefiting materially and politically from its ties to both the Soviet Union and the USA" (Singh, 2006, p. 52; emphasis added).

Such attitudes underpin the "incoherence and indistinctiveness of India's foreign policy [at the time] due to the absence of a well-defined and well-articulated policy framework" (Jain, 2008, p. 42). Abid Husain, the former Indian ambassador to the United States, has offered one of the most revealing metaphors for this hankering after the passing away of the comfortable certainties of the Cold War. He recounted how "One economist described India as a tiger in a cage. When the cage is open, the tiger would show its real strength. The cage is now open but the tiger refuses to come out of the cage" (Husain, 1993). The reference to a "post-Cold War Blues" in India's foreign policy making indicates New Delhi's reluctance to venture out of the cognitive cage of the defunct Cold War world order.

At the same time, it is also intended to suggest the central dilemmas facing the repositioning of India's foreign policy: (i) the dissolution of the Soviet Union and (ii) the need to acknowledge the failure of nonalignment. These two mutually reinforcing dynamics evinced the third underlying predicament—(iii) the increasing tension between "militarism" (i.e. coercive international stance) and "moralism" (i.e. cooperative international stance) during the re-evaluation of India's external relations. In other words, the "post-Cold War Blues" becomes shorthand for the strategic practice of "*unrealpolitik*"—a behavior rooted in the legacy of colonial rule that leads Indian foreign policy makers to doubt their capacity to frame national interests (Kumar, 2008, p. 215).

The dissolution of the Soviet Union

A number of commentators have pointed out that there was "nothing as traumatic" for post-Independence India as the collapse of the Soviet Union (Mohan, 2004, p. 117). Some have even argued that since Moscow had become New Delhi's "most reliable fall-back option" (Menon and Nigam, 2007, p. 166), "the shock for India was greater than for most outside the erstwhile Communist Bloc" (Chiriyankandath, 2004, p. 199). Consequently, the "loss of Indo-Soviet relations to the inevitable march of history threw [India's] foreign policy into a chaotic situation" (Naik, 1995, pp. 173–5).

In this respect, the formulation of foreign policy was compounded not only by the unfavorable international environment, but also by its domestic impact. According to Sumit Ganguly, the 1991 financial crisis was an outcome of "the Soviet collapse [which] undermined India's autarkic approach to economic development, which, in turn, had serious consequences with respect to its foreign policy options" (Ganguly, 2003/2004, p. 43). These attitudes reinforce the perception of a serious blow to India's international identity and foreign policy formulation as a result of the dissolution of the Soviet Union.

The failure of nonalignment

Nonalignment has been the most distinctive feature of India's post-Independence foreign policy. Conceived by Jawaharlal Nehru, nonalignment became the cornerstone of India's foreign policy independence that revealed a "mindset of operating autonomously [while] disregarding other models" (Rana, 2007, p. 47). K. Misra has argued that owing to its South Asian origins, the notion of nonalignment reflects "the cultural psyche" and "the ways of thinking of the Indian people." As he points out, despite its negative construction (i.e. "not an alignment"), nonalignment is not a negative concept, but a positive endeavor "in favor of national reconstruction. . . [and] espousing to transform the international order" (Misra, 1981, pp. 26–37).

This activist framing of nonalignment can, therefore, be read as an avatar of India's normative power. It offered an alternative paradigm of world politics prompted by a vision of a *Pax Indica* around the principles of *Panchasheela* (Upahyaya, 2009, p. 77). While the international allure of nonalignment waned after the 1962 war with China, its impact on Indian strategic culture has prevented New Delhi from "internalizing a balance of power doctrine and making it part of its thinking about international relations" (Mehta, 2009, p. 220). Instead, India continued to project itself as a viable third way between Soviet communism and American capitalism.

Thus, in pragmatic terms, it was the melting of Cold War bipolarity (as the governing logic of the international system) that turned nonalignment into an irrelevant model for world order. Such a dramatic shift had profound consequences for the templates of India's normative power. In this setting, "India found itself [confronted with] a deep dilemma—how to adjust its non-aligned policy to the imperatives of a geopolitical shift in the post-Cold War scenario" (Jain, 2008, p. 30). At the same time, the obsolescence of nonalignment posed an unexpected challenge to the long-standing Nehruvian tradition in Indian foreign policy making. Consequently, India's policy-making anxiety in the immediate post-Cold War environment attests to the challenge of addressing the gaping fissures at the very core of the country's strategic culture.

The tension between "moralism" and "militarism"

The context provided by the disintegration of the Soviet Union and the failure of nonalignment underscored the need for a "basic change of philosophy" (Lal, 2006, p. 98) in India's foreign policy making. Yet, while the agreement on the need for transformation has been nearly universal, its content and direction became a subject of contestation for the better part of the 1990s. At the heart of the debate has been the friction between a "Kautilyan tradition" and an "Ashokan tradition" (Ahmed, 1993, pp. 216–26). The former refers to the model of regional geopolitics codified in the ancient text by Kautilya, *Arthśāstra*; the latter (is a modified version of Nehruvian idealism, which) emphasizes that India is "the world's most important democracy" (Mohan, 2004, p. 57).

The choice for New Delhi seemed bifurcated between an aggressive foreign policy behavior and an apprehensive international agency preoccupied with the protection of the country's volatile borders and precarious social order. The inability to address this tension in the immediate post-Cold War period has underscored the continuing contradictions of India's strategic culture between "the amoral realities of world politics and the moral norms which we aim at" (Basu, 2007, p. 222). Thus, while India's strategic culture has traditionally been comfortable with holding divergent view points, such an eclectic attitude produced a confusing "normative schizophrenia" in New Delhi's international outlook (Kumar, 2008, p. 212).

Therefore, in the immediate post-Cold War environment, New Delhi's attempts to construct a foreign policy in accordance with the shifting climate of international life seemed frustrated by the inability to meaningfully accommodate the desire for a more assertive role on the global stage and the concerns over the defense of its territorial integrity (Mohan, 2004, p. 208). In its struggle to come to terms with the uncertainties of the post-Soviet era, India has unsuccessfully pursued a "two-track approach that was, on the one hand, aimed at resurrecting the vital elements of its economic and military relations, and, on the other, searching out alternatives in the West" (Jha, 1997, p. 76). It is these attempts to follow a 'business-as-usual' pattern of behavior – by turning a blind eye to the ambiguities, contradictions, and inconsistencies of New Delhi's international agenda – that have contributed to the disarray in India's external relations in the immediate post-Cold War period.

1998 and after: Nuclear assertiveness

The testing of nuclear weapons is never a small affair. However, the actual event tends to grow in magnitude when the state undertaking the test has refused to formally accede to the nuclear nonproliferation regime and is in a nearly permanent state of attrition with one of its (equally armed) neighbors. The five nuclear devices detonated by India during 11–13 May 1998 at the Pokhran range confirmed this point. The tests set off widespread criticism and, at the same time, prompted concerns about a nuclear arms race in South Asia. Seemingly unfazed by the international censure (and in a stark contrast to its coy external stance during the early 1990s), the brazen geopolitical discourse of India's nuclear detonations indicated a marked departure from its previously noncommittal and largely conciliatory attitude. In a nutshell, *they were aimed to provoke*.

By flaunting its ability for "pre-emptive response," New Delhi has publicized its ability to independently chart the course for the ship of state in global politics (Basu, 2007, p. 207–22). Such nuclear assertiveness had to reassert the *Indianness* of its strategic culture. Thus, securing the country's strategic objectives becomes dependent on the particular "metaphors of 'Indianness'"—which form "'loose' drivers (organic predispositions)" that distinguish Indian approaches to international politics (Jones, 2006, p. 4). The 1998 nuclear tests have, therefore, become an important cutoff point in India's post-Cold War development. They reveal its progress toward "a more focused sense of itself in the world" which formed the backbone of "a more aggressive and self-confident foreign and security policy" (Lak, 2008, p. 245).

At that time, the Indian Foreign Minister, Jaswant Singh (1999, p. 44), proclaimed that "nuclear weapons remain a key indicator of state power. Since this currency is operational in large parts of the globe, India was left with no choice but to update and validate the capacity that had been demonstrated. . . in the nuclear test of 1974." This assertiveness seems to have been borne out of a long-standing frustration with New Delhi's marginalization in the international system. In this respect, India's post-1998 foreign policy stance indicates a qualitatively different interpretation both of the country's role in international life and the character of the international system.

The end of the post-Cold War foreign policy ambiguity

The 1998 nuclear tests have indicated an end in India's ambivalence between "militarism" and "moralism." The detonations demonstrated New Delhi's decision "to rely more on power politics and less on morality and unilateral restraint in the pursuit of Indian interests" (Kapur, 2006, p. 23). The choice of militarism reflects the interpretation of post-Cold War international relations as increasingly "confrontational and anarchic in nature" (Budania, 2003, p. 81). Reinforcing this point, Indian commentators ascertain that the vacillation between "a self-righteous pacifist approach [and] unilateral action does not take us anywhere":

> Any individual may face death bravely for his absolute principles. Can a country, or those who have the responsibility for its security, take a moral stand, on behalf of its people, which binds the future generations to an inequitable world order? This is where the nuclear option comes. There is no contradiction between working persistently and patiently towards a nuclear weapons free world and developing the nuclear option in the interim, *in the world as it is*. (Udgaonkar, 2001, p. 1792; emphasis in original)

Thus, by opting for Kautilya's geopolitical agenda, India intends to offer an emphatic projection of its "self-confidence" (*Hindustan Times*, 1998). Such a shift in foreign policy formulation has to indicate that New Delhi "can play its condign and productive role in global and regional affairs without being subservient to hegemonic powers" (Jain, 2008, p. 220).

Adopting an assertive foreign policy stance

The resolution of the foreign policy debates that have plagued the formulation and practice of India's post-Cold War international relations has also facilitated an increasingly more assertive external policy. According to C. Raja Mohan (2004, pp. 205–7), a veteran Indian journalist and commentator, this development suggests the recovery of a "forward foreign policy" approach pioneered by Lord Curzon. This "Curzonian school" of Indian foreign policy re-appropriates the "Indocentric" approach advocated by the former British Viceroy. Its strategic narrative displays the belief that "'strength respects strength' in foreign policy" (Chaulia, 2002, p. 221).

Thus, a critical aspect of the message sent by the 1998 nuclear tests is that "Indians are finally emerging from the mindset of dominated people, staking a claim to their rightful place in the global village" (Rai and Simon, 2007, p. 242). The discourse on and the desire for foreign policy independence has long been part and parcel of New Delhi's international relations. Yet, Indian policy-makers have seemed reticent to engage in a behavior that might be (mis) interpreted as the escalation of tensions in an already conflictual geopolitical environment.

Moreover, the Cold War provided an additional layer of structural constraints which limited India's room for independent foreign policy maneuver. The nuclear tests (at least discursively) appear to have lifted the perception of such constraints and have revealed India's willingness to insert its national interest on the global agenda (regardless of the opinions and expectations of other international actors). It is in this respect that the 1998 nuclear tests have become a symbol for the tectonic shift in the post-Cold War foreign policy of India.

Breaking with the imperatives of nonviolence

A central feature of the post-1998 foreign policy stance has been a criticism of the perceived "softness" of Nehru's "pseudo-secularism," which "twisted India's strategic culture into all kinds of absurdities" and ultimately led to "enfeebling a once fierce nation" (Chaulia, 2002, p. 220). In this context, the post-1998 assertiveness of India's forward foreign policy approach represents not merely a break with Nehruvian principles of international relations, but also with Gandhi's commitment to the imperatives of nonviolence. The assertion is that "a country with non-violent values has little chance to enter the major-power system" (Nayar and Paul, 2003, p. 105).[7]

The nuclear language of 1998 proclaims India's willingness to use force as a result of the accumulation of military capabilities that can ensure India's security objectives (Bajpai, 2005, p. 253). The shift indicated by the 1998 nuclear tests was "the result of unilateral military-political actions" pursued on the basis "of practical geopolitical considerations rather than the idealism of Nehru's peace policy" (Kapur, 2006, p. 5). At the same time, they attest to India's idiosyncratic understanding of *realpolitik*—one which intimates that national security can be achieved in "essentially unilateral terms" (Latham, 1998, p. 137).

The narrative outlines of the "Look North" policy

Most commentators maintain that India's engagement with Central Asia is a function of the country's historical interactions with the region. Thus, the "long-standing historical ties encompassing the political, cultural, economic, and religious dimensions" constitute the basis for the international relations between New Delhi and the individual Central Asian states (Bal, 2004, p. 4). Commentators have intimated that "the return of Central Asia to the world" has tended to "generate considerable romance" in New Delhi about rekindling the historic links between India and Central Asia (Muni and Mohan, 2007, p. 66). Confirming such romantic visions, the Bollywood actor Shashi Kapoor has proclaimed that "India and the beautiful countries of Central Asia *share the language of the heart* and a centuries-old culture. We have more in common with Central Asia than [with any other place in the world]."[8]

These (re)visions of New Delhi's involvement in the region have been underpinned by the conviction that "the glorious history of Indian cultural and intellectual achievement" (Kachru, 2007, pp. 207–31) offers a shortcut into the security governance of Central Asia that can substitute the establishment of a deliberate practice of shared interaction. Attesting to the conceptual confluence between "Brand India" and "normative power India" in New Delhi's post-1998 "prism of perception," such proclamations aver that "cultural diplomacy is rooted in geopolitics" (Bhattacharyya, 2004).

Such an attitude reflects a crucial element of India's security governance—the evocation of history for the fulfillment of strategic needs (Scott, 2009, p. 127). This pattern follows the cognitive map of a strategic culture, which assumes a position of superiority because of its "ageless and rich civilization." Jones argues that the collective consciousness of India's past bolsters its "natural claim to greatness." Hence, its prominence in international life is assumed to be an outcome of the legacy of the past—an entitlement that does not have to be earned, proven, or demonstrated (Jones, 2006, p. 7).

New Delhi's "Brand India"-type of normative power in Central Asia is, therefore, often framed in the language of a "civilizational state that should deploy its culture (part of its inherent greatness) as a resource or valuable diplomatic asset, and others [i.e. the Central Asian states] must become cognizant of the moral quality of the Indian foreign and strategic policy" (Mitra, 2003, p. 414). This realization is one of the underlying features in the post-1998 transformations in India's foreign policy, and it helps explain why India does not unveil initiatives that bring together Central Asian states and New Delhi around shared practices. In short, the perception of such "civilizational greatness" (if not superiority) demands that others recognize New Delhi's centrality by voluntarily subscribing to India's vision—indeed, India need not initiate socializing interactions as other states will want to be associated with the reputation of its ancient history and culture.

It is this context that backstops the articulation of the "Look-North" policy. Its discursive engagements with the roles played by India in Central Asia emphasize the need for the development of a proactive and assertive engagement in the region. Yet, the narrative exploitation of the legacies of the past by Indian foreign policy elites discloses a strategy that aims "to remind the new generation in Central Asia that India is not new to them but rather a very old friend if seen in the historical perspective. This creates a 'love at first sight' situation exhorting these past civilizational entities to recognize each other" (Jain, 2008, p. 210).

The conviction in such a "natural" and "self-evident" relationship underpins the strategic rationale of New Delhi's relations with Central Asia. Thus, the "Look North" policy becomes an expression of India's aspiration to establish itself as a model for a secular, multiethnic order that can be transported to the region. It should be reminded that the narratives of the "Look North" policy did not emerge in a vacuum, but were profoundly implicated by the post-Cold War trajectories of India's foreign policy making. The following sections sketch out these dynamics.

India's engagement in Central Asia before 1998

The "post-Cold War Blues," which infected India's international affairs during the 1990s made India's relations with Central Asia one of the most conspicuous aspects of its foreign policy ambiguity during this period. The uncertainty that has dominated this period had two important effects:

> One was that there emerged a new Central Asia, independent and sovereign, freed from the control of the former Soviet Union, and looking forward to a greater and dynamic engagement with the rest of the world, particularly Asia. The second was a sort of crisis of confidence in India's foreign policy perspective resulting from the collapse of the Cold War framework of global politics and the consequent erosion of the former Soviet Union as a source of foreign policy support. (Muni 2003, 102)

However, India's failure to engage Central Asia more convincingly is an outcome not only of the "post-Cold War Blues," but also of the formulation of New Delhi's external relations *in reaction to* Pakistan's foreign policy strategies. The memory and the construction of a historical narrative of independent Indian statehood has been profoundly scarred by the communal divisions that flared during the partition of British India. The trauma of that experience has left an indelible mark on the strategic culture of the country. In "Indian perceptions," therefore, Pakistan has "vested interests" in pursuing a "quest for strategic depth vis-à-vis India in Central Asia" (Joshi, 2007a, p. 150). The assertion is that the "philosophy [of Pakistan's interactions with the region] appears to have always focused on a prescriptive approach as to what *should* happen in or to the Central Asian states within the overall backdrop of deep antagonism against India" (Bal, 2004, pp. 332–3).

The security governance suggested by these discourses of the "Look North" policy has positioned India merely as a "*non-Pakistani* alternative" for Central Asia (*Hindustan Times*, 2008). Thus, the persistent preoccupation with Islamabad's policies in Central Asia and the "ill-conceived [and] ill-executed treatment [of the region] as a counterpoise between India and Pakistan" (Singh, 1999, p. 111) have tended to befuddle New Delhi's foreign policy making during this period. In this setting, the framework of India's "Look North" policy appears unable to obviate both the legacy of mistrust between India and Pakistan and the very real geographic barrier posed by Pakistan-occupied Kashmir.

The experience of India's engagement with Central Asia during the pre-1998 period illustrates that Pakistan "remains an important obstacle to a more productive cooperation with the region" (Muni and Mohan, 2005, p. 66). At the same time, however, Indian commentators have noted that since "neither India nor Pakistan is an immediate neighbor of Central Asia," the wrangling between New Delhi and Islamabad for Central Asia can be described as an "avoidable small game" (Dietl, 1997, p. 134). Such statements reveal the narrative oscillation and strategic tensions underscoring the articulation of an Indian-led framework for the security governance of Central Asia for much of the first post-Cold War decade.

India's engagement in Central Asia after 1998

The post-1998 foreign policy perceptions of Central Asia have been informed by the realization that despite the proclamations of the region's significance, New Delhi has been relegated to a somewhat marginal spectator as a result of its "wait-and-watch-and-hope-for-the best" approach (Mahalingam, 2004, p. 133). To rectify this trend, "India's 'forward' Central Asian policy" has emerged in the post-1998 period "as an integral component of its growing military, nuclear, and economic power" (Jain, 2008, p. 210). The 1998 nuclear tests have made possible a discursive shift in foreign policy formulation, which has provided a "conceptual 'model', 'window', 'lens', and 'frame of reference' through which Central Asia must be viewed" (Bal, 2004, p. 354). Thus, the stated overarching objective of India's "Look North" policy is the promotion of "peace and mutual prosperity" (Sinha, 2004, p. 9).

This intent, however, has been buttressed by the twin ambitions of (i) maintaining "the democratic and secular ethos" of the region, because it "binds India and Central Asia together" (Joshi, 2004, p. 210); and (ii) evolving "measures that would safeguard the stability and integrity of Central Asian republics and save them from getting divided and opposing one another"

(Asopa, 2007, p. 188). At the same time, confirming the (assertive) pragmatism of its post-1998 foreign policy, India has also developed a policy resting on the principles of strategic bilateralism in an attempt to overcome its marginalization in the region. The narrative construction of a security governance mechanism for Central Asia embedded in the narratives of the "Look North" policy (as revealed by these three discursive strategies) is detailed in the following sections.

Experience of managing diversity within a secular and democratic polity

Indian commentators have noted that the (violence accompanying the) dissolution of the Soviet Union and the Federal Republic of Yugoslavia has "eroded the legitimacy of multiethnic, multi-lingual, and multi-religious states" (Dixit, 2004, p. 24). This observation informs the (tacit) conviction that India is one of the few remaining countries that shares the characteristic features of the now defunct socialist federal arrangements (Kavalski and Zolkos, 2008). Consequently, such a realization underpins the responsibility of its foreign policy making to assert the viability of India's state-building project by demonstrating the relevance and experience of successfully managing its internal diversity through the institutional arrangements of a secular and democratic polity. In this context, the assertion usually is that India is not "multicultural by accident," but "multicultural by design" (Manohoran, 2003, p. 330). Thus, India's strategic objective in the region is to "work for the rise and consolidation of democratic and secular polities in Central Asia, because the spill-over of the rise of religious extremism may threaten India's own internal stability and security" (Muni, 2003, pp. 98–9).

Yet, New Delhi's involvement in Central Asia is not about proselytizing the values of democracy (at least not explicitly) but about "letting regional states see what India stands for and what it offers" (Jawahar, 2002). India's involvement in Central Asia appears to be animated by a sense of security governance exercised through the "power of example" (Mehta, 2009, pp. 210–19), but without an attempt to engender communities of practice around specific behaviors or standards. Thus, while democracy is constructed as a desirable value, India (owing to the constraints of its strategic culture) does not integrate democracy-promotion into its external agency; instead, New Delhi asserts that it is "a matter for other states to recognize [the benefits of democracy] and act in accordance" (Jones, 2006, p. 7). Consequently, unlike China's and the EU's normative power which are premised on the power of *active* example (i.e. socialization), India's normative power is based on the power of *passive* example (i.e. an expectation that others will follow New Delhi's lead without providing any inducements or reinforcements).

Indian expectations, however, have been frustrated by the realization that while "conversant in the art of governance" (Asopa, 2007, p. 173), Central Asian states are experiencing a pronounced democratic deficit. Indian commentators list multiple (and, oftentimes, contradictory) rationalities in their explanation of the weakness of democratic practices in the region:

- Firstly, there is a near-universal agreement that the Central Asian states "were ill-prepared for independence" (Joshi, 2003, p. 69). According to this assessment, the independence of Central Asian states was an outcome of "the exclusively subjective ambitions of a group of political leaders and their scramble for political power" (Bal, 2004, pp. 301–2).
- Secondly, despite their independence from the Soviet Union, the leadership of the Central Asian states is still "dominated by the former communist party ruling elites who have adopted democratic pretensions" (Muni, 2003, p. 103). This makes it "difficult for [regional leaders] to appreciate something that their cognitive process has never experienced [i.e. democracy]" (Dash, 2007, p. 190).
- Thirdly, the nascent forms of authoritarianism in Central Asia have been contextualized within long-standing indigenous forms, institutions, and processes of power relations. In particular, the reference to the clan-mentality of Central Asian politics points to the quandaries of a political process in which the dynamics of "regional and tribal affiliations" trump the legitimacy of "political vision and program" (Sharma, 2004b, p. 429).
- Fourthly, the post-Soviet transition of the Central Asian states has been profoundly disrupted by the nexus between drug trafficking, organized crime, and Islamic fundamentalism (Mahapatra, 2005, pp. 168–9).

The confluence between and simultaneity of these dynamics seems to infer that there is "little prospect for a radical departure from the present scenario" (Dash, 2007, p. 204). Paradoxically, however, such realization does not seem to instigate a deliberate practice of regional security governance (for instance, by emulating China). Thus, just like the EU, India's engagement in Central Asia is driven by a perception that it is a "force for good" in world affairs, because—as the Prime Minister, Manmohan Singh asserts—"the world today wants

India to do well."[9] However, owing to its *passive* power of example, India still appears unable to set the standards for 'normal' in global life (regardless of its desire to do so). This realization suggests that despite the underlying assertiveness, India's Central Asian policies are not completely divorced from the conceptual and policy inconsistency that marked India's pre-1998 engagement in the region. In particular, they demonstrate the lack of both capacity and will to initiate communities of practice in the region.

Encouraging regional cooperation in Central Asia

Intertwined with the narrative modalities of secularism and democracy, the "Look North" policy also stresses the significance of regional cooperation to the stability and prosperity of Central Asia. The proposition of Indian commentators is that "India should try [to] forge a collective security arrangement and a collective project for the development of all the countries of the region regardless of their policy slant in favor of this or that great power" (Asopa, 2007, pp. 173–88). New Delhi's call for "greater political cooperation among the Central Asian states" rests on the perception of a "host of common specificities" that they share (Gidadhubli, 2007, p. 171).

This insistence on maintaining the unity of Central Asian states reflects Indian perceptions of the pragmatic benefits from (even a rudimentary form of functional) cooperation which "transforms conventional aspirations into more open, dynamic, and wider practices of peaceful coexistence, collective responsibility, and development" (Lama, 2005, pp. 134–5). The regional character of "these flows" facilitates the "forging [of] linkages and bonds of solidarity" among the participating states (Pant, 2005, p. 181). The fear is that without regional integration, history might be repeated and Central Asia may lose "its creative capacity [just like it did] during the sixteenth century, owing to its internecine warfare, internal instability, and external aggressive policy" (Haidar, 2003, p. 260).

In this respect, there seems to be a significant level of disappointment among Indian commentators that "the political leadership of these countries has been unable to evolve a mind-set that could be truly characterized as Central Asian" (Behera, 2003, p. 210). Yet again, despite such realization, there appears to be little desire in New Delhi to provide a framework that might instigate such collaborative practices in the region. Instead, the lack of regional integration is blamed on the selfish pursuit of narrow personal gains by nepotistic state-elites, which (more often than not) are disguised under the narrative cloak of (ethno-) national interests. Thus, Indian commentators have noted that the failure of Central Asian states to establish a robust framework for regional cooperation illustrates their "poor governance" (Pillai, 2003, p. 249).

Such statements infer the bankruptcy of India's *example* to act as a lodestone for Central Asian elites in the absence of tangible and deliberate practices of socialization. In this setting, while the discourses of the "Look North" policy reveal India's aim to attract Central Asia to its sphere of influence, in a Kautilyan fashion, it also resents the regional security governance strategies of other international actors. Some Indian commentators have propounded that the alleged "homogeneity [of the region] is quite deceptive" and hinders the comprehension of the "diversity, which is articulated in many different ways" in the convoluted dynamics of Central Asian politics (Sharma, 2007, p. 123). The suggestion is that India needs to accompany its regional approach with "country-specific" strategies targeting individual Central Asian states (Dash, 2007, p. 205). This understanding informs the discussion of India's bilateralism in the region in the following section.

Making use of strategic bilateralism in Central Asia

As already suggested, the narratives of the "Look North" policy indicate a desire to encourage regional cooperation among the Central Asian states. Such proclamations notwithstanding, India's engagement in the region has been paralleled by a significant level of bilateral relations between New Delhi and the Central Asian capitals. Pragmatically speaking, the development of strong bilateral relations with some countries in the region reveals New Delhi's attempts to overcome the constraints imposed by its latecomer status in Central Asian affairs, which has further compounded the effects from the lack of a direct physical access to the region (Kavalski, 2007b, p. 854). Thus, India has adopted an approach aimed at making up for lost time with respect to the Central Asian agency of other international actors (especially, China).[10]

In this respect, it is Tajikistan that—to all intents and purposes—has become the posterchild of New Delhi's bilateralism in Central Asia. The construction of Tajikistan as India's "gateway to Central Asia" (Asopa, 2003, p. 153) is of complex provenance in the narratives of the "Look North" policy. The hackneyed point of departure seems to be the observation of "millennia-old," "civilizational relationship" between Tajikistan and the subcontinent (Kaushik, 2003, pp. 30–7). At the same time, many commentators assert that Tajikistan is "the first Central Asian republic [to] realize the importance of building a broader national identity based on institutions" and not on an exclusive ethnicity—a state-building strategy akin to that of India (Sharma, 2003, p. 73).

Strategically speaking, however, it is the shared perception of external threats that appears to motivate India's bilateral relations with Tajikistan. Indian commentators explain that the civil war which ravaged the country during the 1990s has been "*caused* by a skillful exploitation of the inter-regional/inter-clan rivalries by forces of Islamic fundamentalism supported by the Pakistan-backed Mujahideen in Afghanistan" (Kaushik, 2003, pp. 39–40; emphasis added). In this respect, from the point of view of New Delhi, India and Tajikistan having "suffered a lot on account of onslaughts of the dark forces of religious extremism active in Afghanistan *must work together*" (Warikoo, 2003, p. 151; emphasis added).

Thus, while demonstrating the balance-of-power attitude informing India's post-1998 policy toward Central Asia, commentators tend to establish a link between New Delhi's logistic and military support for the anti-Taliban Northern Alliance through Tajikistan since the mid-1990s. Such assistance was articulated as a strategy for "strengthening Tajikistan's secular forces in their war against Islamic fundamentalism" (Asopa, 2007, p. 173). For instance, there have been allegations that India's military outposts in the country have been set up as early as the mid-1990s (Bedi, 2002, p. 17). Framed as an offer of "humanitarian assistance," in 2000, India has formally acknowledged the establishment of a military hospital on the Tajik-Afghan border at Farkhor and the widening of a military air-strip near Dushanbe for transport aircraft (Singh, 2003, p. 201). More recently, India—still "quietly, very quietly"—has deployed at least one helicopter squadron at its "Ayuni" air-base in Tajikistan to bolster its already existing rapid response capabilities (Pandit, 2007). As one commentator pointed out, such developments clearly demonstrated that New Delhi was shedding its image as "the white elephant of Asia" and also that "India's strategic aspirations have now finally come of age" (Aroor, 2007).

The discourses of the "Look North" policy legitimize this military outreach by maintaining that "the nation's strategic interests lie far beyond [its] borders"—a realization, which is "compelling New Delhi to consider the possibility of sending troops abroad *outside of the UN framework*" (Mohan, 2007, p. 395; emphasis added). A. K. Anthony, the Minister of Defense, has confirmed this assertive stance during a 2007 Army Commanders Conference by acknowledging that India will "play a role commensurate to its stature, potential, and aspirations. It need not be overemphasized that our strategic interests extend far beyond the South Asian region."[11] Thus, India's military presence in Tajikistan becomes one of the clearest indications of the presumed Kautilyan logic of its post-1998 foreign policy. As the Foreign Secretary, Shri Shivshankar Menon, has suggested, it is part of a strategy for "ensuring a peaceful periphery" through the expansion of "circles of engagement starting with the immediate neighborhood, West Asia, Central Asia, Southeast Asia, and the Indian Ocean."[12]

In this respect, India's post-1998 involvement in the region exposes an underlying "revisionist" foreign policy stance—through which New Delhi aims to *revise* the existing patterns in its international environment in order to facilitate the exercise of its own agency (Mohan, 2004, p. 80). Thus, the intense ties with Tajikistan reveal India's attempt to carve out a space for its stakes in Central Asia. Yet, the assertiveness backstopping this proactive bilateral arrangement still remains framed by the anti-Pakistan logic that dominated the pre-1998 period. For instance, the emergence of a strategic triangle between India, Tajikistan, and Afghanistan indicates not merely an attempt to gain a strategic beachhead in the region, but "to encircle Pakistan."[13]

The engrained tendency to cultivate counteralliances with Pakistan's neighbors (Jones, 2006, p. 26) confirms the cognitive rut of a strategic culture unable to conceive an alternative approach to the region (based on the *active*—rather than the *passive*—power of example). In other words, India's bilateral relations with Tajikistan fail to demonstrate socializing propensity that might become the cornerstone of a more encompassing community of practice. For instance, the much-flaunted "Indian" air-base in the country was lost in 2011 when Tajikistan decided to discontinue the informal arrangement with India (Kucera, 2011). The suggestion, therefore, is that until India overcomes the constraints and tensions of its strategic culture, it is unlikely to develop a meaningful security governance mechanism that would sway the region in tune with New Delhi's normative power.

In lieu of a conclusion: The lack of influence of the "Look North" policy

The preceding discussion has engaged the implications of the "Look North" policy for India's security governance of Central Asia. It has demonstrated that New Delhi's agency in the region is informed by a strategic culture imbued with a desire for establishing "a more perfect world." In particular, the discourses of the "Look North" policy intimate that "India cannot wait until the rest of the world comes to its way of seeing things or at least acknowledges India's right to do things its own way"—the implication being that "*in a more perfect world*, [New Delhi's] importance would be self-evident [because in] such a world each major power [would] act responsibly to keep order and promote justice in *its part of the world*" (Singh, 2006, pp. 50–2; emphasis added).

Such articulations reveal a proclivity toward a narrative projection of India as a blueprint for Central Asian development. However, this discursive desire for "a more perfect world" is not backstopped by a deliberate practice that can turn such diplomatic rhetoric into reality through the socialization of regional states. Instead, New Delhi appears to have been either unable or unwilling "to face up to the challenges and opportunities of a dynamic security environment" (Mitra, 2003, p. 400). The proclamations of India's external agency in Central Asia have not been matched by comparable transformations in the ideational and institutional makeup of New Delhi's foreign policy formulation. Thus, despite the proliferation of discourses on India's rise to global prominence, the absence of a readily available Indian vision of global politics—a *Pax Indica*, if you will—prevents New Delhi from living up to the expectations generated by such narratives.

On the one hand, India—despite all the assertions to the contrary—still seems unable to overcome the South Asian demarcation of its agency because of its "unfulfilled longing for identity" (Mehta, 2009, p. 217). This seems to be compounded by the lack of consensus on "what constitutes the national interest" (Kumar, 2008, p. 255). On the other hand, the (nuclear) assertiveness of the post-1998 foreign policy stance tends to view normative power from the associated unease about "soft vulnerability"—that is, the possible fate of seeing others doing what you *do not* want (Hymans, 2009, p. 259). It is because of this anxiety that Indian observers tend to interpret the normative power of the EU as a "convenient escape from confronting emerging challenges" (Mohan, 2004, p. 74).[14] Radha Kumar explains such attitude as a legacy of colonialism and its impact on Indian strategic culture, which has made it "unable to distinguish between normative and non-normative Western behavior" (Kumar, 2008, p. 216).[15]

Yet, it is precisely because it does not have a convincing normative power that Central Asian states do not follow New Delhi's lead. Thus, while Indian foreign policy makers seem to understand that the practice of security governance is relational, they nevertheless insist that its stability depends on the preponderant availability of military capacities. Consequently, in the absence of a power of attraction, India still has not managed to develop into "*a kind of a model* for other countries" (Dutt, 2000, p. 205). Instead, India's security governance of the region has been "indistinct and incoherent" because of its underlying "*lack of vision*" (Alexander, 2004, p. 357).

Thus, while India has a number of influential individuals and businesses, as an international actor, the country does not have an *influential* normative power that could establish India as an alternative to existing models of order. Such an assertion should not be misinterpreted as an allegation that India does not have a respected and significant history and cultural heritage. However, the international recognition of this legacy (just like the recognition of its nuclear capabilities) does not amount to *influence*. The discussion of New Delhi's agency in Central Asia has demonstrated that despite the visibility of "Brand India," the narrative construction of India's current external affairs does not project a specific (if any) vision of a world order that would distinguish if from the other participants in the "new great game." Consequently, the international identity of New Delhi has no distinct attributes that Central Asian states might be tempted to emulate.

The question that emerges from the discussion of New Delhi's agency in Central Asia is whether India can "offer an alternative vision of a new world order" (Bhattacharjea, 2008, p. 10), just like the EU and China have done. In other words, the analysis of India's external affairs still does not seem to offer a convincing response to the query whether India "*can change enough*" to become a pole of attraction in an international environment marked by "extreme turbulence" (Kachru, 2007, p. 14). The current setting seems to suggest that India would retain its relative position of *no influence* for some time to come—at least, until it manages to infuse its agency with a normative power that can successfully translate the imperatives underpinning its strategic culture to Central Asia. For the time being, however, India's foreign policy making is likely to remain "a rainbow of contradictions" (Rai and Simon, 2007, p. 158).

Conclusion: The (struggle for) recognition of adaptive normative powers

I become a friend to every person
suffered from this a thousand torments,
Gained nothing, wondered through the world,
I am comforter and am afflicted.

MUHAMMAD MUQIMIY[1]

Introduction

This investigation has been about the place of Central Asia in world politics and the way international affairs affect Central Asia. At the same time, this book has also inquired into the place of the region—both actual and perceived—in the study of global life. Thus, yielding to the suggestion that international relations scholars are historians of world affairs (Puchala, 2003, pp. 1–14), this volume traces the security governance strategies extended to Central Asia by normative powers. This study proposes that the region has been consistently treated as a *context* for the agency of external actors. To that effect, this book has undertaken a parallel assessment of the normative power of the EU, China, and India in Central Asia.

The "immediate" (i.e. observable) corollary of such investigation is that the contextual effectiveness of normative power is a product of design, rather than chance. In particular, the contingency attendant in the promotion of security governance mechanisms impacts the provisions and frameworks of the institutional and ideational makeup of normative foreign policy agency. Yet, the recognition of the contingency of the Central Asian context does not imply that anything is possible, but that what is possible emerges in the context of active and deliberate interaction. It is deliberate practices that change attitudes and assist mutual adaptation. Thus, the cases of normative powers included in Part II of the volume have indicated that their agency in different global locales is relative to their flexibility, contextual atunement, and capacity for "overture to the 'Other'" (Kavalski and Zolkos, 2008, p. 158).

This chapter begins with a summary of the main propositions advanced by this inquiry. The overview of the analytical framework of the volume offers a conceptual snapshot of the main propositions relating to the notion and practices of normative power and security governance. The outline of the cognitive frameworks and strategic cultures of normative foreign policy actors provides the intellectual setting for the assessment of the EU's, China's, and India's agency in Central Asia. The summary initially assesses the individual effects from the involvement of Brussels, Beijing, and New Delhi in the region and then provides a parallel analysis of their normative power in Central Asia. Such a comparative assessment offers an idiosyncratic "translation" of the EU's, China's, and India's relations with Central Asia through inferences drawn from the distinct cognitive frameworks of their strategic cultures.

This chapter also draws attention to a unique feature that becomes conspicuous from the parallel study of normative foreign policy actors—the functional interdependence between normative powers and their environments. In particular, the emphasis on the relational character of security governance draws attention to the dynamics through which the demand for recognition affects the construction of an actor as a normative power. Thus, the security governance projects of the EU, China, and India in Central Asia reflect a nascent "struggle for recognition" of their normative power status. In this respect, this chapter suggests that the parallel assessment of normative powers *in context* has significant implications for the analysis of their interactions with one another. The claim is that the explanation of the possible trajectories in the relations between international actors are best deciphered not through the study of their bilateral interactions but through the examination of the character of their associations with third parties. The chapter concludes with a preliminary investigation of what *acting politically* under the conditions of a "struggle for recognition" might actually mean?

Overview of the analytical propositions

This book has contended that it is the rise of normative powers that makes Central Asia one of the most emblematic features in the fluid post-Cold War geographies of global life. In this respect, the proposition is that the pervasive uncertainty of the regional spatialization reflects the overlapping security governance strategies of various international actors. This study has explicitly concentrated on the agency of the EU, China, and India. The suggestion is that it is the practices initiated by such normative foreign policy actors that become significant to the trajectories of Central Asian affairs. In other words, even if local, regional interactions are nevertheless enmeshed in global networks of relations.

The analysis of Part I captures this complexity in the historical and cognitive contextualization of the region on the mental maps of world politics. Trawling through a warren of designations and experiences, Chapter 1 infers that Central Asia emerges as a web of discourses and desires that arrange the patterns of international relations within a particular global locale through the relational and interactive aspects of geopolitical labels. This proposition draws attention to the construction of Central Asian affairs as a contested site for the transmission of competing rules produced by distinct and overlapping regimes of security governance extended by normative foreign policy actors. The ensuing increasing awareness of vulnerability to distant causes conveys a sense of unpredictability prompted by the catalytic effects of small events, whose consequences are felt later, elsewhere, and by others (Kavalski, 2008b, p. 426).

The reference to the "new great game" therefore acknowledges the multidirectionality of such processes. In particular, this term has become shorthand for the rival images of appropriateness that are extended to the region by normative powers such as the EU, China, and India. At the same time, the notion of the "new great game" recognizes the increasing autonomy in the selection of priorities by the Central Asian states. The onus is not only on the external actors, but also on the regional polities as they (have to) indicate whose image they are adopting (or adapting to). Therefore, the discussion of the "new great game" in Chapter 1 challenges entrenched perceptions of the alleged passivity of Central Asian states that depicts them as incapable of independent agency in international life. On the contrary, the region is turning into "a fully-fledged international player in its own right" and is pivotal to the emergence of a "New Silk Road," which exposes that "all roads no longer merely run through Central Asia, they run to it" (Carls, 2009, p. 1).

All five of the Central Asian states have demonstrated their panache for bandwagoning-for-profit and pick-and-choose strategies (Kavalski, 2010b, c). Thus, while regional polities might find themselves compelled to indicate their preferred model of externally promoted behavior, they are not constrained to comply with its injunctions for long and, in fact, oftentimes swing their preferences to another external pole of attraction. These dynamics have tended to assist the proliferation of external normative agency in Central Asia. In this respect, the location of Central Asia in the pattern of global politics is neither fixed nor stable. Hence, the security governance developed by normative foreign policy actors is relative to the provision of credible commitments in a relational setting.

Chapter 3 develops the argument that effective security governance mechanisms are embedded within communities of practice. This proposition uncovers the fundamental fluidity and self-organization of the dynamics of international socialization. As a result, the visions of order that frame the external promotion of norms are contingent on the ability to develop deliberate practices that can maintain their appeal. Thus, "as communities of practice generate knowledge, they [also] renew themselves" (Wenger and Snyder, 2000, p. 243). Especially, as the case of China (in Chapter 6) reveals, the security governance of normative foreign policy actors conceives of "communities as fields of practice" through which actors acquire their intersubjective meanings and the capacity to act as agents (Adler, 2005, p. 6).

At the same time, it is the *awkwardness* of Central Asian polities that opens the region to the agency of the EU, China, and India. As already demonstrated, it is the demand for recognition of their newly independent status in international life that underpins the willingness of Central Asian states to interact with a wide array of international actors. As the analysis of Part II indicates, the involvement of the EU, China, and India in the region aims at having conditioning effects on state behavior. In this respect, Chapter 2 outlines the analytical framework for approaching the agency of distinct normative powers. The contention is that the proliferation of normative foreign policy actors reinforces the sensitivity to the complexity of global politics marked by diverse understandings of what the 'proper' framework of international affairs should be.

Thus, in terms of the Central Asian agency of the EU, China, and India, the notion of normative power allows for engaging with the underlying ideational motivations of their strategic cultures. In other words, strategic culture provides the grammar of cognition within and through which normative power is practiced. Since the term "strategic culture" comprises "deep-seated norms, beliefs, and ideas about an actor's role in the world, its perception of security threats, and the legitimate means and ends for the use of force" (Meyer, 2007, p. 2), the suggestion is that normative powers are complex actors whose impact cannot be reduced to the level of either individual, or agency, or rules of engagement, or policy representation, or particular belief systems and emotions, or any other facet of their decision-making. On the contrary, the whole represented by normative powers is truly more than the sum of its part (Kavalski, 2007b). Thus, while it does not necessarily assist in the predilection of specific policy choices, an awareness of an actor's strategic culture makes available an understanding of the broader context of beliefs, attitudes, and emotions within which policy-making occurs.

In this setting, the assessment of the Central Asian agency of the EU, China, and India has offered insights into their regional policies and not their (grand) foreign policy designs (although an inference can easily be drawn). At the same time, the Central Asian agency of the EU, China, and India facilitates the understanding of how their security governance engages with the regional "lived realities" (Raddon, 2007, pp. 61–5). Thus, while related, the *particular* Central Asian and the *general* international relations of normative foreign policy actors reflect distinct conceptualizations of identity, interests, and effort that are contingent on contextual interpretations. Normative powers, therefore, should be perceived as neither the "goodies" nor the "baddies" of global life. Instead, as the analyses of the EU, China, and India in Part II have demonstrated, they are merely *powers*. Yet, because it is framed by their strategic culture, the *power* of normative foreign policy actors resides in their ability to influence other actors through the capacity to make some policy choices more attractive than others (but without recourse to or the threat of force). In other words, the power of normative powers is relative to their ability to influence perceptible alterations in the behavior, emotions, and beliefs of other actors. It is this recognition of and demand for such dispositional change that calls attention to the frameworks of security governance extended by normative powers.

Security governance, as Chapter 3 explains, emerges as a system of deliberate practices aimed at regulating, coordinating, and managing the collective existence of actors (Adler and Greve, 2009, p. 64). The instances of the EU, China, and India evidence that the security governance of normative powers simultaneously rests upon and reveals asymmetric relationships. In this respect, Chapter 3 demonstrates that, in practice, security governance is about the ways in which normative foreign policy actors manage such relations of asymmetry. The analytical claim of the volume is that it is through the deliberate practice of *doing things together* with other actors that normative powers are able to influence the policy-making behavior of target states through the process of socialization. To paraphrase from Norbert Elias, the deliberate practice of security governance reveals that normative power is about the exertion of influence over others as it is about exerting influence over oneself.[2] Strategically speaking then, security governance is about the practices that become prevalent in a particular region. Socialization ensures their persistence via the interactions and relationships established through communities of practice. Thus, Part I of the volume proposes that by instigating communities of practice, normative powers indicate credible commitments and deliberate efforts to socialize other actors into promoted models of behavior as scripted by the cognitive frameworks of their strategic culture.

Main findings

The findings from the application of the analytical propositions of Part I to the Central Asian experience of extraregional actors both confirm some expectations from already acknowledged trajectories and suggest a few new trends. This section will first focus on the outcomes from the analysis of the individual agency of the EU, China, and India in Central Asia before engaging in parallel assessment of their normative power in the region. It has to be reiterated that the assumption of this volume is that all the three of them are normative foreign policy actors. In this respect, the investigations of Part II confirm that the EU, China, and India are engaging Central Asian states from either the position or the intention to be (and, thereby, the rhetorical disposition of) normative powers. However, despite this similarity, the Central Asian agency of the EU, China, and India has indicated diverse abilities to influence perceptible alterations in the behavior, emotions, and beliefs of regional states.

Individual assessment of the Central Asian agency of normative foreign policy actors

This book has investigated *when* (i.e. under what conditions) and *how* (i.e. through what processes) have normative foreign policy actors been able to promote effective security governance mechanisms. By focusing on the strategic culture that informs their international agency, the proposition has been that it is by initiating communities of practice that normative powers gain the capacity to shape definitions of the "normal." It is through the deliberate practice of security governance and the ongoing commitment to "respect the other" (in the context of an asymmetric relationship) that normative foreign policy actors are able to socialize target states. The suggestion is that such relationships do not and should not be based on consensus (or consensual hegemony) to have socializing effects. Instead, the repeated and deliberate practice of interaction provides a shared framework through which different issues are discussed. As argued in Chapter 3, security governance "need not entail any socialization to a norm, but merely repeated exposure to how things are, and are not, done" (Hopf, 2010, p. 542). Bearing these propositions in mind, the following sections consider the individual effects of the normative power of the EU, China, and India in Central Asia.

The European Union

To begin with, for the EU, Central Asia clearly poses the fundamental challenge of approaching a post-Communist region outside of the established frameworks for enlargement and enlargement-like initiatives. In particular, the focus on strategic culture points out that the ontology of Brussels' policy-making as a knee-jerk reaction to entrenched cultural predispositions (deriving from the securitization of the integration project) makes it very difficult for the EU to alter its foreign policy behavior—especially, when such change is promptly needed. Thus, in terms of Brussels' global outreach, the development of sophisticated security governance mechanisms through the Europeanization of candidate and neighborhood countries seems to undercut the operational effectiveness of the EU's normative power in "out-of-Europe" areas.[3] In fact, as the experience of Central Asia indicates, the security governance of the EU seems to be severely constrained by the novel need to compete with other normative powers.

It would appear that Brussels' "cultural instincts" toward envisioning regions as nascent security communities (Kavalski, 2008a) are ill-suited to the dynamic political context of Central Asia. Likewise, the EU's predilection to position itself as a security community builder does not seem to curry it any favors (let alone influence) in the region (Delcour, 2011, p. 153). In fact, the EU finds itself in the unusual situation where it not only is not a magnet for the Central Asian countries, but it also is in the uncomfortable (and qualitatively new) position of vying for the attention of awkward states that appear spoilt for choice by the many suitors involved in the "new great game." At the same time, the reticence and uncertainty that marks the EU's engagement in Central Asia during the 1990s offers probably one of the clearest indications of the difficulty for both sides of the Cold War divide to alter their cognitive patterns and conceptual vocabulary, carefully groomed during the decades of antagonism and confrontation.

As Chapter 4 shows, while the security governance of Brussels has traditionally been characterized by the dynamics of inclusion and exclusion, Central Asia—unique among all the other post-Communist regions—is subject to explicit *exclusionary* exclusion. Thus, while the EU has practiced exclusionary forms of security governance both as punishment and as setting (negative) examples for quite some time now, these can be interpreted as forms of *inclusive* exclusion—that is, those excluded are still subject to a form of socialization by the EU. In contrast, the EU's *exclusionary* exclusion is not characterized by any deliberate practice of educating others and promoting compliance. Instead, as the instance of the Central Asian states demonstrates, those subject to *exclusionary* exclusion are simply ignored. The inference then is that Brussels seems disinterested in the transformation of Central Asian countries and, instead, appears bent on leaving them to find their way through the fluid maze of regional affairs—that is, Central Asian states are the kind of polities that the EU will neither consider as targets for meaningful socialization nor feel the "moral" compulsion to Europeanize.

Such an inference seems confirmed by the reactive 'disaster mentality' that characterizes the EU's actorness in Central Asia—especially after the terrorist attacks on the United States on 11 September 2001. It reveals the effects of failure (rather than success) in temporarily altering the international behavior of normative foreign policy actors. Thus, the underdeveloped Central Asian agency of the EU has found itself in a situation where it was forced to jump-start (belatedly) in the early 2000s its regional approach. Regardless of such (already undertaken or projected) shifts in its approach, Chapter 4 demonstrates that Brussels still remains disconnected from the region, because it has not altered the substance of its security governance practice. To borrow from Steve Wood's taxonomy, the EU's normative power in Central Asia fails to deliver, because it still is not a deliberate "actor" for the security governance of the region. Instead, its pre-1999 initiatives establish it as a "passive pole," while its post-1999 involvement positions it as a "pragmatic reactor" (Wood, 2011, p. 246). In this respect, the EU's search for a "new" strategy for Central Asia (and also for its external affairs beyond enlargement and enlargement-like initiatives) demands a serious reflection upon the impact, substance, and practices of its own normativity.

China

As Chapter 5 has revealed, China—with its deliberate and thoughtful engagement in Central Asia—seems to occupy almost the opposite end on the continuum of normative agency from the EU. Again, it is the focus on its strategic culture that helps uncover the intriguing intersection between the discursive memory of the past with the contexts of the present and the anticipated tasks of the future. The idiosyncratic confluence between these modalities seems to animate the patterns of China's security governance in the region. It would seem, therefore, that Beijing recollects a security governance approach premised on the practices of interaction rather than explicit norms of appropriateness. Such conceptualization is informed by China's unique experience of modernization which promotes awareness that Beijing should not inflict its experience upon others by force, but by making China attractive to them.

In this setting, the proposition of Chapter 5 is that owing to the specificities of its historical trajectory, its idiosyncratic polity, and its power constellations, China advances a particular understanding of prescribed and proscribed behavior in international life that predisposes it to act in a normative way in Central Asia. In fact, China's foreign policy can be read as an attempt to rectify the discursive legacy of 'the century of humiliation' by projecting a self-conscious international identity dispelling the specters of the past; yet, whose socializing rhetoric and deliberate practice proclaim that others need not experience humiliation either. The conceptualization of the international role(s) of China as a shaper of norms intimates procedural socializing mechanisms as a consequence of its deliberate efforts to practice credible commitments.

In Central Asia, this pattern of security governance mechanisms has been framed by the Shanghai Cooperation Organization (SCO). At the same time, Chapter 5 indicates that the perception of SCO as the lodestone of a new *Pax Sinica*—that is, an ambitious strategy for regional domination through the establishment of a Sinocentric (regional/world) order—is a major oversimplification. The assertion of Chinese domination tends to reflect Western strategies of narrativizing historical experience, which conjure up images of thinly veiled quasi-imperialistic visions of regional security governance.[4] In fact, to the extent that there exists a Central Asian version of a *Pax Sinica*, it reveals that sovereignty is a social structure whose meaning emerges in the process of interaction (Murray, 2008, p. 250).

Thus, by indicating the overlapping contexts of China's normative power, Chapter 5 has demonstrated that the institutionalization of SCO affords Beijing an opportunity to project itself as a blueprint for the future trajectories of Central Asian states. In particular, by providing an active community of practice in the region, Beijing assists in developing a sense of belonging to a group of shared social norms and values. Consequently, China's normatively driven engagement in the region has exhibited socializing effects. Moreover, in acknowledgment of the fact that "'newly emerging powers' are an increasingly important force in international politics" (Glosny, 2010, p. 101), Beijing's influence in the region has been assisted by the ability to articulate self-reflexive security governance policies premised on the centrality of sovereignty and the economic benefits of China's peaceful development.[5] In this respect, the logic of relationships underpinning China's normative power reveals that Beijing's authoritative status in Central Asia is an outcome of its strategic culture, which assists "others in becoming the true authors of their lives" (Rosemont, 2011, p. 1).

India

The discussions in Chapter 6 have indicated that India's "Look North" policy occupies a position in-between the EU and China on the continuum of external normative agency in Central Asia. The analysis reveals that for the better part of the 1990s, India's foreign policy formulation has remained in the grips of conceptual tensions, strategic uncertainty, and geopolitical constraints which hampered the extension of a coherent policy toward Central Asia. Not unlike the experience of the EU's "reverse-realist paradigm," India's "post-Cold War blues" was marked by a palpable "unrealpolitik" behavior. This situation, however, has changed as a result of the May 1998 nuclear tests and the subsequent discursive overhaul of India's external affairs premised on a much more assertive (if not aggressive) foreign policy stance. The brazen geopolitical discourse of India's nuclear tests has indicated a noticeable departure from its previously noncommittal and largely conciliatory attitude.

The focus on the cognitive structures of New Delhi's international relations elicits the absence of a "big idea" in India's strategic culture. It also paves the way for an unusual style of security governance—one in which New Delhi does not establish shared practice with other actors. India, therefore, does not place emphasis on developing *relationships* with others, but expects to be accorded *respect* for its military (and economic) prowess.[6] Chapter 6 has also revealed that it is the perception of a competitive South Asian strategic environment that prevents India from extending a security governance approach to Central Asia that rests on the exercise of normative power. Instead, the nuclear assertiveness of its post-1998 foreign policy projects the image of a self-aggrandizing state. In particular, the uncritical convergence between "normative power India" and "Brand India" has reinforced the hiatus between external and domestic perceptions of India's international agency. Such analysis refers us back to the propositions of Part I on the entrapment of strategic culture, which—like a ghost chasing its victims down a preordained path—directs policy making into already scripted terrains.

In this setting, the articulation of India's normative power is based upon the power of *passive* example—that is, an expectation that others will follow New Delhi's lead without the provision of inducements, reinforcements, or credible commitments. Not surprisingly, India's post-1998 involvement in Central Asia exhibits its underlying revisionist foreign policy stance. Thus, despite the proliferation of discourses on India's rise to global prominence, the narratives of its "Look North" policy reveal the absence of a readily available Indian vision of global politics—a *Pax Indica*, if you will—which prevents New Delhi from living up to the expectations that such proclamations have generated.

This is one of the clearest indications of India's difficulty to fashion a post-Western international relations theory and practice for itself (Behera, 2007, p. 342). At the same time, the case of India also reveals that normative foreign policy actors are just as likely to engage in competitive security scenarios as in cooperative ones. Owing to the complexity and uncertainty of her outlook, India still remains a very "distant background" for the interests of Central Asian countries, which projects to the region merely "a rumor of economic power and technological accomplishment" (Wimbush, 2011, p. 261).

Parallel assessment of the Central Asian agency of the European Union, China, and India

The introductory chapter of this volume emphasized that the eclectic research program adopted by this investigation differentiates itself from the (post-) positivist epistemology, which is often associated with more mainstream approaches to comparative politics. This assertion notwithstanding, it certainly does not warrant (let alone advocate) "abandoning comparative historical analysis in favor of relentless presentism" (Nexon, 2009, p. 290). Instead, this study insists that a parallel narrative analysis can break through the generalizing straitjacket of the individual agency of normative foreign policy actors by offering contextual understandings of their emerging roles in world affairs relative to the particular (but not *ahistorical*) instances of their agency.

This means that the comparative assessment of the EU's, China's, and India's discursive policy formulations on Central Asia are analyzed in juxtaposition with one another. Consequently, the parallel examination of the normative foreign policy agency of Brussels, Beijing, and New Delhi has provided heuristic lenses for the identification, encounter, and understanding of "significant absences," "omissions," and "non-events" in their engagement of the awkward states of Central Asia (Kavalski and Zolkos, 2007, p. 389).

Thus, to borrow from a different context, such an approach confirms the observation that

> To the extent that specific formal properties of relational contexts [such as the agency of normative powers] endure across time and space, we should expect to see similar mechanisms and processes at work. But these dynamics will be concentrated with [and, thereby, be impacted by] other factors—differences in content, agent-level decisions, adjacent

> processes, other nested relational structures—to produce historically variable outcomes.[7]

The parallel assessment of the Central Asian agency of the EU, China, and India makes explicit nascent developments that are only now beginning to draw the attention of observers. Their actorness seemingly confirms the observation that "cultural global interdependence and trans-regional similarities are more important than tendencies towards regional cultural cohesion" (Teló, 2007, p. 14). Yet such observation holds true only to the extent that culture is perceived as a vessel of particular "civilizational" propensities (which need not necessarily be essentialized). Yet, if one is to interpret strategic culture as a representation of a particular international security identity which frames the agency of a normative foreign policy actor, then the analysis shifts to the norms and values purveyed through the deliberate practices of security governance.

As this book has demonstrated, such practices of security governance are about the construction of "responsible subjectivity" (Gheciu, 2008, p. 23). The agency of normative foreign policy actors reveals not only the power to define what is normal, but also what is real—that is, "what is," "what matters," and "what we should care about." As Ken Booth has eloquently posited, although "human life takes place in a material world in which things happen regardless of our thoughts, in its social dimension it takes place importantly according to 'facts by human agreement'" (Booth, 2007, pp. 183–4). Thus, the security governance practices indicated by normative powers such as the EU, China, and India reflect a deliberate attempt to manage the "intensified search for *one* stable identity (regardless of its actual existence)."[8]

In this respect, despite (or probably because of) the normativity of their agency, the Central Asian involvement of the EU, China, and India reveals that these normative foreign policy actors still perceive one another from the position of "the other-as-enemy"—that is, their regional interactions with one another follow "an ethos of survival, as an enemy that must be survived" (Odysseos, 2007, p. 2). Of course, the intensity of such antagonism differs among the EU, China, and India, and is dependent on the spatial, temporal, and issue-specific contexts of their encounter in Central Asia. What is significant for this study, however, is the *presence* of this enmity rather than its particular occurrences. It appears to emanate from the contending trajectories for the "directedness" of the security governance process through which different normative powers attempt to impact the manner in which target states pursue their interest (Adler et al., 1991, p. 14).

At the same time, such rivalry could be explained from the alleged existence of distinct Western/Occidental and Eastern/Oriental strategic cultures (Choudhury, 1977, p. 189; Gray, 1999, p. 63; Scobell, 2002, p. 17). While not necessarily redolent of the hackneyed logic of the "clash of civilizations," the proposition is that different culturally conditioned ways of seeing and representing reality do matter. One Chinese commentator has suggested that the relationship between the different external actors in Central Asia suggests a qualitatively new pattern of international relations, in which they "will not be completely enemies or adversaries, but neither will they be completely friends or partners."[9] Moreover, as Chapters 2 and 3 have demonstrated, such differences play a not so insignificant role in the construction of security governance practices by normative foreign policy actors. Thus, the EU's "western," China's "eastern," and India's "hybrid"[10] modalities do inflect their perceptions of one another in Central Asia.

Such antagonism is also relative to their ability to influence Central Asian affairs. As suggested in Chapter 3, such capacity depends on the willingness of normative foreign policy actors to offer ongoing credible commitments to target states. As the instances of the EU, China, and India show, such actorness is contingent upon the deliberate practice of security governance—a process, which is not necessarily enjoyable for the normative foreign policy actor and, thereby, demands strong motivation (if not perseverance) for the initiation of regularized (oftentimes monotonous and repetitive) activities of socialization.[11]

One need only consider the EU's over decade-and-a-half long accession-driven socialization of East European countries (which has not ceased even after their membership of the Brussels-based bloc) to begin appreciating the enormity of the task. Likewise, China's deliberate practices of confidence-building through the "Shanghai Five" mechanism in the 1990s have contributed to the formalization of this relationship and precipitated the establishment of the SCO. Even then, however, Beijing did not cease its efforts to provide ongoing credible commitments—as a matter of fact it intensified them—which explains its unlikely (from the point of view of 1991) centrality in regional affairs in fewer than two decades after the collapse of the Soviet Union.

On this basis, it would appear that the EU's security governance of Central Asia depicts it as a normative foreign policy actor that lacks both a motivation for and a policy practice of socialization (beyond its enlargement and enlargement-like initiatives). This finding corroborates the suggestion that the EU has only recently begun to articulate a vision of its "grand strategy" (Vennesson, 2010), which might also explain why there is still no activist "global power Europe" (Meyer, 2007, p. 30). China, on the other hand, emerges as an extremely motivated actor with a well-developed deliberate practice of security governance. In this setting, India seems to be rhetorically motivated to socialize Central Asia, but owing to its strategic reliance on the power of *passive* example, it has not extended any meaningful practice for the security governance of the region. Furthermore, in contrast to the normative power of the EU and China in Central Asia which is motivated by "*debelled*" values (Adler, 1991, p. 142), India's *bellicose* post-1998 foreign policy has become the key ingredient in the articulation of its "Look North" policy.[12]

Thus, the parallel assessment of the Central Asian agency of the EU, China, and India outlined in Part II suggests that (i) the EU's lack of deliberate practice is indicative of involvement in the region for its own security which is not accompanied by "respect for the other" in Central Asia; (ii) China's ability to initiate a regional pattern of cooperation and its successful consolidation within the SCO suggests that while prioritizing its own security, its deliberate practice of security governance is informed by "respect for the other;" and (iii) India's interactions with Central Asia reveal that while it has barely scratched on the surface of committed engagement, New Delhi is clearly prioritizing its own security and self-aggrandizement.

Such an outline confirms that the socializing tendencies of security governance emerge from the cumulative impact of decisions regarding cooperative actions.[13] Yet, as this book has evidenced, at the end of the day, such a cumulative impact rests on deliberate practices. Unreflective practice, on the other hand, denies normative powers the agency to influence others. Hence, the effective security governance of normative foreign policy actors is relative to their socializing commitment. The analyses included in Part II evidence that only China and (to a very small extent) the EU have Central Asian policies that gesture toward such deliberate socialization. In the case of China, it has already become an ongoing practice, while in the case of the EU, it is barely rhetoric. India has neither the rhetoric nor the practice but only a discursive desire for influence.

At the same time, according to the explanation provided in Part II, the EU and India seem to treat Central Asia merely as a derivative of their other (and more important) interests, which prevents the prioritization of the region in their foreign policy purview. Both Brussels and New Delhi, therefore, tend to treat Central Asia as a context for addressing other issues which do not allow them to relate to the abilities, experiences, and concerns of regional states. In this respect, China appears to be the only actor to engage the region on its own terms. The parallel assessment of the normative underpinnings of the Central Asian agency of Brussels, Beijing, and New Delhi highlights the idiosyncratic "translation" of this involvement through the distinct cognitive frameworks of their strategic cultures. At the same time, it also points to the functional interdependence between normative foreign policy actors and their environments. Such emphasis on the relational character of security governance draws attention to the dynamics through which the demand for recognition affects the construction of an actor as a normative power.

Normative power and the "struggle for recognition"

The contestation between the fledgling normative powers of the EU, China, and India in Central Asia draws attention to one of the crucial aspects of world affairs—the feature that the basic ontological condition of international actors is relational (i.e. the content of their existence as actors is constituted intersubjectively during the process of interaction) (Murray, 2008, p. 252). As has already been amply suggested throughout this book, the exercise of normative power is simultaneously a tool for and predicated upon the *recognition* of an actor's perception about its status on the global stage. Normative powers need to be perceived as legitimate—that is, their agency depends on the validation by target actors (usually through different types of compliance or conformity). Thus, the security governance projects of the EU, China, and India in Central Asia reveal a *desire to be recognized* as actors that are capable to define the ramifications of the 'normal' in international life. The acknowledgment of this nascent struggle for recognition suggests that the contestation between normative powers moves beyond their relative capability.

In other words, the answer to the question "Who or what exists politically as a normative power?" is "Those actors that are *recognized* as normative powers." Recognition, in this setting, is indicated by the specific attitudes, dispositions, and behavior of target states. This is what Joseph Nye (2008, p. 85) had in mind when he stressed that "power depends on context." This then raises the question: "Under what conditions are target states willing to grant such recognition"? The answer provided in this study is that normative powers are granted recognition when they deliver credible commitments to the intended target. Thus, the most credible incentive appears to be "the inclusion of the interests and/or ideas dominant in another country" into the security governance project of the normative power (Schrim, 2010, p. 199). Furthermore, this claim attests to the "constitutive vulnerability" of international actors "to the unpredictable reactions and responses of others" (Markell, 2003, p. 36). Such reciprocity and mutual adaptation does not deny the fact that the relationship is asymmetrical; yet, the ability to be (or, at least, act like) a normative power is premised on having others (in this case, the Central Asian states) acknowledge the status of the EU,

China, and India as normative powers by voluntarily following their lead. This assertion confirms Alexander Wendt's observation that "it is through recognition by the Other that one is constituted as a Self in the first place" (Wendt, 2003, p. 599).

For instance, the case of India (discussed in Chapter 6) demonstrates that on a basic instrumental level, the challenge for normative powers is to find the most effective way for utilizing "the protective color of philanthropy for [the] external legitimation [of the] national interest" (Mehta, 2009, p. 218). New Delhi's discursive and policy inability to link its self-image of a rising power to a strategy that can translate this perception to the outlook of other actors attests both to the significance and to the difficulty of achieving recognition. This is what makes the development of normative principles based on national interests "one of the most complicated transitions" (Kumar, 2008, p. 212).

In this respect, the pattern (and perception) of international anarchy is animated by the "status insecurity" of actors, whose provenance is tied to a combination of factors such as their geopolitical location, the demands for foreign policy reorientation, the detachment/exclusion from international organizations, etc (Webber, 2007, pp. 4–5). Such status insecurity also stems from the uncertainty associated with the intersubjective constitution of identity in global life. Michelle Murray cogently argues that owing to the inherent insecurity of the struggle for recognition, international actors attempt to take control over the process of meaning-creation, by anchoring their identity to explicit material practices (Murray, 2008, p. 249). For instance, the EU's desire for recognition is grounded in the practices of the common market, China's—in the government-led model of development, and India's—in the nuclear-armed assertiveness of its ancient civilization.

The struggle for recognition among normative powers is not merely "a part of," but becomes constitutive of the complex systemic logic of global life. As Headley Bull has asserted, great powers need to be "*recognized* by others to have certain special rights and duties" (Bull, 1977, p. 196; emphasis added). Likewise, Hans Morgenthau has suggested the significance of recognition in his avowal that the "prestige of a nation is its reputation for power. That reputation, the reflection of the reality of power in the mind of the observers can be as important as the reality of power itself. *What others think about us is as important as what we actually are*" (Morgenthau, 1965; emphasis added). Thus, "the primary motivation of subjects in 'anarchy' [is] to gain knowledge of the self, or self-certainty" (Murray, 2008, p. 249). The construction of such knowledge emerges *through* and *in* interaction. Recognition does not merely contribute to an actor's status; it also projects a particular international identity based on self-certainty within an interactive international society (Honneth, 1995).

Thus, the international identity of an actor is not so much about capabilities (as India seems to discover), but mostly about recognition—which is both an outcome and a reassertion of an actor's normative power. Status is, therefore, contingent upon the intersubjective construction of identity, which "is not (only) threatened by others, but also possible because of them [as] they are always already involved *in* [an actor's] identity" (Wæver, 1996, p. 127). Consequently, anarchy is not just "what states make of it," but what reaction actors engender in their struggle for recognition.

In line with the argument developed in Part I (especially in Chapter 2), the suggestion here is that the desire for recognition is also framed by the strategic cultural images that actors hold about one another. In this setting, recognition reflects "the preconceived stereotype of the strategic disposition of another nation, state, or people that is derived from a selective interpretation of history, traditions, and self-image" (Whiting, 1998, p. 19). Yet, the significance of the cognitive framing of international interactions need not presage the inevitable "tragedy of great power politics" (Mearsheimer, 2001). On the contrary, while subject to incremental and gradual change, strategic cultures nevertheless *do* change. And as the case of China (in Chapter 5) indicates, it is the very deliberate practice of external relations that *represents* an actor. The interactive process that emerges from the practices of international relations can, therefore, both alter the perceptions of others and exhibit a qualitative change in an actor's behavior.[14]

In particular, China's "logic of relationships" suggests that positions of authority are not merely reflective of a "prior epistemological order of shared values, and self-other relations," but "depend on an ever-receding horizon of pre-existing shared meanings" (Bially-Mattern, 2005, p. 53). Such attention to the "logic of relationships" of China's normative power indicates that conventional models of security governance—such as the EU's logic of appropriateness and, especially, India's logic of consequences—say very little about the legitimacy of socializing actors; instead, such models draw attention to the effectiveness of their foreign policy agency (Lynch, 2002, p. 189).

Thus, the analysis of the cases in Part II evidences that recognition *by* others rests on recognition *of* others. Again, it is the instance of China that offers the clearest example of the "cardinal value" of respect for the other. Respect encourages expectations of reciprocity. It also delegates certain responsibilities to the normative power-granting respect. But such delegation is both tentative and revocable (Appleby, 1954, p. 96). Thus, the reference to normative power indicates an actor's ability to show consideration for the effects of its actions on others (Womack, 2008, p. 266). At the same time, respect goes beyond the mere acknowledgment of an actor's "equal membership rights" and involves "an appreciation about what is distinct and valuable" about this actor (Nel, 2010, p. 965).

India, as Chapter 6 shows, appears to be positioned on the opposite end from China when it comes to indicating "respect for the other"; thus, its Central Asian agency demonstrates that a great power status entails not only speaking and posturing like one, but also being *recognized* as such by others.[15] Such recognition derives from the deliberate capacity to act like a normative power. Thus, as Chapter 2 has elicited, the ability to exercise normative power offers the most reliable path to the coveted recognition of a "great power" status.

To maintain its credibility, a reflexive normative foreign policy actor has to engage in (and maintain) a deliberate practice of security governance which shows care (i.e. preparedness to make oneself vulnerable). That is why this volume has drawn attention to the patterns of socialization provided by communities of practice. Such dynamics acknowledge that it is through the interactions with others that an actor establishes its position as a normative power. The inference is that normative agency emerges in a community not in a vacuum. Especially, interactions based on respect have the potential to become 'generative relationships'—cascades of constructive feedback that "induce cognitive interpretations of the world which lead to actions which cause structural change, which generates possibilities for new generative relationships" (Lane and Maxfield, 1996, p. 222). As one Chinese commentator put it, the strategic aim of the logic of relationships is to develop "more high-quality friends in the world" (Yan, 2011, p. 260).

The recognition as a normative foreign policy actor, thereby, is impacted by (as well as dependent upon) an actor's sense of obligation—the policy choice of expanding the practice of "self-interest" to include "an interest in the welfare of others" (i.e. "responsibility to one's own welfare is defined as responsibility to others") (Crawford, 1991, p. 455).[16] Such an (almost *emotional*) "ability to attribute mental states to others" is crucial for achieving recognition as it assists with the prediction and explanation of behavior—that is, "imagining the mental states of others involves an ability to represent those mental states to oneself" (Mercer, 2010, p. 10). The psychological processes underpinning these interactions stress the deliberate efforts of a normative power, which in turn enhances the credibility and recognition of its security governance.

The dependence of the recognition *by* others as a normative power on an actor's recognition *of* others appears to be an emerging property of contemporary global politics. In particular, such development draws attention to the significance of emotions in generating international behavior. As Axel Honneth suggests, the current successful patterns of security governance "no longer appear to be [guided by] the elimination of inequality, but the avoidance of degradation and disrespect; its core categories are no longer 'equal distribution' or 'economic equality', but 'dignity' and 'respect'" (Honneth, 2001, p. 43).

In this setting, the relationship pattern of communities of practice engenders an environment in which "expectations are 'shared'" because of the "shared emotional experience" that they engender (Sasley, 2011, p. 460). Thus, it is through the performance of normative power—that is, the establishment of interactions based on respect, obligation, and mutuality, which are maintained through communities of practice—that actors engender relationships to acquire the status they desire. It is no longer victory in war (or at least, not just war) that accords actors positions of influence. Instead, such recognition is a product of deliberate and sustained, not episodic, relationships, which an actor initiates.

Conclusion: Acting politically as adaptive normative power

The analytical engagement with the roles enacted by normative powers in Central Asia has demonstrated that the practices of security governance that prevail in a particular area are relative to the historically specific legitimation of promoted norms, the contextual recognition of the normative foreign policy actor, and its ability to maintain resilient and credible commitments. Thus, in line with the propositions of the introductory chapter, this volume has confirmed the continuing treatment of Central Asia—of course, with different effects—as *context* by the agency of international actors. With respect to the normative power of the EU, China, and India, the region has become one of the more prominent contexts of their "struggle for recognition." It is in this way that Central Asia emerges in their normative foreign policy agency as an intersubjective background of expectations, attitudes, and narratives that participate in the articulation and practices of their security governance (Adler, 2006, p. 40).

This study suggests that the parallel assessment of normative powers *in context* has significant implications for the analysis of their interactions with one another. The claim is that the explanation of the possible trajectories in the relations between international actors are best deciphered not through the study of their bilateral interactions but through the examination of the character of their associations with third parties. In other words, the contention of this investigation is that the "true" nature of the EU↔China, EU↔India, and China↔India relations is not going to emerge from the study

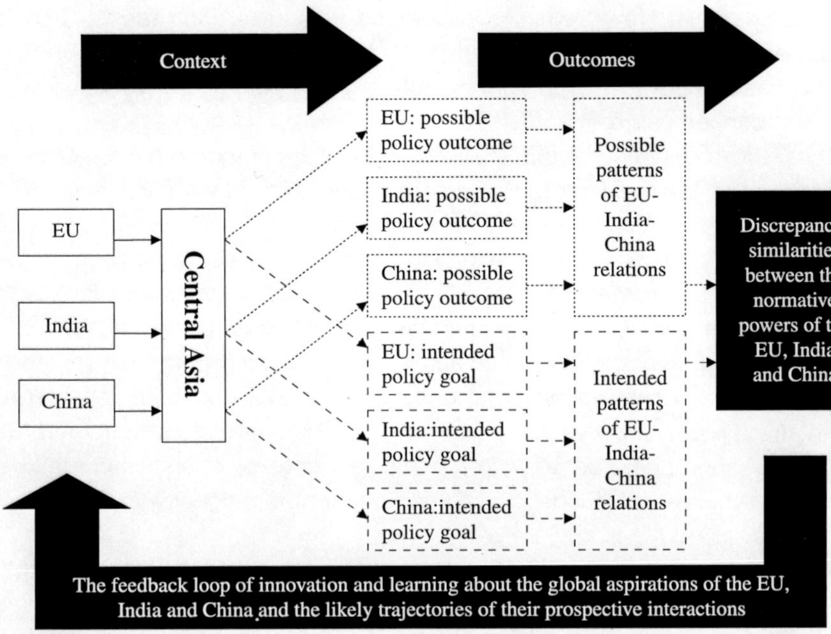

Figure 3 *The complexity of EU-China-India interactions in Central Asia.*

of the bilateral interactions between Brussels↔Beijing, Brussels↔New Delhi, and Beijing↔New Delhi, but through the parallel assessment of their agency in different global contexts (for instance, as the one provided by Central Asia).

Figure 3 offers a visual representation of this proposition. At the same time, it also sketches out a prolegomenon to the conceptual context of complex security governance (outlined in Chapter 3) that provides the foundation for the possible comparative analysis of the normative foreign policy agency of the EU, China, and India in Central Asia. Borrowing from a different context, the claim here is that the international behavior of normative powers is "a function of the intrinsic properties of the system on the one hand [i.e. their strategic culture], and the thing reacted to, on the other [i.e. the context of their agency]" (Iriye, 1979, p. 115).

Therefore, the question here is to what degree the policies of the EU, China, and India engage with the context of Central Asia. Although a full-scale functional assessment of the push-and-pull factors would be difficult (if not impossible) to conduct (not least because of the ongoing transformation of these moving targets), this should not prevent analytical modeling of possible scenarios (Figure 3 instances one of these options). At present, it seems that Beijing appears to project a better contextualized regional policy than either Brussels or New Delhi. As suggested, this assertion reflects China's awareness of its own agency in Central Asia—a self-reflexive dimension that the EU has still not indicated convincingly in the region and India has barely begun to conceptualize.

Thus, the suggestion of this study is that the agency of external actors is tied to their ability to adjust to the dynamic processes at work in the context to which they are applied. In other words, it takes the deliberate practice of *adaptive normative power* to have the legitimacy of one's security governance recognized by target states (especially in terms of indicating compliance with promoted rules and norms). Reflecting the suggestions provided in this book, the inference draws attention to an actor's ability to adapt to transformations in its internal and external environment (Kavalski, 2007a, p. 440). In order to act in strategically effective ways, normative powers need to understand the patterns of appropriate behavior in a particular context—it is such contextual atunement that can persuade local actors to grant them agency (Barkin, 2010, pp. 56–7).

Adaptive normative powers have the capacity to change the context that they engage and this occurs only when they become part of it. In this respect, the parallel assessment of the normative foreign policy agency of the EU, China, and India in Central Asia elicits not merely the fact that these powers offer "different *perspectives*" on the security governance of the region, but also the fact that they enact "different *realities*" of the regional context (Kavalski, 2007a, p. 446). This is what the complexity of security governance outlined in Chapter 3 emphasizes—the possibility of a Central Asian "multiverse" as a result of the regional overlay between the agency of different normative foreign policy actors.

Thus, the call for a parallel assessment of the agency of international actors presented in Figure 3 suggests that contexts—such as Central Asia—emerge as a "nexus of relevant events," whose intersecting incidents are simultaneously partly impression, partly constructions, and partly experience (Smith and Jenks, 2006, p. 52). Such an approach also promises analytical tools both for explaining and understanding discontinuities that conventional analyses of bilateral relations tend to leave out. The focus on the *adaptive propensity* of normative powers, therefore, makes possible the engagement with an actor's "capacity to respond to the moment of contingent interaction" (Kavalski, 2008b, p. 434). For instance, the analyses in Part II suggest that the security governance of Central Asia demands policy-heterogeneity—that is, the simultaneous maintenance of diverse strategies (as well as the willingness and ability to develop new ones) in response to the contingencies of the regional context. Normative power then demands adaptive security governance strategies that do not strive for the perfect way to "optimize" their agency, but for "satisfice"—the production of "local solutions by changing and improving themselves relative to what other agents are doing" (Schmitt, 1997, p. 110). According to Hayward Alker (2011), such adaptive capacity to satisfice involves an actor's willingness to rearrange both memories and international structures.

This understanding informs the interpretation of the nascent global roles of the EU, India, and China. Consequently, the model of security governance that emerges from Figure 3 demands the deliberate practice of continuous adaptability to the nascent vulnerabilities embedded in the context of Central Asia. It is this capacity to "satisfice" that underpins the effectiveness of normative power. As the instances of the EU, China, and India discussed in Part II have revealed, resilience competences (i.e. effective adaptations) are relational and contingent on the contextual intelligence (Nye, 2008) of normative foreign policy agency.

Thus, the outline of the complexity of security governance in Chapter 3 (and visually rendered in Figure 3) indicates that adaptive normative powers have to continually renew, reassert, and reconfirm their *exapted* resilience—in the sense that the recognition of normative foreign policy actors is relative to their ability to convince target states that they are both adapted (and adaptable) to present circumstances and to the untimely contingencies of the future (Grosz, 2004, p. 11). Adaptability, therefore, becomes a key feature of a resilient security governance strategy. Moreover, the suggested "struggle for recognition" elicited by the normative foreign policy agency of the EU, China, and India in Central Asia also draws attention to the normative query of this investigation—namely, what *acting politically* under the conditions of such complexity might actually mean?

As Part II of this book reveals, acting politically in the fluid and uncertain context of Central Asia entails taking responsibility for leaving an impact, for forcing things in one direction rather than another, "since there is no way of guaranteeing in advance whether an act is good or bad. . . [thus] in a specific situation, one must run the risk that the effects of one's actions turn out bad" (Wæver, 2004, pp. 1–5).[17] Thus, following the suggestion of adaptive normative power, acting politically reflects an ability "to make *choices* in context, which in turn affect the context"; in fact, this is what the deliberate practice of security governance entails—the capacity of normative foreign policy agents to "both react appropriately to unforeseen events and actually generate those events [by] acting creatively and innovatively" (Montuori, 2005, pp. 240–52).

Provoked by the parallel assessment of normative foreign policy agency of the EU, China, and India in Central Asia, such understanding of political action elicits the "negative capabilities" of security governance—the "capab[ilities] of being in uncertainty, Mysteries, doubts without any irritable reaching after fact and reason" (Keats, 1970 [1818], p. 43). The negative capabilities demanded from the security governance practices of normative powers reveal the ability to think "under fire," which underwrites the capacity to live with ambiguity, to remain "content with half-knowledge," and, therefore, to engage in a nondefensive way with change, while resisting the impulse (merely) to react (French, 2001, p. 482). Such a mode of security governance indicates an ability to maintain the deliberate practice of socialization despite the pervasive uncertainty of outcomes (Kavalski, 2009b, p. 546).

Returning to the cases presented in this study, acting politically in Central Asia would entail the deliberate practice of security governance which does not seek to control the complexity of the region, but actively engages it through the development of adaptive normative foreign policy that acknowledges the subjectivity of regional actors. It has to be recognized that the contestation between the normative foreign policy agency of the EU, China, and India in Central Asia is part of a "broader unfinished struggle for recognition" animating contemporary global life (Nel, 2010, p. 956). As already indicated, it is by demonstrating "respect for the other" in the setting of asymmetric relationships that one's status as a normative power gains recognition. Thus, returning to Muhammad Muqimiy's nineteenth-century lament in the epigraph to this chapter, it is only though genuine relations (of "friendship") that Central Asians can expect to "gain" meaningfully from their interactions with external actors. Otherwise, the region will merely remain "afflicted" by external agency—regardless of whether it is of the normative power type or not.

Notes

Introduction

1 While from a different perspective, Martha Olcott intuits the treatment of the region as a *context* for external actors when she suggests that, "[t]he identities and the languages of the peoples of Central Asia have changed over the millennia, as each fresh group of conquerors, usually from the East, has swept into this boundless, difficult-to-defend space. While unity has generally evaded the Central Asians, the maintenance of control over this territory, and its preservation intact, has been a constant goal of those living in the region. Although many individuals were rarely forced out; rather they were absorbed into the newcomers, in turn absorbing the newcomers as well, maintaining some aspects of their previous identity, in their language, or in the words they injected into their new language, in tribal identities and customs, blood ties and kinship patterns" (Olcott, 1994, p. 21). Apart from hinting at the contextual framing of Central Asia by the agency of external actors, Olcott also offers a vivid description of the dynamics of *localization* in the region, which will be discussed at length in Chapter 3.

2 This understanding of self-other relations in international politics follows the discussion of Odysseos (2007, p. xiii).

3 This statement paraphrases Björn Hettne's and Frederik Söderbaum's (2000, p. 461) claim on the "rise of regionness."

4 For a cogent critique of the "EU-as-an-actor" approach, which can also be applied to China and India, see White (2004).

5 Nye's extended definition frames soft power in co-optive terms as the "ability of a nation to structure a situation so that other nations develop preferences or define their interests in ways consistent with one's own nation. This type of power tends to arise from such resources as cultural and ideological attraction as well as the rules and institutions of international regimes" (Nye, 1990, p. 191).

6 In a similar way, Emanuel Adler contends that "[t]here is thus a major difference between 'soft power', conceived as a culturally based foreign policy tool to be used on behalf of the national interest. . . and normative power, which relies on the ability to attract states to become members or partners of a political community, access to which depends on the adoption of a set of norms, practices, and institutions" (Adler, 2010, p. 75).

7 This aspect is engaged in greater detail in Chapter 3.

8 This statement borrows from the analytical observations of Daniel Nexon (2009, pp. 23–5).

9 Sergei Kortunov cited in Hansen (2005, p. 50).

10 Already in the early 1990s commentators were beginning to hint that Russia's withdrawal from the region is creating a power vacuum. This has produced an interesting speculative exercise on who is the likely international actor that might be able to fill Moscow's shoes. For instance, Lillian Harris (1993, p. 128) has suggested that "the vacuum may not yet be apparent, but—at the risk of writing off the Russians too soon—China is presently the only power in the region with the military might and the incentive to attempt to fill it should it occur."

11 *Kommersant*, 23 August 1995 cited in Freedman (1998, p. 31).

12 See Michael Emerson (2005) and the European Commission's website on its relations with Russia: http://ec.europa.eu/external_relations/russia/index_en.htm.

13 Cohen (2001, p. 1) in fact goes on to insist that the landmark "Treaty for Good Neighbourliness, Friendship and Cooperation" which the two countries signed in July 2001 was underpinned by similar "anti-Western sentiments" as its 1950 predecessor signed by Mao Tse-tung and Joseph Stalin. During a meeting between the then Russian President Putin and his Chinese counterpart, Hu Jintao, the two countries issued a joint declaration opposing attempts "to impose models of social and political development from outside" and urging states to renounce "striving for monopoly and domination in international affairs and attempts to divide nations into leaders and those being led" (*USA Today*, 2005).

14 Statements like this are redolent of Beijing's sentiments during the 1950s and 1960s when it accused the Soviet Union of "imperialism" (Kavalski, 2009a, p. 180).

15 In this respect, the analysis presented here concurs with Ruth Deyermond's suggestion that war-like interactions in Central Asia are unlikely for the time being, because the external actors involved are barely acting as regional challengers and the alleged "regional hegemon [i.e. Russia] is unwilling and/or unable to mount a challenge" (Deyermond, 2009, p. 173).

16 For methodological applications of eclecticism, see Katzenstein (2005, p. 136) and Kavalski (2008a, p. 5). Rudra Sill and Peter Katzenstein define analytical eclecticism as "any approach that seeks to extricate, translate, and selectively integrate analytical elements—concepts, logics, mechanisms, and interpretations—of theories or narratives that have been developed within separate paradigms but that address related aspects of substantive problems that have both scholarly and practical significance" (Sil and Katzenstein, 2010, p. 10).

17 The rudiments of the narrative splicing approach were first articulated in Kavalski (2010a, pp. 7–12).

18 Friedrichs (2004, p. 8) offers further elaboration of the institutional, intellectual, and structural contexts that assisted the American outlook of mainstream International Relations (IR) theory.

19 Since it is not the intention of this study to offer a detailed accounted of EIR's diversity, it will not be addressed here. For further investigations, see Bretherton and Vogler (2006), Hay and Mennon (2005), Hill and Smith (2005), Friedrichs (2004), Kavalski (2005a, 2006c, 2008a), Kelstrup and Williams (2000), Laffan et al. (1999), Smith (2004), and White (2000).

20 The following discussion of EIR follows (mainly) the propositions of the so-called Copenhagen School of EIR (Hansen, 1996; Wæver, 1998, 2000, 2002; Zolkos, 2005).

21 Methodologically, such engagement with the strategic culture of normative powers acknowledges that "cultural and historical influences on international relations decision-making often go unanalyzed because their causal impact is difficult to theorize and define. Yet, they remain crucial for an understanding of relations between states, for history and cultural presupposition influence not just strategic and military considerations (when and why force was considered legitimate or necessary option or response), but also how peaceful intercourse with other states should be conducted (including diplomacy, trade, and the treatment of foreign nationals)" (Stuart-Fox, 2003, p. 4). However, this book goes beyond (or at least intends to) the mere acknowledgment of the difficulty to make culture and history count in the study of world politics. Instead, it argues that the notion of strategic culture allows for gauging when, where, and how culture and history matter.

22 Nexon (2009, p. 45) also elaborates the ways through which "claims making" and "discourse" go on to "construct, reproduce and alter social relations." In a similar fashion, this investigation suggests that the security governance practiced by normative powers emerges in a dialogical relation with target states rather than as a hegemonic monologue. In other words, security governance is about building a particular kind of community—a community of practice.

23 Concurring with Richard Ned Lebow's observation, the necessary qualification here is that such narratives can oftentimes appear metafactual and highly abstract social constructions. Yet, such caveat also acknowledges that observations are almost invariably "the products of the narratives and interpretations embedded within them" (Lebow, 2010, p. 58).

24 Collin Gray (2006, p. 11) uses Lawrence Freedman's statement to indicate that the discourses of strategic cultures "can be molded purposefully into a narrative cunningly contrived for the purpose of popular persuasion." For a more detailed engagement with such "mythmaking" quality of narratives, see Kavalski (2010a, pp. 48–57) and Snyder (1991).

25 It needs to be qualified that—in line with Andre Gunther Frank's (1992, p. 55) suggestion—"the origins of the state" both generally and in Central Asia, in particular, are beyond the scope of the current investigation. The intention here is to draw attention to the *awkwardness* of Central Asian statehood and, in the process, discuss its implications for the international politics of the region. For instance, Daniel Nexon (2009, p. 298) points out that the states of Central Asia "remain essentially composite polities where much governance is carried out through highly autonomous intermediaries—such as regional governors, clan networks, and other forms of patron-client relations—and processes of 'globalization' create everincreasing connection between their fates and those of the citizens of other states."

26 Many international relations scholars have passionately critiqued such pandering to the Westphalian framework of the study of world affairs. For instance, Berenice Carroll (1972, pp. 597–8) has insisted that "To begin with, we must note that the widespread emphasis upon the nation-state as the unit of study. . . reflects an *acceptance* (however unwilling) of the continued primacy of the nation-state in the international system. . . This acceptance masquerades as 'realism' or dispassionate recognition of 'things as they are'. . . But all such realism is at the same time self-fulfilling prophecy. It reinforces the perpetuation of things as they are, at least in their basic outlines, turns attention and energy from efforts to achieve radical change, and confines scholarly intelligence to solving problems or proposing 'incremental' alterations in policy within the limits of what may be understandable and acceptable to decision-making elites." Likewise, others have insisted that it is the power politics emerging from such Westphalian beliefs that underscores the "recurrent cycles of war, breakdown, and reconstruction" (Ikenberry, 2001, p. 17), which intuits that "traditional methods of engaging the sovereign state are insufficient to prevent the types of conflict that threaten peace today" (Lefkon, 2003, p. 679). It is in this context that one needs to read Alexander Wendt's eloquent statement that "anarchy is what states make of it." On this issue, see Kavalski and McCullock (2005).

27 Likewise, Chris Ford's analysis of Chinese strategic culture emphasizes that it "shuns rule-ethics. . . in favor of a context-specific solution" (Ford, 2010, p. 257). As the concluding chapter of this book will demonstrate, such security governance approach backstops China's *recognition* as normative power.

28 As Chapter 3 indicates, such framing of the security governance of normative powers should not be taken as an indication that the communities of practice that they initiate "*are* necessarily progressive. Rather, as representations of *an* (rather than *the*) idea of progress, new and novel practices, because they may be perceived as better, or less bad, than others," may help attract political entities to a particular normative power's definitions of the "normal" (Adler, 2010, p. 69; emphasis in original).

29 My introduction and references to Abbott's thought derive from their brilliant engagement to the context of early modern Europe by Daniel Nexon (2009, p. 46).

Chapter 1

1 In fact, Wilfrid Blunt's statement can be read as a reincarnation of Lord Curzon's nineteenth-century proposition that, "In Central Asia the position of affairs changes not every hour, but every minute. Therefore, I say, Vigilance, vigilance, vigilance. . . It [Central Asia] is the blank leaf between the pages of an old and a new dispensation; the brief interval separating a compact and immemorial tradition from the rude shock and unfeeling Philistinism of nineteenth-century civilization. The era of the Thousand and One Nights, with its strange mixture of savagery and splendor, of coma and excitement, is fast fading away, and will soon have yielded up all its secrets to science. Here in the cities of Alp Arslan, and Timur, and Abdullah Khan, may be seen the sole remaining stage upon which is yet being enacted that expiring drama of realistic romance" (Curzon, 1889, pp. x–xii).

2 What Frank Lee Holt has in mind here is that the presence of Alexander's armies "did not signal a permanent break in [the] ancestral ways of life" of Central Asia peoples (Holt, 1988, p. 52).

3 It needs to be acknowledged that such fourfold periodization of Central Asia's entanglement in the dynamics of world affairs—into pre-Islamic, Islamic, Russian/Soviet, and post-Soviet—is undertaken merely for the purposes of brevity and clarity. This, however, should not be taken as a denial of the overlap between trends across the four periods, nor as a rejection that other actors and/or processes have shaped the Central Asian experience. For instance, the Chinese incursion into the region can be traced back at least to the Islamic period (if not much earlier). However, even the history of the Chinese involvement in the region confirms the treatment of Central Asia as a context for the strategic goals of external-to-the-region actors/agency. As some have pointed, "[t]raditionally, China adopted a dual policy to protect the Chinese heartland combining the carrot of economic opportunity with the stick of forward defence. Central Asian kingdoms were alternatively bribed by gifts and access to trade under cover of the tribute system, and subject to punishing raids and military occupation" (Stuart-Fox, 2003, p. 228).

4 While this view is maintained by a number of commentators, its significance should not be overplayed. As Seymour Becker insists, "[a]lthough Central Asian cotton had acquired a new importance for Russia on the eve of conquest, and considerable sentiment existed for an advance into Central Asia to protect and promote Russian manufacturing and trading interests, the influence of these factors on policy-making was minimal" (Becker, 1968, p. 22).

5 A circular of 9 November 1864 written by Prince Gortchakov offers a glimpse into the narrativization of such *mission civilisatrice*: "The position of Russia in Central Asia is that of all civilized States which are brought into contact with half-savage, nomad populations, possessing no fixed social organization. In such cases, it always happens that the more civilized State is forced, in the interest of the security of its frontier and its commercial relations, to exercise a certain ascendancy over those whom their turbulent and unsettled character makes most undesirable neighbors. . . The [Russian] Imperial Government thus found itself, in spite of all its efforts in the dilemma. . . either to permit the continuance of a state of permanent disorder, paralyzing to all security and progress, or to condemn itself to costly and distant expeditions leading to no practical results and with the work always to be done anew; or, lastly, to enter upon the undefined path of conquest and annexation which has given England, the Empire of India, by attempting the subjugation by armed force, one after another, of the small independent States, whose habits of pillage and turbulence, and whose perpetual revolts, leave their neighbors neither peace nor repose" (cited in Lloyd, 1997, pp. 127–8). The conclusion to Chapter 2 undertakes a detailed discussion of the impact of such civilizing propensities on the security governance mechanisms extended to Central Asia by normative foreign policy actors.

6 For the narratives of the "great game," see Hopkirk (1992), Meyer (2003), Meyer and Brysac (1999), and Paine (1996).

7 For a good overview of "Russian colonization," see Breyfogle et al. (2007).

8 Adeeb Khalid goes on to argue that unlike the civilizing projects of colonialism, the Soviet domination of Central Asia was different, because "it matters a great deal whether [the powers of the state are] deployed to exclude people from politics or to force their entry into it, whether it is used to assert inequalities or to preach world revolution" (Khalid, 2006, p. 251).

9 The section on "The awkwardness of Central Asian polities" in this chapter discusses at length some of those ideological features of Soviet statehood and their impact on state-building in the region. Others, however, have interpreted the Soviet domination merely as a continuation of the Russian colonial project of oppression: "The Russian object was first, under a cloak of separate race-consciousness, to break down and weaken the natural ties joining the limbs of Turkestan, and then to bring each severed part not into relation with other parts but into subjection to the outside force, Russia" (Caroe, 1967, p. 148).

10 A number of commentators have insisted in this context that "all five states are now considered *less* free than the Soviet Union was in the last year of its existence. And they are all considered either similar to or even *worse* than the pre-*demokratizatsiia* Soviet one-party system of the late 1980s. The region, simply put, has witnessed a considerable deterioration in its political climate since sovereignty in 1991" (Hansen, 2005, p. 46; emphasis in original). Already in the 1990s observers were drawing attention to the fact that "developments in the [post-Soviet] Asian zone appear to be nothing else than the construction of policed, national authoritarian regimes. For the first time in decades, non-Communist political refugees are fleeing, not from, but to, Russia, mainly from Central Asia. None of these republics has an open, legal, and civilized political opposition, and election can certainly not be described as free. And none of them has a free press or an independent court system" (Kulchik et al., 1996, p. 27). These issues are further elaborated in the discussion of the *awkwardness* of Central Asian statehood.

11 Reflecting the flimsiness of the Central Asian designation, Owen Lattimore defines the region as "a circle with a radius of a thousand miles, centering on Urumchi, capital of Sinkiang [Xinjiang], [which] encloses more different kinds of frontier than could be found in any area of equal size anywhere else in the world." He goes on to describe the various linguistic, cultural, and political frontiers enmeshing the region (Lattimore, 1950, p. 3).

12 Dennis Sinor cited in Frank (1992, p. 47).

13 As one commentator noted, "before the end of the Cold War, it was difficult to talk about the regional actorness of [Central Asia] independent of the policies and identities of the Soviet Union" (Korkmaz, 2010, p. 357).

14 On Turkmenistan, see Sabol (2010).

15 Paul Ricoeur cited in Bowden (2009, p. 99).

16 This suggestion borrows from Kathleen Collins' prescient observation that the Central Asian region shares important features with political developments and state-making dynamics in sub-Saharan Africa and the Middle East (Collins, 2009, p. 277).

Chapter 2

1 Cited in Raugh (2004, p. 151). In practice, the expression "tournament of the shadows" was the Russian version of the British term the "great game." For more on this issue, see Meyer and Brysac (1999) as well as the discussion in Chapter 1.

2 For a detailed discussion of these issues, see Tocci (2008, p. 15).

3 The "civilizational" aspects of normative powers will be discussed further in the conclusion of this chapter.

4 Carroll (1972, p. 589) points out that a mere comparison of the definition of power in the Oxford and Webster's dictionaries from the 1930s to 1970s illustrates such alteration in the meaning of the concept. Therefore, Carroll argues that in some sense the original meaning of *power as ability* can be retrieved through negation—that is, that power indicates a framework of "*noncontrol*" or a situation of "deliberate suspension of control" (Carroll, 1972, pp. 601–2; emphasis added).

5 This understanding of the power of attraction borrows from Haas (1992, pp. 27–8).

6 Moreover, Rummel treats the meaning of influence as a product of intersubjective interaction centered on a symbolic perception of binding expectations: "power like money is itself 'worthless', but is accepted in the *expectation* that it can later be 'cashed in', this time in the activation of binding obligations" (Rummel, 1976, p. 187; emphasis original). In a similar fashion, but not so perceptively, Barnett and Duvall (2005, pp. 55–7) advance the concept of "productive power" which concerns "the social process and the systems of knowledge through which meaning is produced."

7 On this aspect, see Gray (1984), Booth (1990, p. 126).

8 The texts by Gray (1984), Poore (2003), and Johnston (1995) are especially helpful.

9 For a good overview of this reductive view, see Murray (1999) and Kier (1995).

10 Martin Stuart-Fox justifies such substitution by arguing that the "principal way in which cultural factors influence the way states and nations relate to one another derives from how their foreign policy elites understand the world. This worldview, which a foreign policy elite shares for the most part with the broader political elite, includes both how the world is constituted

(believed to be in a descriptive sense) and how it should be constituted (in an ideal and prescriptive sense). . . Worldview shapes and is shaped by culture, while its temporal dimension defines how time and history are understood. Both culture and history contribute significantly to our sense of identity. How we think about ourselves as belonging to a community or a national group, and how we think about others, using what metaphors and analogies, drawing upon prejudices and stereotypes, are important cultural influences on international relations. Culture also influences decision-making processes through the education and socialization of political elites, the politics of personal power and ambition, and the functioning of national institutions (parties, parliaments, ministries of foreign affairs, etc.). Analysis of such influences on the behavior of states and nations towards each other reveals many of the presuppositions underlying foreign policy decision and action. These presuppositions include values, norms, and expectations with respect to the proper conduct of international affairs. Together they constitute what I shall call *international relations culture*" (Stuart-Fox, 2003, p. 5).

11 More recently, Huiyun Feng (2007, p. 8) has employed the notion of "operational code construct" to assist his analysis of Chinese strategic culture. Akin to the notion of cognitive structure, the operation code construct (i) represents "a psycho-cultural construct that incorporates cognition, character, and culture" and (ii) provides "a perspective that bridges the gap between motivation and cognition as mechanisms of political choice." Like the term "cognitive structure", the operational code construct incorporates "'philosophical' and 'instrumental' beliefs. Philosophical beliefs refer to the assumptions and premises made by an actor regarding the fundamental nature of politics and political conflict and the image of the opponent; the general prospects for achieving one's fundamental nature of politics and political conflict, and the image of the opponent; the general prospects for achieving one's fundamental political values; the extent to which political outcomes are predictable; the extent to which political leaders can influence historical developments and control outcomes; and the role of chance instrumental beliefs, on the other hand, have to do with questions of correct strategy and tactics, such as the best approach for selecting goals for political action; how such goals and objectives can be pursued most effectively; the best approach to calculation, control, and acceptance of the risks of political action; the matter of 'timing' of action; and the utility and role of different means for advancing one's interests." For the purposes of this study, the propensities of the operational code construct will be subsumed with the notion of cognitive structure.

12 Confirming this proposition, Chris Ford has suggested that the insights gleaned from history "spell out the causal sinews of the world as it exists at *all* times, making them fundamental reference points for decision-making at any, and every, point" (Ford, 2010, p. 14).

13 Likewise, at roughly the same time, Adda B. Bozeman (1976) has mounted a powerful critique of the lack of attention in conventional analyses to the impact and significance of local—especially, ideational and cultural—conditions. As she put it, "no allowance [is] made for the possibility that war-related phenomena might be, *perhaps even predominantly*, aspects of locally prevalent values, images, traditions, and mental constructions. . . This failure in the perception of reality has been aggravated by a widespread acquiescence in essentially irrational trends—the inclinations, namely to dissociate values from fact, to treat values as if they were norms and to assume that privately or locally preferred values are also globally valid norms. These intellectual developments have contributed not only to many recent foreign policy errors, but also to widespread uncertainties about America's roles in world affairs. They also suggest that the United States has begun to resemble Don Quixote: like the Knight of the Mournful Countenance, it is fighting windmills and losing its bearings on the real world" (Emphasis added).

14 See Kavalski (2008a).

15 See also Bowden (2009), Chandler (2004), and Paris (2002). A powerful critique of the benign underpinnings of normative power in international politics was articulated by K. J. Holsti (1991, p. 27) in his comparison of Western models of development to colonial practices: "The diffusion of Western culture and economic patterns to other areas of the world has proceeded unabated for more than three centuries. Its forms, often violent and oppressive, have always been tempted by a faith in the ultimate benefits that the underdeveloped world would receive through the processes of cultural and economic interaction. While apologists for colonialism did not deny the strategic, prestige, and economic advantages accruing to the metropolitan states, they would point out simultaneously that natives were *also receiving benefits, including employment, stable government. . . the introduction of education, democracy, and modern health facilities*" (Emphasis added).

16 In fact, one can draw parallels to the patron-client relations (quite familiar to Central Asian actors) described by Daniel Nexon (2009, p. 41). Such patronage perspective on normative powers would come to suggest "'asymmetrical, quasi-moral relation[s]' in which [an actor] 'directly provides protection and assistance (patronage) and/or influences persons who can provide these services (brokers), to persons (clients) who depend upon. . . such assistance'. In other words, patronage. . . encourages cooperation and is effective in moving people to action." From this perspective, the neo-trusteeship relationship established by such patron-client linkages suggests that when analyzing the agency of normative powers "we need not rely on 'logics of appropriateness' or 'logics of consequence' to understand, at least in a general sense, the political implications that follow when patrons shift their allegiances. Their clients may act out of logics of appropriateness, such as their loyalty to their patron, their sense of honor, or whatever. They may also act out of logics of consequence, such as recognition that breaking from the patron will result in an immediate loss of status, security, and economic resources. Both decision-making processes may often be at work" (Nexon, 2009, p. 41). The suggestion here is that such a patronage-based approach to normative powers can help elicit interesting aspects of their socializing dynamics. Owing to the limitations of space and the objectives of the current investigation, these possibilities are only hinted here, but not developed in the book.

Chapter 3

1 K. J. Holsti (1991, p. 4) has challenged such proclamations of the beginning of a "new world order" by pointing out the continued pervasiveness of "security dilemmas, the use of force and war." He, therefore, propounds that "the end of the Cold War has not fundamentally changed the international system, but only certain fissures and cleavages in it."

2 Rober Cox (1981, p. 126) offers a persuasive analysis of the practical aspects of cognition.

3 See also his earlier commentary in Rosenau (1979).

4 In contrast, Keith Suter (2003, p. 166) suggests that "most warnings in the name of global security have proved to be false alarms. Apparently created to encourage global governance, these warnings are overstatements of problems. The world can survive without the global governance remedy." On the development of "global security governance" both as an alternative to and a sub-category of "global governance", see Ba and Hoffman (2005), Kirchner and Sperling (2007), Hough (2004), and Wood and Dupont (2006).

5 For an instance of a prescient "empirical" study (especially in the North American sense of this term) of the problem of establishing causality and predicting/controlling future events (see Blyth 2006).

6 See also Buzan (1983) and Sheehan (2005).

7 It needs to be reminded that the discourses and practices of *security as control* have also decontextualized human-human interactions. The claim, however, is that these have been accorded significant attention by security studies (see Booth 2007), while the effects of the detachment between human and natural systems remain largely unaddressed.

8 Despite his criticism of complexity thinking, Wæver (2004, pp. 1–5) unwittingly confirms its inkling that the cognitive structures of security need to be construed in terms that reflect the requirement "to react as rarely as possible, and to avoid situations and relationships that would condemn one to suspend as it were, one's 'freedom' and initiative and to become a mere re-agent."

9 This definition of security governance bears resemblance to meaning of progress in the field of international relations: "progress [involves] changes in the policies and relations of states that reduce conflict or increase cooperation so as to further security, welfare, or human rights, understood as a reduction in violence, misery, or human rights violations. In other words, progress in international relations implies the pursuit of the national interest of states in ways that further human interests. This does not mean that actors must relinquish their national interests or their power. Rather, it implies that actors apply their power differently from the way they used it in the past and invest time and resources in finding solutions to problems from which individuals across borders suffer" (Adler et al., 1991, p. 9).

10 As the following section will demonstrate, the practices of socialization consider the security governance of normative powers as a particular form of civilizing in the name of security. To borrow from a different context (and as

already indicated in Chapter 2), colonization can be perceived as an early and a very crude form of security governance by which those deemed uncivilized were to become civilized through tutelage that was intended to provide them with the correct means of organizing society (Bowden, 2009, p. 79). In this respect, while contemporary forms of security governance are still about the introduction of a particular kind of polity and a framework for its international relations, socialization occurs through leadership by example; in contrast, imperial models of socialization are "introduced" via colonizing enforcement and the submission of the target. The former logic is amply demonstrated by the Central Asian agency of the EU, India, and China. As outlined in Part II of the book, such a framing of security governance is intimated by the dynamics of exclusion and inclusion. For instance, Webber asserts that the regulatory mechanisms of security governance rest on a demarcation between those who are allowed and those who are not permitted to engage in its system of relations. Both dynamics have important socializing effects and are underpinned by the worldview of a normative power. As Webber argues, security governance relies "on a sharp differentiation between 'self' and 'other'. This distinction is one of inclusion—that which belongs—and exclusion—that which is alien. The included is seen in positive light: the internal structure offers order stability, safety, security. The external disorder vibrates with threat, risk, and danger" (Webber, 2007, p. 16). As indicated in Chapter 1, the awkwardness of Central Asia is a crucial contributing factor for the rise of normative powers in the region—they are there to contain both the real and perceived sources of insecurity emanating from the excluded context of Central Asia, by introducing a framework of predictability through regional security governance mechanisms, intended to include Central Asian states into particular practices and patterns of international behavior. Thus, while Central Asia may have traditionally been perceived as a "closed space"—both due to Soviet rule and the unwillingness (and inability) of normative powers to extend their practices—today, the region undergoes multiple processes of opening up, which have transformed it into an "invited space" through the socialization of external actors. See Carventa (2007), for further elaboration of "closed" and "invited" spaces.

11 See the discussion of "cognitive structure" in Chapter 2.

12 Webber (2007, p. 62) nearly stumbles upon this insight.

13 As Chapter 5 shows, China appears to indicate the most sophisticated awareness (and atunement) to this reality. Beijing's ability to initiate and maintain a regional community of practice in post-Soviet Central Asia reflects the significance of relationships for the socialization into and the localization of externally promoted norms. In this setting, the focus on the practices of localization helps us "unbundle the behavior [of] the producers of events from our judgment of it, and consider it as their actions with their intentions" (Womack, 2008, p. 294). Such resonance between promoted and local standards of behavior, however, can only emerge in the relational environment provided by communities of practice—something that the normative powers of both the EU (Chapter 4) and India (Chapter 6) still have to come to terms with. The construction of compliance, therefore, requires not only an instrumental perspective on state behavior in response to external factors, but also the recognition by local stakeholders of the appropriateness of promoted norms. For a further discussion of the dynamics of localization in Central Asia, see Nourzhanov (2010) and Wilkinson (2010).

Chapter 4

1 Such an inquiry borrows from the analysis of EU foreign policy offered in Michael Smith (2009, p. 596).

2 The designation of the EU as a "new political system" comes from Simon Hix (2008). He develops the label of "new political system" as an indication of the uniqueness of the Brussels-based bloc in international life, where the EU bears similarities to several other entities—for instance, (federal) states and international organizations—yet, at the same time, is different from all of them not least because of its idiosyncratic codecisional framework of governance. The difficulty to pin down the nature of the EU's polity has led some to label is as a "non-identifiable political object" (Nanclares, 2001, p. 624) or a "unique but non-unitary actor" (White, 2000, p. 24). Others have referred to the Brussels-based community as a "postdemocracy," which reflects "a search for new realism in our idea of actual social reality. . . we are no longer thinking the reality merely of this nation or that, but of a new global social reality, a social reality of all social realities, national and international, a reality far exceeding all previous social reality in complexity and diversity and its potentiality for good and evil" (Allott, 2003, p. 326). See also Kavalski (2009b), Kavalski and McCullock (2005).

3 Going back to the proposition of the EU's civilizing demand for compliance in Central Asia (developed in the conclusion of Chapter 2), it is worth noting that Jennifer Mitzen explains this demand as "a crucial function of the EU deliberate routines. . . to manage or tame the anarchic space. . . because the habit of deliberation tames anarchy 'inside', it also produces the potential to civilize EU relations with the 'outside'. . . This does not mean that the EU will be an effective actor, or even successfully implement a given policy. But it does mean that it will be difficult to take security actions that are inconsistent with an internationally accepted notion of what it means to be civilized" (Mitzen, 2006, p. 281).

4 European Commission, "European Neighborhood Policy: Strategy Paper," [COM(2004)373 final], Brussels.

5 Holsti goes on to argue that "the policy implication must be that the states system is not compatible with the continued existence of mankind. If there is indeed and automacity to war, driven by differential growth rates, if there are cycles, and if hegemonies must inevitably replace each other through the device of major wars, then we are left with few possibilities for human intervention. They are reduced essentially to two: either we must stop differential growth rates, or we must organize the world on some basis other than that of sovereign nation-states" (Holsti, 1991, pp. 204–5).

6 *Agence Europe*, 10 November 1999.

7 The understanding of Europeanization offered here should not be assumed as an indication of a uniform agency across the board of external affairs. On the contrary, it is assumed merely as the *direction* (if not the underlying trend) of "Europe-induced changes" in an otherwise "messy," "institutionally cumbersome," and "diverse" process. See Jan Zielonka (2007, p. 70).

8 Some have argued that the socialization propensities of the Europeanizing project reflect "the cultural foundations of security" that have come to dominate the intersubjective understandings, identities, and interactions in the continent (Gheciu, 2008, p. 14).

9 It would be ahistorical to suggest that a framework of normative appropriateness emerged in a given time. However, perceptions of order (and, hence, the interpretations of identity, which they articulate) are often led by an emphasis on these individual years, which see the accumulation of significant events. Thus, the events in Kosovo during 1999 provided the context in which the EU, in order to preserve its salience (i.e. the credibility of its normative power), had to reiterate the order-promoting capabilities of its strategic culture by extending its zone of peace (see also Efegil (2009, p. 74)).

10 European Commission, "Wider Europe: A New Framework for Relations with Our Eastern and Southern Neighburs," [COM(2003)104 final], Brussels.

11 It is in this context—especially, the nearly-decade-long experience of Yugoslav dissolution—that one should read Emanuel Adler's claim that "[p]ushed by disappointment and pulled by learning. . . Europe chose to reinvent itself as a new political and economic 'zone of prestige' and 'network of attraction' that might once again magnetically attract the world. Europe's power to change the world thus lies not only with what it was, but what the world may now become with the help of its refurbished normative political practices" (Adler, 2010, p. 72).

12 In fact, Ian Manners has gone as far as acknowledging that the development of the *ESS* indicates a "sharp turn away from the normative path of sustainable peace towards the full spectrum of instruments for robust interventions" (Manners, 2006b, p. 189).

13 European Commission, *TACIS Regional Cooperation: Strategic Considerations 2002–06 and Indicative Programme 2002–03* (Brussels: European Commission, 2001, p. 3).

14 European Council, *European Union and Central Asia: Strategy for a New Partnership* (Brussels: General Secretariat of the Council, QC-79-07-222-29-C, 2007), p. 5. Emphasis added.

15 Chris Patten, Speech made on 6 September 2002.

16 European Council, *European Union and Central Asia: Strategy for a New Partnership* (Brussels: General Secretariat of the Council, QC-79-07-222-29-C, 2007), p. 5.

17 For more information on this issue, see Song (2011, p. 54).

18 This interpretation borrows from Janice Bially-Mattern (2005, p. 43).

19 In effect, the then US Vice-President Albert Gore has denoted this rationale during the early stages of NATO's Kosovo campaign: "We are at a fork in the road. This first way lies bombing, continued and accelerated. However, if the Yugoslav president took the other fork, he might maintain some sovereignty over Kosovo and benefit from long-term assistance to the region" (Norris 2005, p. 850)." In the current version there are plenty of typos and incomprehensible signs.

20 For an extended discussion of this issue, see Kavalski (2008a).

21 This reality seems to conform to R. Cullen's suggestion that "the West bears no responsibility for helping overcome the problem created by [Soviet] colonialism there" (Cullen, 1994, p. 134).

22 In his analysis Sergei Prozorov relies heavily on Bahar Rumelili (2007).

23 For further information on this, see Johns (2003).

24 For the purposes of this study, the Black Sea Synergy and the Eastern Partnership programs are treated as coterminous. The reason is that the aim here is to make a larger point about the EU's *enlargement-like* socialization of some of the ENP countries aimed at bringing them in closer association and collaboration with already existing member states as well as candidate countries. In this setting, the underlying aim of both the Black Sea Synergy and the Eastern Partnership programs is to send a message to the ENP countries involved in these projects that they are perceived and treated as *peers* of the EU member states and candidate countries. In this respect, the EU has effectively established an "ENP-plus" club of quasiintegration in the "shadow of enlargement" (Henderson and Weaver, 2010; Magen, 2006; Schäffer and Tolksdorf, 2009). It is the context of these programs that makes the EU's *exclusionary* (nonsocializing) exclusion especially palpable and conspicuous.

25 One needs, however, to agree with Alexanda Gheciu's observation on the paradox of the ENP: "on the one hand, it is explicitly aimed at preventing the emergence of new dividing lines in Europe, and on the other hand, in the name of the Union, it seeks to create new types of (albeit more mobile) fences around the EU, and between partners of the Union and third countries" (Gheciu, 2008, p. 67). These inferences bring us back to the notion of "yoking" outlined in the introductory chapter of this book and, especially, Central Asia's role in this process.

26 European Parliament, "Resolution on the Commission approach, A4-0158/95," *Official Journal of the European Communities*, 15 September 1995, p. 0215.

27 For more information, see the TACIS website: http://ec.europa.eu/comm/external_relations/ceeca/tacis/index.htm.

28 TACIS website: http://europa.eu/legislation_summaries/external_relations/relations_with_third_countries/eastern_europe_and_central_asia/r17003_en.htm

29 Bertie Ahern, speech at a press conference for the Declaration on Combating Terrorism, Brussels, 25 March 2004. Emphasis added.

30 All references from the European Security Strategy come from: http://www.consilium.europa.eu/showPage.aspx?id=266&lang=en.

31 European Commission, "Strategy paper (2002–06) and Indicative Program (2002–04) for Central Asia," Brussels, 12 October 2002.

32 European Council, "Council joint action 2005/588/CFSP," (2005) 199 *Official Journal of the European Union*, pp. 100–1.

33 European Council, "Council joint action 2005/588/CFSP," p. 100. Emphasis added.

34 See the discussions within the European Commission on the future scenarios for the TACIS program at http://ec.europa.eu/comm/external_relations/consultations/cswp_tacis.htm. It needs to be acknowledged that DCECI is probably the clearest signal the EU's distancing from Central Asia. In practice, DCECI severs even if only a rhetorical link between the European integration project and the post-Soviet space, which was implicit in the TACIS programming.

35 European Council, *European Union and Central Asia: Strategy for a New Partnership* (Brussels: General Secretariat of the Council, QC-79-07-222-29-C, 2007), pp. 8–14.

36 European Council, *European Union and Central Asia: Strategy for a New Partnership* (Brussels: General Secretariat of the Council, QC-79-07-222-29-C, 2007), p. 28.

37 For more information on this topic, see Delcour (2011, p. 103).

38 Quoted in Yazdani (2008, 248; emphasis added).

39 See "Council Joint Action 2008/760/CFSP" and "Council Decision 2009/956/CFSP."

40 On the definition of the EU as a "bit player," see S. Neil MacFarlene (2004, p. 14).

41 These inferences borrow from Thomas Diez (1999, pp. 609–10).

42 In other words, while the EU has managed to establish itself as a viable (and, largely, attractive community of practice on (and for) the European continent, it appears that the influence of its normative power remains constrained both by geography and by perceptions of normative proximity (which, for the time being at least, remain also spatially circumscribed). That is why "Europe's security community of practice" persists as a distinctly *European* phenomenon with little traction in "out-of-Europe" areas. Thus, what the EU has been able to establish on the continent—"the knowledge that constitutes normative power like-mindedness, the community of practitioners, including both practice producers and users; and practices embodying knowledge the community develops and maintains. . . [bound by] a sense of shared enterprise and mutual engagement, together with national and supranational physical, institutional, and cultural resources invested in normative power" (Adler, 2010, p. 76)—remains hardly transportable to other global locales. What remains overlooked in the genesis of this community of practice is that it was not initiated by Brussels, per se, but was an outcome of the EU's response to the application bid of post-Communist states. Thus, owing to the overlap between NATO and EU membership, the European security community of practice emerged as a result of the lack of an alternative pole of attraction in the continent. Thus, the EU's normative power is very much a product of these circumstances (rather than an inherent quality), which also comes to explain the difficulty of the EU to divest itself of this experience and develop alternative practices (from enlargement and enlargement-like initiatives) for its security governance.

Chapter 5

1 A number of commentators have insisted that China's influence in Central Asia remains an unlikely proposition, simply because Southeast Asia offers a much more "natural" beachhead for Chinese influence (not least because Beijing is not constrained by any other power there). In support of this position, its proponents argue that apart from Southeast Asia, all other neighboring regions have "historically. . . resisted any form of Chinese political influence. Traditionally, Chinese influence was greatest along the Silk Road—into Central Asia. . . But any influence Beijing hopes to exert among the Central Asian republics. . . will face strong competition from both Russia and political Islam. Moreover, Xinjiang hardly provides an ideal base from which to project Chinese influence, any more than Tibet does for the South Asian sub-continent. . . For now and into the future, the coastal provinces of Central and Southern China are where the country's economic development is, and will be focused, not Xinjiang. Even given competition from the US and Japan, Southeast Asia offers far more inviting opportunities for Chinese political and economic ambitions than does Central Asia" (Stuart-Fox, 2003, p. 225). As argued in this chapter, China's growing significance in Central Asia—as well as in Southeast Asia and other global locales (Kavalski, 2009a)—attests to the capacity and flexibility not only of its "omni-directional" foreign policy, but also of its nascent normative power. The contention is that one needs to engage with China's normative power not on Manners' terms, but on China's terms.

2 In spite of such depictions, as late as 1998, Hooman Peimani (1998, p. 4) has insisted that China "is not considered a player in the ongoing rivalry [in Central Asia] since its impact has not been on the whole of the region."

3 On the current trends toward *decentering* the field of IR, see Nayak and Selbin (2010) and Cudworth and Hobden (2011).

4 It will be demonstrated shortly that China's interactions with Central Asia are one of the most conspicuous instances of this project.

5 George R. Barmé traces the origins of the term *guqing* to the ancient text on the Warring States Period, *Zhanguo ce*. As he points out, the "term was used variously as a pretext for rejecting the influence of the West. . . because Western institutions and practices did not conform to the national situation," or it "harks back to Mao Zedong's 1939 dictum: "A clear understanding of the national situation of China [*Zhingguode guqing*] is the primary basis for appreciating all questions relating to the Chinese revolution" (Barmé, 2000, p. 446). Other commentators have noted that *guoqing* has been variously translated as either "national identity" or "national essence" (Liu, 1996, p. 80). What makes *guoqing* significant to this study is its closeness to the concept of strategic culture. As Arif Dirlik points out, *guoqing* is "a term that does not exclude culture, but is not reducible to it either, as it captures simultaneously material conditions and the intangible elements that make up a nation's particularity" (Dirlik, 2011, p. 145).

6 Commentators have cautioned, however, that even such zero-sum calculus represents (nothing more and nothing less than) a "realism with Chinese characteristics." Hence, inferences about the Chinese predilection to recourse to violence in conflict resolution need to be tempered with understanding of the particular contextual milieu of a specific policy, rather than subject to generalization (Callahan, 2001, p. 80).

7 From a slightly different perspective, Michael Glosny has argued that China basically has no option but subscribe to the dominant rules regulating the international society, because "under the constraints imposed in a unipolar world, the rising power [i.e. China] is likely not only to cooperate with the dominant state, but to be especially careful so that its unilateral actions or relationships with others are not perceived as a potential challenge" (Glosny, 2010, p. 106).

8 For a detailed account of this trend, see Ai (2011). Such tendency to pivot foreign policy articulations in China's traditions has been labeled by some as "restoration nationalism" (Wang, 1996, p. 7). Other commentators have been less sanguine about the promise of Chinese traditions. For instance, Jürgen Osterhammel (1995, p. 160) has ascertained that "[a] genuine Chinese paradigm for the understanding of international relations seems to be lacking. Chinese traditions offer a variety of normative ideas on the conduct of relations between the empire and its neighbors, but none has much relevance for understanding the post-imperial world." Much more explicitly, Chris Ford draws attention to the historical absence of the notion and practice of sovereign coequality in Chinese strategic culture. As he stresses "with the single exception of Buddhism," all other Chinese traditions lack "a meaningful concept of coequal, legitimate sovereignties pursuant to which states may coexist over the long term in *non*hierarchical relationships." Ford, therefore, asserts emphatically that Chinese strategic culture is framed by the "effective denial of the existence of what we would call today *international relations*" (Ford, 2010, p. 57 and p. 103; emphasis in original).

9 Cited in Ding (2010, p. 264).

10 Chris Ford goes on to explain that "as inhabitants of an insular political system and the inheritors of a monist political ideology that conceives of international order in fundamentally hierarchical terms, idealizes interstate order as tending toward tributary universalism. . . modern Chinese statesmen would seem to carry heavy cultural baggage" (Ford, 2010, p. 273).

11 "China tries to dodge Darfur bullets report" at http://www.alertnet.org/thenews/newsdesk/N19151974.htm.

12 As it will be pointed out in the concluding chapter, the logic of relationships is crucial to the recognition of China's normative power in Central Asia. Paraphrasing Confucian dictum, status or *wei* (defined as "a positioning in the primary ontocosmology which should underlie any other constructed or developed system, for it is most fundamental and has everything to do with the very existence of a thing and its worth. In this sense, *wei* can be said to define the worth and 'raison d'être' of anything, particularly those of the human person") reflects a "situation in which a thing finds itself [and] is both a position and a stage which constitutes, confines, and defines the thing" (Cheng, 1996, pp. 149–57).

13 Robert Jervis cited in Loke (2009, p. 202).

14 It has to be indicated that a fruitful line for future inquiry is provided by the interaction between Brantly Womack's "logic of relationships" and the notion of *guanxi* (relationship). Wenshan Jia defines *guanxi* as "the web of relationships that functions as the set of interlocking laces which connects people of different *wei*s [positions/status] together." *Guanxi*, therefore, emerges as "the context, means, and the motive for *wei*. *Guanxi* literally means connections across barriers. *Guan* means barriers and *xi* means connections. First of all, the concept of *guanxi* makes the awareness of the audience and community possible. *Wei* differentiates people from each other, which functions as a barrier, but the very meaning of *wei* resides in the connections embedded in the complex hierarchy of different *wei*s. People strive for *wei* in order [to gain] communal respect or for power over and above the community. . . *wei* and *guanxi* are two philosophical constructs that reflect the Chinese way to know about reality (ontology), the Chinese way to interpret reality (phenomenology), and the Chinese values about humanity (axiology). In other words, the Chinese worldview holds that hierarchy and relationality constitute the substance of humanity" (Jia, 2006, pp. 49–54). Likewise, Lucian Pye has stressed that "the particularistic basis of the relationship is not a guide as to what it may be applied toward. Indeed, the very power of *guanxi* is that its workings are not limited to its ostensible basis, but rather it can be universally directed and used for multiple and diverse purposes." Pye stresses that within the Chinese strategic culture, "the structuring of human relationships has such a vivid quality as to be a very substantive part of physical reality. In practice, *guanxi* in action has thus structured authority and given order and form to Chinese governance. . . The very pragmatic, utilitarian character of *guanxi* can help it to serve the function of institutionalizing power relationships, and thereby give the system a degree of stability" (Pye, 1995, pp. 43–55). Such statements indicate the promise and potential for the explanation and understanding of Chinese strategic culture offered by a prospective synergy between "the logic of relationships" and *guanxi*.

15 Such explanation again brings us back to the Confucian underpinnings of Chinese strategic culture. As Henry Rosemont points out, for "Confucius, unless there are at least two human beings there are no human beings." In other words, unless an actor is engaged in relations with others, that actor has no agency (and is, therefore, not an actor). Actorness emerges in the process of interactions. Thus, the logic of relationships emphasized here suggests that definitions of the "normal" emerge in the context of "reciprocal relationships, best generalized as holding between benefactors and beneficiaries. The roles are thus clearly hierarchical, but each of us moves regularly from benefactor to beneficiary and back again, depending on other(s) with whom we are interacting, when, and under what conditions." It is this emphasis on the dialogical and contextual nature of Chinese strategic culture that allows Rosemont to infer that *recognition* as an actor (in our case, a normative power actor) depends on the capacity for reflection—namely, "the way in which we live these relational roles are the means whereby we achieve dignity, satisfaction, and meaning in life" (Rosemont, 2006, pp. 11–17).

16 For more on this aspect, see Kavalski (2009a, pp. 1–18).

17 In an interesting recent development, some commentators have inferred the "logic of relationships" of Chinese security governance by drawing attention to Beijing's practices of "third culture building to improve international relations." The proposition is that through the open patterns of deliberate and continual interactions, new perceptions about oneself and others, about reality, about the framing of decision-making, and about the ways of managing emotions—that is, a "third culture" bringing together elements of the cultures of the interacting actors as well as new ones emerging in the process of interaction—are being created and re-created. This dynamic makes "Chinese political discourse on foreign policy *deeply relational*" (Jia, 2009, pp. 322–5; emphasis added).

18 Cited in Cui and Li (2011, p. 149).

19 Cited in Ai (2011, p. 89).

20 *Xinhua News Agency*, 14 March 2004.

21 In this setting, some have even gone as far as to claim that the narrative of "peaceful development is a strategy of smart balancing" (Wang, 2011, p. 197).

22 For example, President Hu Jintao's opening remarks at the 2006 FOCAC Summit in Beijing offer a good example of the identity politics underpinning China's normative outreach: "In the long course of history, the Chinese and African peoples, with an unyielding and tenacious spirit, created splendid and distinctive ancient civilisations. In the modern era, our peoples launched unremitting and historic struggle against subjugation, and have written a glorious chapter in the course of pursuing freedom and liberation, upholding human dignity, and striving for economic development and national rejuvenation." For the full text, see: http://www.china.org.cn/english/features/focac/187678.htm.

23 Shaoguang Wang quoted in Shih (1993, p. 35).

24 On these narratives, see Cabestan (2010, p. 26), Dillon (2005), Kavalski (2007b, 2007c, 2009a), Ong (2001), and Tubilewicz (2007). Some commentators have suggested that the "securitizing moment" of these threats has been the establishment of SCO in June 2001 (Cui and Li, 2011, p. 146).

25 Zhao Gancheng quoted in Glosny (2010, p. 128).

26 In a similar fashion, Harald Bockman construes the contemporary Sino-Central Asian relations as a rekindling of the ancient 'tributary' system in which the "foreign relations between the empire and the people in the surrounding areas were perceived as an external expression of the principles of social and political order that existed within the Chinese state and society. These relations were accordingly regarded as non-egalitarian and hierarchically order, just like Chinese society itself. Because of this, *we cannot talk about international relations or foreign policy as such, but only* *of a hierarchically ordered world with China as its center*" (Bockman, 1992, p. 184; emphasis added).

27 Likewise, another commentator has observed that SCO rather than "an informal grouping of Asian states (without formal institutional rules, but with a common understanding, usually defined as a 'regional spirit') is more akin to a formal (western-style) regional cooperation organization" (Korkmaz, 2010, pp. 360–1). While the analysis of this book concurs that SCO represents an idiosyncratic regional grouping, it does not find such juxtaposition between "Asian" and "Western" forms of regionalization particularly productive. If anything, SCO's uniqueness derives from the fact that it features from both—for instance, a "Shanghai Spirit" institutionalized in a formal regional organization.

28 Statement by the Chinese Ministry of Foreign Affairs cited in Pan (2007, p. 61)

29 *Xinhua News Agency*, 11 October 2002.

30 *EurasiaInsight*, 29 April 2002.

31 It is worth pointing out here Chris Ford's poignant observation on the Chinese category of guest (*ko*). As Ford demonstrates, this is a "perhaps deliberately ambiguous" designation, which is "intriguingly connected with ideas of foreignness and barbarian status" (Ford, 2010, pp. 91–2).

32 Description on the 2010 Shanghai Expo website available at http://en.expo2010.cn/c/en_qy_tpl_209.htm.

33 Cited in Pan (2007, p. 65).

34 Chinese observers themselves have commented on the constraints of Western perspectives—for instance, some ascertain that "the research conducted by Western IR scholars is unavoidable restricted by the national and cultural environment in which they are nested" (Yuan Ming cited in Dirlik, 2010, p. 143).

35 Cited in Rosner (2010).

36 Ruan Zongze quoted in Munro (2006, p. 328).

Chapter 6

1 This chapter benefits from suggestions developed earlier in Kavalski (2009e, 2010a).

2 For a detailed analysis of India's narratives of self-aggrandizement, see Kavalski (2010a, p. 75).

3 Cited in Ogden (2011, p. 5; emphasis added).

4 Such acknowledgment also refers to the issue of applying Western frameworks of international politics for explaining and understanding the external interactions of non-Western actors. See Acharya and Buzan (2007), and Kavalski (2009a, 2010a).

5 Cited in Nayar and Paul (2003, p. 47). Again, the origins of such "post-dated self-image" can be traced back to the framing of post-Independence Indian strategic culture by Jawaharlal Nehru, who had insisted already during the 1930s that "fate has marked us for big things" cited in Gordon (1995, p. 1). Reflecting on the peremptory tone of such statements, Pavan Varma utilizes their language to caution that "[o]ver the years the Indian leadership, and the educated Indian, have deliberately projected and embellished an image of India that they know to be untrue, and have willfully encouraged the well-meaning but credulous foreign observer (and even more foreign scholar) to accept it. What is worse, they have fallen in love with this image, and can no longer accept that it is untrue. . . India is much too important today, and its potential far too significant in the coming decades, to be held hostage to this simplistic mythmaking" (Varma, 2004, p. 4).

6 Arundhati Roy cited in Gandhi (2003, p. 291).

7 In fact, Baldev Raj Nayar and T. V. Paul go as far as to suggest that it was the 1962 war with China that "dethroned Gandhi in favor of Kautilya" in Indian strategic thinking (Nayar and Paul, 2003, p. 254).

8 Cited in *Hindustan Times*, 15 April 2006; emphasis added.

9 Manmohan Singh, "Speech on the 60th anniversary of India's independence," 15 August 2007, available at: http://pmindia.nic.in/speeches.htm.

10 On the complexity of India's encounter with China in Central Asia, see Kavalski (2010a, pp. 133–66).

11 Cited in Scott (2009, p. 122).

12 Cited in Kumar (2008, pp. 252–3).

13 Indian Ministry of Defence officials cited by Scott (2009, p. 128).

14 On the complexity of EU-India relations, see Kavalski (2008c).

15 Also, perhaps counter-intuitively, such attitudes are said to confirm the "Gramscian hegemony" of Western international relations theory over Indian perspectives on world affairs (Behera, 2007, p. 341). India, therefore—especially, its *realpolitik* practices—offers one of the most conspicuous confirmations for the suggestion that "The internalization of Eurocentrism in non-Euro-American societies has even created an ironic situation where they appear as perpetrators of Eurocentrism when Euro-Americans are in the process of renouncing it" (Dirlik, 2002, p. 261).

Conclusion

1 In a letter to a friend from 1880 cited in Allworth (1967, p. 408).

2 Norbert Elias' original claim is that "It is not hard to grasp the idea that what we attempt to conceptualize as social forces are in fact forces exerted by people over one another" (Elias, 1978, p. 17).

3 As Chapter 4 demonstrates, this is not least because the EU has had very few incentives (as well as time) to develop such capacities while the preparations for the "Big Bang" East European enlargement were still underway and, consequently, because of the preoccupation with the protracted ratification of the Lisbon Treaty.

4 Kirill Nourzhanov has eloquently revealed that "Western critical IR theory [is] focusing on issues that do not necessarily capture the reality of threats on the ground" when it comes to providing "any cogent threat assessment in Central Asia" (Nourzhanov, 2009, p. 100). The claim of this investigation is that the analytical propositions of European International Relations (EIR) theory can travel beyond the boundaries of Europe. Thus, they are good at conceptualizing the roles of external agency, even if they are not always good when it comes to the explanation of such international agency (on the latter see Wilkinson, 2007).

5 Recently, some commentators have begun to argue that rather than a one-off, such development is indicative of the broader pattern of Chinese foreign policy. As Stephen Roach has suggested, it is this pattern of relations that makes China "*so different*." As he put it, "unlike the West, where the very concept of strategy has become an oxymoron, China has embraced a transnational framework aimed at resolving its sustainability constraints. Moreover, unlike the West, which is trapped in a dysfunctional political [and we can also add economic] quagmire, China has both the commitment and the wherewithal to deliver on that strategy" (Roach, 2011; emphasis added). While the current analysis is more tempered in its assessment, it concurs with Roach's point that China's experience is *sui generis* and needs to be taken on its own terms, rather than Western ones.

6 This is perhaps part of the real reason why Samuel Huntington described India as "lonely" and "friendless" cited in Nayar and Paul (2003, p. 205).

7 This claim follows Daniel Nexon (2009, p. 65). His inference (while premised on an entirely different experience) is especially pertinent to the comparative analysis of the Central Asian agency of normative powers as it allows to position (as well as acknowledge) the variability of such actorness in different global locales. As Nexon postulates, "Actors are frequently positioned within multiple networks, which gives rise to sometimes complementary and sometimes contradictory structural forces. An actor may be central to a particular political network, but peripheral with respect to a different network. In addition, the content—the meanings and symbols—of the social relations that make up a networks have important influences on its structural dynamics" (Nexon, 2009, p. 44).

8 Kinnvall (2006, p. 35; emphasis in original) offers an extremely erudite engagement with the ontological security (and insecurity) of rising powers.

9 Zhao Huasheng cited in Jackobson et al. (2011, p. 12).

10 On the East-West hybridity of India's purview, see Alatas (2006, p. 101).

11 This claim paraphrases a proposition by Ericsson et al (1993, p. 371).

12 This is an important point not least because it reflects a particular articulation of India's external outlook, which has gained popular, policy, and scholarly prominence in the post-1998 period. The peculiar Indian framing of normative power exclusively through the logic of consequences suggests that the definitions of the normal demand the existence of effective military capabilities. For instance, Baldev Raj Nayar and T. V. Paul (2003, p. 58) evidence this attitude with their assessment that "without hard-power resources, the articulation of norms becomes a hollow exercise, as powerful actors tend to ignore options that are not congruent with their interests." It is for this reason that normative power of the EU tends to provoke "disdain in India" (Cameron et al., 2005, p. 46). That is why, a prominent Indian commentator has asserted that "Europe's self-perception of its post-modern orientation is in essence a convenient escape from confronting emerging challenges" (Mohan, 2004, p. 76).

13 This statement paraphrases Michael E. Smith's claim that institutionalization refers to "the cumulative impact of decisions regarding cooperative outcomes' as well as the 'process by which norms or shared standards of behavior, are created and developed" (Smith, 2004).

14 Chapter 2 has, therefore, suggested that it is the ability of actors to change their behavior for the purposes of maintaining their identity as normative powers that underpins the agency of a normative foreign policy actor. Expanding on this claim, the case-studies of Part II confirm Brian Greenhill's proposition that social interactions in the international domain produce sets of shared understandings about an actor's international behavior. He, therefore, distinguishes between the need for recognition and other desires that feed into the complex pattern of global politics. Greenhill argues that the need for recognition "constitute[s] the individual as *a particular type of actor*," while in the process "chang[es] the make-up of the individual concerned" (Greenhill, 2008, p. 348; emphasis added).

15 Michael Brittingham draws a similar conclusion in his assertion that "if a state continues to act like a great power and is *accepted* as one by others, it may also become contested if the state no longer takes up the responsibilities associated with a great power or it is no longer clear that the state in question can live up to the role" (Brittingham, 2007, p. 92).

16 This statement demands the qualification that such mutually constitutive act of recognition should not be misunderstood as the root of collective identity formation—while a possible (long-term) outcome, recognition should not be assumed to play "such a deeply transformative role" (Greenhill, 2008, p. 346). Likewise, Ole Wæver argues that the mutuality of recognition asserts neither that "we are one big whole (not the cosmopolitan 'they too are [like] us'), nor that we will be the more ourselves the more we negate them and negate other identities in ourselves. [David] Campbell talks of 'radical interdependence' as 'the sense in which the origin of an agent or subject—whether that agent or subject be an individual or a state—is to be found in the relationship between Self and Other, and not in the uncovering of some autonomous sovereign ground of being removed from that relationship'" (Wæver, 1996, p. 127).

17 For a detailed discussion of the notion of acting politically under the conditions of complexity, see Kavalski (2008b, pp. 442–3).

Bibliography

Acharya, A. (2004). How ideas spread? Whose norms matter? *International Organization*, 58(1), 239–75.

—(2009). *Whose ideas matter? Agency and power in Asian regionalism*. Ithaca, NY: Cornell University Press.

Acharya, A. & Buzan, B. (2007). Why is there no non-western international relations theory. *International Relations of the Asia-Pacific*, 7(3), 287–312.

Adam, B. (1998a). Values and cultural timescapes of science. *Cultural Values*, 2(2), 388–93.

—(1998b). *Timescapes of modernity*. London: Routledge.

Adams, L. (2008). Globalization, universalism, and cultural form. *Comparative Study in Society and History*, 50(3), 614–40.

Adler, E. (1991). Seasons of peace: Progress in postwar international security. In E. Adler & B. Crawford (Eds), *Progress in postwar international relations* (pp. 128–73). New York: Columbia University Press.

—(1997). Seeking the middle ground: Constructivism in world politics. *European Journal of International Relations*, 3(2), 319–63.

—(2005). *Communitarian international relations: The epistemic foundations of international relations*. London: Routledge.

—(2006). Communitarian multilateralism. In I. Newman, R. Thakur, & J. Tirman (Eds), *Multilaterlaism under challenge? Power, international order, and situational change* (pp. 34–55). Tokyo: United Nations University Press.

—(2008). The spread of security communities: Communities of practice, self-restraint, and NATO's post-cold war transformation. *European Journal of International Relations*, 14(2), 195–230.

—(2010). Europe as a civilizational community of practice. In P. J. Katzenstein (Ed.), *Civilizations and world politics: Plural and pluralist perspectives* (pp. 67–90). New York: Routledge.

Adler, E. & Barnett, M. (1996). Governing anarchy. *Ethics and International Affairs*, 10(1), 63–98.

Adler, E. & Barnett, M. (Eds). (1998). *Security communities*. Cambridge: Cambridge University Press.

Adler, E. & Greve, P. (2009). When security community meets balance of power: Overlapping regional mechanisms of security governance. *Review of International Studies*, 35(1), 59–84.

Adler, E., Crawford, B. & Donnelly, J. (1991). Defining and conceptualizing progress in international relations. In E. Adler & B. Crawford (Eds), *Progress in postwar international relations* (pp. 1–42). New York: Columbia University Press.

Ahmed, I. (1993). *State and foreign policy: India's role in South Asia*. New Delhi: Vikas Publishing.

Ai, J. (2011). *The political use of tradition in contemporary China*. Unpublished PhD Thesis: University of Melbourne.

Alagappa, M. (Ed.). (1998). *Asian security practice*. Stanford, CA: Stanford University Press.

Alatas, S. F. (2006). *Alternative discourses in Asian social science*. New Delhi: Sage.

Alexander, P. C. (2004). *Through the corridors of power: An insider's story*. New Delhi: HarperCollins.

Alker, H. R. (2011). The powers and pathologies of networks: Insights from the political cybernetics of Karl W. Deutsch and Norbert Wiener. *European Journal of International Relations*, 17(4), 679–703.

Allen, D. & Smith, M. (1990). Western Europe's presence in the contemporary international arena. *Review of International Studies*, 16(1), 19–37.

Allison, R. (2004). Regionalism, regional structures, and security management in Central Asia. *International Affairs*, 80(3), 463–83.

Allison, R. & Johnson. L. (Eds). (2001). *Central Asian security: The new international context*. London: Royal Institute for International Affairs.

Allott, P. (2003). The emerging international aristocracy. *New York University Journal of International Law and Politics*, 35(2), 309–38.

Allworth, E. (Ed.). (1967). *Central Asia: A century of Russian rule*. New York: Columbia University Press.

—(1994). *Central Asia*. Durham, NC: Duke University Press.

Al-Qahtani, M. (2006). The Shanghai cooperation organization and the law of international organizations. *Chinese Journal of International Law*, 5(1), 129–47.

Alvarez, J. E. (2005). Do States Socialize. *Duke Law Journal*, 54(3), 961–74.

Anderson, J. (1997). *The international politics of Central Asia*. Manchester: Manchester University Press.

Appleby, P. H. (1954). Managing complexity. *Ethics*, 64(2), 79–99.

Aris, S. (2009). Spreading the "Shanghai Spirit": A Chinese model of regionalization in post-Soviet Central Asia. In E. Kavalski (Ed.), *China and the global politics of regionalization* (pp. 153–64). Farnham: Ashgate.

—(2011). *Eurasian regionalism: The Shanghai cooperation organization*. New York: Palgrave Macmillan.

Aroor, S. (2007). India's base at Ayuni. *India Today*, 21 July.

Asopa, S. K. (2003). Regional interests in Tajikistan. In M. Singh (Ed.), *India and Tajikistan: Revitalizing a traditional relationship* (pp. 155–96). New Delhi: Anamika Publishers.

—(2006). *Struggle for spheres of interest in Trans-Caucasia-Central Asia and India's stakes: An appraisal of India's Central Asia policy*. New Delhi: Manak Publications.

—(2007). India and post-Soviet Asia: An appraisal of India's Central Asian policy. In J. N. Roy & B. B. Kumar (Eds), *India and Central Asia: Classical to contemporary periods* (pp. 172–89). New Delhi: Concept Publishing.

Ba, A. & Hoffmann, M. (Eds). (2005). *Contending perspectives on global governance*. London: Routledge.

Bajpai, K. (2005). Indian strategic culture. In M. R. Chambers (Ed.), *South Asia in 2020: Future strategic balances and alliances* (pp. 253–6). Carlisle, PA: Strategic Studies Institute.

Bal, S. N. (2004). *Central Asia: A strategy for India's look-north policy*. New Delhi: Lancer Publishers.

Baldwin, D. (1997). The concept of security. *Review of International Studies*, 23(1), 5–26.

Barbalet, J. (2011). Market relations as *wuwei*: Daoist concepts in analysis of China's post-1978 market economy. *Asian Studies Review*, 35(3), 335–54.

Barkin, J. S. (2010). *Realist constructivism: Rethinking international relations theory*. Cambridge: Cambridge University Press.

Barmé, G. R. (1999). *In the red: On contemporary Chinese culture*. New York: Columbia University Press.

— (2000). *In the red: On contemporary Chinese culture*. New York: Columbia University Press.

— (2009). China's flat earth: History and 8 August 2008. *China Quarterly*, 197(1), 64–86.

Barnett, M. & Duvall, R. (2005). Power in international politics. *International Organization*, 59(1), 39–75.

Bassin, M. (1999). *Imperial visions: Nationalist imagination and geographical expansion in the Russian far east, 1840–65*. Cambridge: Cambridge University Press.

Basu, R. (2007). *Globalization and Indian foreign policy*. Jaipur: Vital Publications.

Bechev, D. (2011). Enlargement—alive and kicking. *ECFR Sofia View*, 9 December.

Becker, S. (1968). *Russia's Protectorates in Central Asia, 1865–1924*. Cambridge, MA: Harvard University Press.

Bedi, R. (2002). India and Central Asia: India's growing presence and role in the resource-rich and strategically significant Central Asian region has important implications. *Frontline*, 19(19), 14–27 September.

Behera, N. C. (2003). Forging new solidarities: Nonofficial dialogues. In M. Mekenkam, P. van Tongeren, & H. van de Veen (Eds), *Searching for peace in Central and South Asia: An overview of conflict prevention and peacebuilding activities* (pp. 210–36). Boulder, CO: Lynne Rienner.

— (2007). Re-imagining international relations in India. *International Relations of the Asia-Pacific*, 7(3), 341–68.

Beissinger, M. R. & Young, C. (Eds). (2002). *Beyond state crisis? Post-colonial Africa and post-Soviet Eurasia in comparative perspective*. Cambridge: Cambridge University Press.

Bezlova, A. (2008). SCO split on Georgia. *IPS News*, 2 September.

Bhadrakumar, M. K. (2004). New regionalism in Central Asia. *The Hindu*, 14 July.

— (2008). India must return to Eurasian energy game. *The Hindu*, 18 February.

Bhattacharjea, M. S. (2008). Does China have a grand strategy? In P. Vohra & P. K. Ghosh (Eds), *China and the Indian ocean region* (pp. 1–19). New Delhi: National Maritime Foundation.

Bhattacharyya, S. (2004). Lure of the silk route. *Hindustan Times*, 19 August.

Bhatty, R. & Auty, R. M. (2006). The effectiveness of western leverage: IFI projects and programs. In R. M. Auty & I. de Soysa (Eds), *Energy, wealth and governance in the Caucasus and Central Asia: Lessons not learned* (pp. 248–60). London: Routledge.

Bially-Mattern, J. (2005). *Ordering international politics*. London: Routledge.

Bigo, D. (2001). The möbius ribbon of internal and external security. In M. Albert, D. Jacobson, Y. Lapid, & D. Bigo (Eds), *Identities, borders, orders: Rethinking international relations theory* (pp. 91–116). Minneapolis, MN: Minnesota University Press.

Bin, Y. (2005). China and Russia: Normalizing their strategic partnership. In D. Shambaugh (Ed.), *Power shift: China and Asia's new dynamics*. Berkeley, CA: University of California Press.

Black, J. L. (2004). *Vladimir Putin and the new world order: Looking east, looking West?* Lanham, MD: Rowman & Littlefield.

Blank, S. (2002). The arming of Central Asia. *Asia Times*, 23 August.

—(2004). Democratic prospects in Central Asia. *World Affairs*, 166(1), 133–47.

—(2005). China in Central Asia: The hegemon in waiting? In A. Cohen (Ed.), *Eurasia in balance: The US and the regional power shift* (pp. 149–82). Aldershot: Ashgate.

Bliesemann de Guevara, B. (2008). The state in times of state-building. *Civil Wars*, 10(4), 348–68.

Blunt, W. (1973). *The golden road to Samarkand*. New York: Viking Press.

Blyth, M. (2006). Great punctuations: prediction, randomness, and the evolution of comparative political science. *American Political Science Review*, 100(4), 1–6.

Bockman, H. (1992). The brewing ethnic conflicts in China and their historical background. In K. Rupesinghe, P. King, & O. Vorkunova (Eds), *A post-communist world: Eastern Europe, Russia, and China* (pp. 183–98). New York: St. Martin's Press.

Bohr, A. (2004). Regionalism in Central Asia. *International Affairs*, 80(3), 485–502.

Booth, K. (1979). *Strategy and ethnocentrism*. London: Croom Helm.

—(1990). The concept of strategic culture affirmed. In C. G. Jacobsen (Ed.), *Strategic power USA/USSR* (pp. 120–31). Basingstoke: Macmillan.

—(2005). Critical exploration. In K. Booth (Ed.), *Critical security studies and world politics* (pp. 1–18). Boulder, CO: Lynne Rienner.

—(2007). *Theory of world security*. Cambridge: Cambridge University Press.

Borrie, J. (Ed.). (2005). *Alternative approaches to multilateralism*. Geneva: UNDIR.

Bowden, B. (2009). *The empire of civilization: The evolution of an imperial idea*. Chicago, IL: The University of Chicago Press.

Bozeman, A. B. (1960). *Politics and culture in international history*. Princeton, NJ: Princeton University Press.

—(1976). War and the clash of ideas. *Orbis*, 20(1), 77–102.

Bretherton, C. & Vogler, J. (2006). *The European union as a global actor*. London: Routledge.

Breyfogle, N., Schroder, A. & Sunderland, W. (Eds). (2007). *Peopling the Russian periphery: Borderland colonization in Eurasian history*. London: Routledge.

Brittingham, M. A. (2007). China's contested rise: Sino-US relations and the social construction of great power status. In S. Guo & S. Hua (Eds), *New Dimensions of Chinese Foreign Policy*. Lanham, MD: Lexington Books.

Budania, R. (2003). The emerging international security system: Threats, challenges, and opportunities for India. *Strategic Analysis*, 27(1), 79–93.

Bull, H. (1977). *The anarchical society: A study of order in world politics*. Basingstoke: Macmillan.
Bunce, V. & Wolchik, S. (2009). Getting real about "real causes." *Journal of Democracy*, 20(1), 69–73.
Buzan, B. (1983). *People, states, fear*. Hemel-Hempstead: Harvester-Wheatsheaf.
Buzan, B. & Wæver, O. (2003). *Regions and powers: The structure of international security*. Cambridge: Cambridge University Press.
Cabestan, J.-P. (2010). Central Asia-China relations and their relative weight in chinese foreign policy. In M. Laruelle, J.-F. Huchet, S. Peyrouse, & B. Balci (Eds), *China and India in Central Asia: A new "great game"?* (pp. 25–40). New York: Palgrave Macmillan.
Callahan, W. (2001). China and the globalization of IR theory. *Journal of Contemporary China*, 10(1), 75–88.
—(2006). History, identity, security: Producing and consuming nationalism in China. *Critical Asian Studies*, 38(2), 179–208.
Cameron, F., Berkofsky, A., Bhandari, M., & Halley, D. (2005). The EU-India relations. *EPC Issue Papers* 35.
Canfield, R. L. (1992). Restructuring in greater Central Asia: Changing political configurations. *Asian Survey*, 32(10), 875–87.
Caporaso, J. & Jupille, J. (1998). States, agency, and rules. In C. Rhodes (Ed.), *The European Union and the world community* (pp. 213–30). Boulder, CO: Lynne Rienner.
Cappelli, O. (2008). Pre-modern state-building in post-Soviet Russia. *Journal of Communist Studies and Transition Politics*, 24(4), 531–72.
Carls, A.-C. (2009). Central Asia: The new silk road's Gordian knot. *World History Connect*, 6(1), 1–18.
Caroe, O. (1967). *Soviet Empire: The Turks of Central Asia and Stalinism*. New York: St. Martin's Press.
Carr, E. H. (1964). *The Twenty Years' crisis, 1919–39: An introduction to the study of international relations*. New York: Harper & Row.
Carroll, B. (1972). Peace research: The cult of power. *Journal of Conflict Resolution*, 16(4), 585–616.
Cassirer, E. (1946). *The myth of the state*. New Haven, CT: Yale University Press.
Ceccarelli, A. (2007). Clans, politics, and organized crime in Central Asia. *Trends in Organized Crime*, 10(3), 19–36.
Chandler, D. (2004). The responsibility to protect? Imposing the liberal peace: A critique. *International Peacekeeping*, 11(1), 59–81.
Chaulia, S. (2002). BJP, India's foreign policy, and the "realist alternative" to the Nehruvian tradition. *International Politics*, 39(2), 215–34.
Checkel, J. (1999). Norms, institutions, and national identity in contemporary Europe. *International Studies Quarterly*, 43(1), 83–114.
—(2001). Why comply? Social learning and European identity change. *International Organization*, 55(3), 553–88.
Checkel, J. (Ed.). (2007). *International institutions and socialization*. Cambridge: Cambridge University Press.
Chen, K. (2002). Why is "great reconciliation" impossible? *Inter-Asia Cultural Studies*, 3(1), 77–99.

Chen, M. (2007). Chinese national oil companies and human rights. *Orbis*, 51(1), 41–54.

Cheng, C. (1996). *Zhouyi* and philosophy of *wei* (positions). *Extreme-Orient, Extreme-Occident*, 18(1), 149–75.

Chiriyankandath, J. (2004). Realigning India: Indian foreign policy after the Cold War. *The Round Table*, 93(374), 199–211.

Chopra, V. D. (1997). India-Russia-China: Changing equations. In M. Rasgotra & V. D. Chopra (Eds), *India's relations with Russia and China: A new phase* (pp. 15–36). New Delhi: Gyan Publishing.

Choudhury, G. W. (1977). *Chinese perceptions of the World.* Lanham, MD: University Press of America.

Christou, G., Crogt, S., Ceccorulli, M., & Lucarelli, S. (2010). EU security governance. *European Security*, 19(3), 341–59.

Chung, C. (2004). The Shanghai cooperation organization. *China Quarterly*, 44(180), 989–1009.

Cini, M. & Bourne, A. K. (Eds). (2006). *European Union studies.* Basingstoke: Palgrave Macmillan.

Cioffi-Revilla, C. (2006). The big collapse. In B. K. Gills & W. R. Thompson (Eds), *Globalization and global history* (pp. 79–95). London: Routledge.

Clapham, C. (1998). Degrees of statehood. *Review of International Studies*, 24(1), 143–57.

Clarke, M. E. (2009). China and the Shanghai cooperation organization: The dynamics of "new regionalism," "vassalization," and geopolitics in Central Asia. In E. Kavalski (Ed.), *The "new" Central Asia: The regional agency of international actors* (pp. 117–48). London: World Scientific.

Claude, I. L. (1965). *Power and international relations.* New York: Random House.

Cohen, A. (2001). The Russia-China friendship treaty. *Heritage Foundation Backgrounder* 1459.

Cohen, A. (Ed.). (2005). *Eurasia in balance: The US and the regional power shift.* Aldershot: Ashgate.

Cohen, A. (2008). *Kazakhstan.* Washington, DC: CACI.

Cohen, S. (2001). *India: Emerging power.* Oxford: Oxford University Press.

Coicaud, J.-M. (2001). Legitimacy, socialization, and institutional change. In C. A. Kupchan, E. Adler, J.-M. Coicaud, & Y. F. Khon, with the assistance of J. Davidson & M. Sucharov, (Eds), *Power in transition: The peaceful change of international order* (pp. 68–100). Tokyo: United Nations University Press.

Coleman, P. T. (2004). Paradigmatic framing of protracted, intractable conflict. *Peace & Conflict*, 10(3), 197–235.

Collins, K. (2006). *Clan politics and regime transition in Central Asia.* Cambridge: Cambridge University Press.

—(2009). Economic and security regionalism among patrimonial authoritarian regimes: The case of Central Asia. *Europe-Asia Studies*, 61(20), 249–81.

Colton, T. J. & Legvold, R. (1992). *After the Soviet Union: From empire to nations.* New York: W. W. Norton & Co.

Cooper, R. (2002). Why we still need empires. *The Observer*, 7 April.

Cortell, A. P. & Davis, J. W. (2000). Understanding the domestic impact of international norms. *International Studies Quarterly*, 2(1), 65–87.

Cox, R. W. (1981). Social forces, states, and world orders: Beyond international relations theory. *Millennium*, 10(2), 126–55.

Crawford, B. (1991). Toward a theory of progress in international relations. In E. Adler & B. Crawford (Eds), *Progress in postwar international relations* (pp. 438–68). New York: Columbia University Press.

Crawford, N. (2002). *Argument and change in world politics.* Cambridge: Cambridge University Press.

Cruz, C. (2000). Identity and persuasion: How nations remember their pasts and make their futures. *World Politics*, 52(3), 275–312.

Cudworth, E. & Hobden, S. (2011). *Posthuman International Relations.* London: Zed Books.

Cui, S. & Li, J. (2011). (De)Securitizing frontier security in China: Beyond the positive and negative debate. *Cooperation and Conflict*, 46(2), 144–65.

Cullen, R. (1994). Central Asia and the west. In M. Mandelbaum (Ed.), *Central Asia and the world: Kazakhstan, Uzbekistan, Tajikistan, Kyrgyzstan, and Turkmenistan* (pp. 130–46). New York: Council on Foreign Relations Press.

Curtis, L. (1922). A criterion of values in international affairs. *Journal of the British Institute of International Affairs*, 1(6), 165–80.

Curzon, G. (1889). *Russia in Central Asia.* London: Longmans and Co.

Dark, K. (2002). The informational reconfiguring of global geopolitics. In Y. Ferguson & R. J. Barry Jones (Eds), *Political space.* New York: SUNY Press.

Das, G. (2000). *India unbound.* New Delhi: Viking.

Das, R. (2009). The prism of strategic culture and south Asian nuclearization. *Contemporary Politics*, 15(4), 396–411.

Dash, P. L. (2007). Central Asia: Tulips have different hews. In J. N. Roy & B. B. Kumar (Eds), *India and Central Asia* (pp. 190–210).

— (2007a). Central Asia: Tulips have different hews. In J. N. Roy & B. B. Kumar (Eds), *India and Central Asia: Classical to contemporary periods* (pp. 190–210). New Delhi: Concept Publishing.

— (2007b). Sixty years of Indo-Russian synergy. *World Focus*, 28(335/366), 473–7.

Delcour, L. (2011). *Shaping the post-Soviet space? EU policies and approaches to region-building.* Farnham: Ashgate.

de Nevers, R. (2007). Imposing international norms. *International Studies Review*, 9(1), 53–80.

Deng, F. M. (1995). Frontiers of sovereignty. *Leiden Journal of International Law*, 8(1), 249–75.

Deng, Y. (2005). Better than power: "International status" in Chinese foreign policy. In Y. Deng & F. Wang (Eds), *China rising: Power and motivation in Chinese foreign policy.* Lanham, MD: Rowman and Littlefield.

Der Derian, J. (1992). *Antidiplomacy.* Oxford: Blackwell.

Deutsch, K., Burrell, S., Kahn, R., Lee, M., Lichterman, M., Lindgren, R., Loewenheim, F., Van Wagenen, R. (1957). *Political community in the north Atlantic area.* Princeton, NJ: Princeton University Press.

Deyermond, R. (2009). Matrioshka hegemony? Multi-leveled hegemonic competition and security in post-Soviet Central Asia. *Review of International Studies*, 35(1), 151–73.

Dietl, G. (1997). Quest for influence in Central Asia: India and Pakistan. *International Studies*, 34(2), 111–43.

Diez, T. (1999). Speaking "Europe:" The politics of integration discourse. *Journal of European Public Policy*, 6(4), 598–613.

—(2001). Europe as a discursive battleground. *Cooperation and Conflict*, 36(1), 5–38.

—(2005). Constructing the self and changing others: Reconsidering "normative power Europe." *Millennium*, 33(3), 613–36.

Diez, T. & Manners, I. (2007). Reflecting on normative power Europe. In F. Berenskoetter & M. J. Williams (Eds), *Power in world politics* (pp. 173–88). London: Routledge.

Dillon, M. (1996). *Politics of security*. London: Routledge.

—(2004). The security of governance. In W. Larner & W. Walters (Eds), *Global governmentality* (pp. 76–94). London: Routledge.

—(2005). *Xinjiang: China's Muslim far northwest*. London: Routledge.

—(2007). Governing terror: The state of emergency of biopolitical emergence. *International Political Sociology*, 1(1), 7–28.

Ding, S. (2010). Analyzing rising power from the perspective of soft power. *Journal of Contemporary China*, 19(64), 255–72.

Dirlik, A. (2002). History without a centre? Reflections on eurocentrism. In E. Fuhs & B. Stuchtey (Eds), *Across cultural borders* (pp. 259–68). Lanham, MD: Rowman and Littlfield.

—(2011). Culture in contemporary IR theory: The Chinese provocation. In R. Shilliam (Ed.), *International relations and non-western thought* (pp. 139–56). New York: Routledge.

Dixit, J. N. (2001). *India's foreign policy and its neighbors*. New Delhi: Gyan Publishing.

—(2004). Emerging international security environment: Indian perceptions with focus on South Asian and Central Asian predicaments. In K. Santhanam & R. Dwivedi (Eds), *India and Central Asia: Advancing the common interest* (pp. 13–25). New Delhi: Anamaya Publishers.

Donnelly, J. (1998). Human rights: A new standard of civilization. *International Affairs*, 74(1), 1–23.

Duffield, M. (2001). *Global governance and the new wars*. London: Zed Books.

Duke, S. (1994). *The new European security disorder*. London: Macmillan.

Dunn, M. (2007). Securing the digital age: The challenges of complexity and IR theory. In J. Eriksson & G. Giacomello (Eds), *International relations and security in the digital age* (pp. 85–105). London: Routledge.

Dutt, V. P. (2000). *India's foreign policy in a changing world*. New Delhi: Vikas Publishing House.

Efegil, E. (2009). The European Union's new Central Asian strategy. In E. Kavalski (Ed.), *The "new" Central Asia: The regional impact of international actors* (pp. 71–88). London: World Scientific.

Ehteshami, A. (1995). *From the Gulf to Central Asia*. Exeter: University of Exeter Press.

Elder, C. D. & Cobb, R. W. (1983). *The political uses of symbols*. New York: Longman.

Elias, N. (1978). *What is sociology?* New York: Columbia University Press.

Elkins, D. J. & Simeon, R. E. B. (1979). A cause in search of its effect, or what does political culture explain. *Comparative Politics*, 11(2), 127–45.

Emerson, M. (2005). EU-Russia: Four common spaces and the proliferation of the fuzzy. *CEPS Policy Brief*, 1/2.

Ericsson, K. A. (2004). Deliberate practice and maintenance of expert performance in medicine and related domains. *Academic Medicine*, 79(10), S70–S81.

Ericsson, K. A., Krampe, R. T., & Tesch-Römer, C. (1993). The role of deliberate practice in the acquisition of expert performance. *Psychological Review*, 100(3), 363–406.

Feng, H. (2007). *Chinese strategic culture and foreign policy decision-making: Confucianism, leadership, and war*. London: Routledge.

Feng, Z. (2008). The Russia-Georgia military conflict: For China does it mean scrambling between a "strategic partnership" and being a "responsible stakeholder"? *Korean Journal of Defence Analysis*, 20(4), 305–18.

Ferdinand, P. (1995). The new Central Asia and China. In P. Ferdinand (Ed.), *The new states of Central Asia and their neighbors* (pp. 95–110). New York: Council on Foreign Relations Press.

Field, H. (2001). Awkward States: European Union enlargement and Slovakia, Croatia, XE "Croatia" and Serbia. *Perspectives on European Politics and Society*, 1(1), 23–46.

Finkelstein, L. (1995). What is global governance. *Global Governance*, 1(2), 367–73.

Flecker, J. E. (1922). The Golden Journey to Samarkand. In G. C. F. Mead & R. C. Clift (Eds), *English verse, old and new: An anthology* (p. 31). Cambridge: Cambridge University Press.

Flockhart, T. (2004). *Uses and abuses of hegemony: Socialization of democratic norms in post-war Germany and post-war Iraq*. Aaborg: SPIRIT.

Flockhart, T. (Ed.). (2005a). *Socializing democratic norms*. Basingstoke: Palgrave Macmillan.

Flockhart, T. (2005b). A mission bound to fail. *Whitehead Journal of Diplomacy and International Relations*, 6(1), 53–68.

Ford, C. (2010). *The Mind of Empire: China's history and modern foreign relations*. Lexington, KY: University Press of Kentucky.

Frank, A. G. (1992). The centrality of Central Asia. *Studies in History*, 8(1), 43–97.

Frazier, D. & Stewart-Ingersoll, R. (2010). Regional powers and security. *European Journal of International Relations*, 16(4), 731–53.

Freedman, L. (2006). *The transformation of strategic affairs*. London: Routledge.

Freedman, R. (1998). Russia's Middle East ambitions. *Middle East Quarterly*, 5(3), 31–40.

French, R. (2001). "Negative capability:" Managing the confusing uncertainties of change. *Journal of Organizational Change Management*, 14(5), 480–92.

Friedrichs, J. (2004). *European approaches to international relations theory: A house with many mansions*. London: Routledge.

Fumagalli, M. (2009). The United States and Central Asia. In E. Kavalski (Ed.), *The "new" Central Asia: The regional impact of international actors* (pp. 149–76). London: World Scientific.

Gabuyev, A. (2009). Cost of the matter. *Kommersant* (FBIS SOV), 23 December.

Gandhi, R. (1996). From Armenia to Almaty: Detachment policy bad for business. *The Times of India*, 26 November.

—(2003). Understanding religious conflicts. In M. Mekenkam, P. van Tongeren, & H. van de Veen (Eds), *Searching for peace in Central and South Asia: An overview of conflict prevention and peacebuilding activities* (pp. 291–302). Boulder, CO: Lynne Rienner.

Ganguly, S. (2003/2004). India's foreign policy grows up. *World Policy Journal*, 20(4), 43–56.

Gareau, F. H. (1981). The discipline of international relations: A multi-national perspective. *Journal of Politics*, 43(3), 779–802.

Gariup, M. (2009). *European security culture: Language, theory, policy*. Farnham: Ashgate.

Gaventa, J. (2007). Levels, spaces, and forms of power: Analysing opportunities for change. In F. Berenskoetter & M. J. Williams (Eds), *Power in world politics* (pp. 204–24). London: Routledge.

Gheciu, A. (2008). *Securing civilization? The EU, NATO, and the OSCE in the post-9/11 world*. Oxford: Oxford University Press.

Gidadhubli, R. G. (2007). Politics of oil and natural gas in Central Asia: Conflicts and cooperation. In J. N. Roy & B. B. Kumar (Eds), *India and Central Asia: Classical to contemporary periods* (pp. 156–77). New Delhi: Concept Publishing.

Gilson, J. (2005). New inter-regionalism? The EU and East Asia. *European Integration* 27(3), 307–26.

Gills, B. K. & Thompson, W. R. (2006). Globalization, global histories, and historical globalities. In B. K. Gills & W. R. Thompson (Eds), *Globalization and Global History* (pp. 1–17). London: Routledge.

Gleason, G. (1997). *The Central Asian states: Discovering independence*. Boulder, CO: Westview Press.

Glosny, M. A. (2010). China and the BRICs: A real (but limited) partnership in a unipolar world. *Polity*, 42(1), 100–29.

Goertz, G. (1994). *Contexts of international politics*. Cambridge: Cambridge University Press.

Goetze, C. & Guzina, D. (2008). Peacebuilding, statebuilding, nationbuilding—turtles all the way down? *Civil Wars*, 10(4), 319–47.

Golden, S. (2006). Socio-cultural aspects of the relationship between the European Union and East Asia, with a particular reference to China. *Asia Europe Journal*, 4(1), 265–94.

Gololobov, I. (2008). The Soviet people. In E. Kavalski & M. Zolkos (Eds), *Defunct federalisms: Critical perspectives on federal failure* (pp. 145–56). Aldershot: Ashgate.

Goodman, R. & Jinks, D. (2003). Toward an institutional theory of sovereignty. *Stanford Law Review*, 55(4), 1749–88.

Gordon, S. (1995). *India's rise to power in the twentieth century and beyond*. New York: St. Martin's Press.

Grabbe, H. (2002). EU conditionality. *International Political Science Review*, 3(1), 249–68.

Gray, C. S. (1984). Comparative strategic culture. *Parameters*, 14(4), 35–9.

—(1999). Strategic culture as context: The first generation fights back. *Review of International Studies*, 25(1), 53–60.

—(2006). Out of the wilderness: Prime time for strategic culture. *US Nuclear Strategy Forum Paper* No. 0004.

Greenhill, B. (2008). Recognition and collective identity formation in international politics. *European Journal of International Relations*, 14(2), 343–68.

Grosz, E. A. (2004). *The nick of time: Politics, evolution, and the untimely*. Durham, NC: Duke University Press.

Gruber, H., Degner, S., & Lehman, A. C. (2004). Why do some commit themselves to deliberate practice for many years—and why so many do not? Understanding the development of professionalism in music. In M. Radovan & N. Dordević (Eds), *Current issues in adult learning and motivation* (pp. 222–35). Ljubljana: Slovenian Institute for Adult Education.

Grzymala-Busse, A. & Jones Luong, P. (2002). The ignored transition: Post-Communist state development. *Weatherhead Center for International Affairs Working Paper* 02.

Gupta, B. S. (1997). India in the twenty-first century. *International Affairs*, 73(2), 309–19.

Guzzini, S. (2004). The enduring dilemmas of realism in international relations. *European Journal of International Relations*, 10(4), 533–68.

Haas, P. (1992). Epistemic communities and international policy coordination. *International Organization*, 46(1), 1–35.

Haass, R. (2003). Sovereignty: Existing rights, evolving responsibilities. Remarks to the School of Foreign Service and the Mortara Center of International Studies, Georgetown University, 14 January.

Haglund, D. G. (2004). What good is strategic culture? A modest defence of an immodest concept. *International Journal*, 59(2), 479–502.

Haidar, M. (2003). India and Central Asia: Linkages and interactions. In N. Joshi (Ed.), *Central Asia—the great game replayed: An Indian perspective* (pp. 257–94). New Delhi: New Century Publications.

—(2004). *Indo-Central Asian relations*. New Delhi: Manohar Publishers.

Haier, M. H. (1995). *The politics of environmental discourse*. Oxford: Clarendon Press.

Hall, T. D. (2006). [Re]periphalization, [re]incorporation, frontiers, and non-state societies. In B. K. Gills & W. R. Thompson (Eds), *Globalization and Global History* (pp. 96–113). London: Routledge.

Hansen, F. S. (2005). A grand strategy for Central Asia. *Problems of Post-Communism*, 52(2), 45–54.

Hansen, L. (1996). Slovenian identity: State building on the Balkan border. *Alternatives*, 2(4), 473–95.

Hao, T. (2010). China's seasonal politics. *OpenDemocracy*, 4 May.

Harris, L. (1993). Xinjiang, Central Asia, and the implications for China's foreign policy in the Islamic world. *China Quarterly*, 133(1), 111–29.

Harrison, N. E. (Eds). (2006). *Complexity in world politics*. Albany, NY: SUNY Press.

Haugen, A. (2003). *The establishment of national republics in Soviet Central Asia*. New York: Palgrave Macmillan.

Hay, C. & Mennon, A. (Eds). (2005). *European politics*. Oxford: Oxford University Press.

Heathershaw, J. (2010). Central Asian statehood in post-colonial perspective. In E. Kavalski (Ed.), *Stable outside, fragile inside? Post-Soviet statehood in Central Asia* (pp. 87–105). Farnham: Ashgate.

Heinzen, B. (2004). Surviving uncertainty. *Development*, 47(4), 4–8.

Henderson, K. & Weaver, C. (Eds). (2010). *The black sea region and EU policy.* Farnham: Ashgate.

Herrmann, R. K., Voss, J. F., & Schooler, T. Y. E. (1997). Images in international relations: An experimental test of cognitive schemata. *International Studies Quarterly*, 41(3), 403–33.

Hettne, B. & Söderbaum, F. (2000). Theorizing the rise of regionness. *New Political Economy*, 5(3), 457–73.

Hill, C. & Smith, M. (Eds). (2005). *International relations of the European Union.* Oxford: Oxford University Press.

Hindustan Times (1998). Sign of self-confidence, say experts. 12 May.

—(2006). Pakistan blocking access to Central Asia. 15 April.

—(2008). India's Afghan road to be ready. 13 July.

Hix, S. (2008). The European Union as a new political system. In D. Caramani (Ed.), *Comparative politics* (pp. 573–601). Oxford: Oxford University Press.

Hoffman, S. A. (2004). Perception and China policy in India. In F. R. Frankel & H. Harding (Eds), *The India-China relationship: What the United States needs to know* (pp. 33–75). New York: Columbia University Press.

Hoffmann, S. (1977). An American social science: International relations. *Daedalus*, 106(3), 41–60.

Holsti, K. J. (1989). Mirror, mirror on the wall, which are the fairest theories of all. *International Studies Quarterly*, 33(3), 255–61.

—(1991). *Change in the international system: Essays on the theory and practice of international relations.* Aldershot: Edward Elgar.

Holt, F. L. (1988). *Alexander the Great and Bactria: The formation of a Greek frontier in Central Asia.* Leiden: E. J. Brill.

Honneth, A. (1999). *The struggle for recognition: The moral grammar of social conflict.* Cambridge, MA: MIT Press.

—(2001). Recognition or redistribution? Changing perspectives on the moral order of society. *Theory, Culture & Society*, 18(2/3), 43–54.

Hopf, T. (2010). The logic of habit in international relations. *European Journal of International Relations*, 16(4), 539–61.

Hopkins, R. E. & Mansbach, R. W. (1973). *Structure and process in international politics.* New York: Harper and Row.

Hopkirk, P. (1992). *The great game: The struggle for empire in Central Asia.* New York: Kodansha International.

Hough, P. (2004). *Understanding global security.* London: Routledge.

Hu, A. (2011). *China in 2020: A new type of superpower.* Washington, DC: Brookings Institution Press.

Hui, V. T. (2005). *War and state formation in ancient China and early modern Europe.* Cambridge: Cambridge University Press.

Hurrell, A. (1993). International society and the study of regimes: A reflective approach. In V. Rittberger (Ed.), *Regime theory and international relations* (pp. 49–73). Oxford: Clarendon Press.

Husain, A. (1993). Opinion. *India Today*, 15 March.

Hussain, I. (2011). The Shanghai framework and Central Asia: Chop-suey governance? In E. J. Kirchner & R. Dominguez (Eds), *The security governance of regional organizations* (pp. 243–72). London: Routledge.

Huysmans, J. (1998). Security! What do you mean? From concept to thick signifier. *European Journal of International Relations*, 4(2), 226–55.
Hymans, J. E. C. (2009). India's soft power and vulnerability. *India Review*, 8(3), 251–63.
Ignatieff, M. (2002). Nation-building lite. *New York Times Magazine*, 28 July.
Ikenberry, G. J. (2001). *After victory: Institutions, strategic restraint, and the rebuilding of order after major wars.* Princeton, NJ: Princeton University Press.
Ikenberry, G. J. & Kupchan, C. (1990). Socialization and hegemonic power. *International Organization*, 44(3), 283–315.
International Crisis Group (2005). Uzbekistan: The Andijon uprising. *Asia Briefing*, 38.
—(2006). Central Asia: What role for the EU. *Asia Report,* 113.
Iriye, A. (1979). Culture and power: International relations as intercultural relations. *Diplomatic History*, 3(2), 115–28.
Jackson, J. (1975). Normative power and conflict Potential. *Sociological Methods and Research*, 4(2), 237–9.
Jain, B. M. (2008). *Global power: India's foreign policy, 1947–2006.* Lanham, MD: Lexington Books.
Jakobson, L., Holtom, P., Knox, D., & Peng, J. (2011). China's energy and security relations with Russia. *SIPRI Policy Paper* 29.
Jawahar, J. (2002). India and Kazakhstan: Significant changes. *SAPRA India*, 24 February.
Jervis, R. (1968). Hypotheses on misperception. *World Politics*, 20(3), 454–79.
—(1997). Complex systems: The role of interactions. In D. S. Alberts & T. J. Czerwinski (Eds), *Complexity, global politics and national security* (pp. 45–72). Washington, DC: National Defense University.
Jha, S. K. (1997). Indo-Russian relations: In the light of new realities. In M. Rasgotra & V. D. Chopra (Eds), *India's relations with Russia and China: A new phase* (pp. 75–96). New Delhi: Gyan Publishing.
Jia, W. (2006). The wei (positioning)–ming (naming)–lianmian (face)–guanxi (relationship)–renqing (humanized feelings)–complex in contemporary Chinese culture. In P. H. Hershock & R. T. Ames (Eds), *Confucian cultures of authority* (pp. 49–64). Albany, NY: SUNY Press.
—(2009). An intercultural communication model of international relations: The case of China. In Y. Hao, C. X. G. Wei, & L. Dittmer (Eds), *Challenges to Chinese foreign policy: Diplomacy, globalization, and the next world power* (pp. 319–34). Lexington, KY: University Press of Kentucky.
Jiang, W. (2006). China makes "great leaps outward" in regional diplomacy. *International Journal*, 61(2), 329–40.
Johns, M. (2003). "Do as I say, not as I do:" The European Union, Eastern Europe and minority rights. *East European Politics and Societies*, 17(4), 682–99.
Johnson, D. D. P. & Madin, E. M. P. (2008). Paradigm shifts in security strategy. In R. D. Sagarin & T. Taylor (Eds), *Natural security: A Darwinian approach to a dangerous world* (pp. 209–39). Berkeley, CA: University of California Press.
Johnston, A. I. (1995). Thinking about strategic culture. *International Security*, 19(4), 32–64.

—(1996). Cultural realism and strategy in Maoist China. In P. Katzenstein (Ed.), *The culture of national security* (pp. 216–68). New York: Columbia University Press.

—(1998a). International structures and foreign policy. In S. Kim (Ed.), *China and the world*. Boulder, CO: Westview Press.

—(1998b). *Cultural realism*. Princeton, NJ: Princeton University Press.

—(1999). Strategic cultures revisited. *Review of International Studies*, 25(4), 519–23.

Jones, R. W. (2006). *India's strategic culture*. Carlisle, PA: Defence Threat Reduction Agency.

Jones, D. & Smith, M. L. (2001). The changing security agenda in Southeast Asia. *Studies in Conflict and Terrorism*, 24(4), 271–88.

Jones Luong, P. (2001). Russia and Central Asia. In R. Allison & L. Jonson (Eds), *Central Asian security: The new international context* (pp. 95–126). London: RIIA.

—(2002). *Institutional change and political continuity in post-Soviet Central Asia*. Cambridge: Cambridge University Press.

Jones Luong, P. (Ed.). (2004). *The transformation of Central Asia*. Ithaca, NY: Cornell University Press.

Jones Luong, P. & Weinthal, E. (1999). The NGO paradox. *Europe-Asia Studies*, 51(7), 1267–84.

Joshi, N. (2002). The Putin visit. *The Hindu*, 11 December.

—(2003). Issues in Central Asian stability. In N. Joshi (Ed.), *Central Asia—The great game replayed: An Indian perspective* (pp. 67–96). New Delhi: New Century Publications.

—(2004). Regional economic cooperation and transport links with Central Asia: An Indian perspective. In K. Santhanam & R. Dwivedi (Eds), *India and Central Asia: Advancing the common interest* (pp. 2013–2213). New Delhi: Anamaya Publishers.

—(2007a). Geopolitical perspectives on Central Asia: An Indian view. In J. N. Roy & B. B. Kumar (Eds), *India and Central Asia: Classical to contemporary periods* (pp. 143–55). New Delhi: Concept Publishing.

—(2007b). India's policy toward Central Asia. *World Focus*, 28(335/336), 440–6.

Kachru, U. (2007). *Extreme turbulence: India at the crossroads*. New Delhi: HarperCollins.

Kang, D. (2003). Getting Asia wrong: The need for new analytical frameworks. *International Security*, 27(4), 57–85.

Kaplan, R. D. (1994). The coming anarchy. *The Atlantic Monthly*, February, 56–76.

Kapur, A. (2006). *India: From regional to world power*. London: Routledge.

Kapur, H. (1997). *India's foreign policy, 1947–92*. New Delhi: Sage.

Karns, M. (2000). Postinternational politics and global governance. In H. Hobbs (Ed.), *Pondering postinternationalism: A paradigm for the twenty-first century?* (pp. 39–69). Albany, NY: SUNY Press.

Karrar, H. H. (2009). *The new silk road diplomacy: China's Central Asian foreign policy since the cold war*. Vancouver: UBC Press.

Katzenstein, P. J. (Ed.). (1996). *The culture of national security*. New York: Columbia University Press, 1996.

Katzenstein, P. J. (2005). *A world of regions: Asia and Europe in the American imperium*. Ithaca, NY: Cornell University Press.

Katzenstein, P. J. & Sil, R. (2004). Rethinking Asian security: A case for analytical eclecticism. In J. J. Suh, P. J. Katzenstein, & A. Carlson (Eds), *Rethinking security in East Asia* (pp. 1–33). Stanford, CA: Stanford University Press.

Kaushik, D. (1997). India and Central Asia: Past and present relations and future hopes. *Contemporary Central Asia* 1(1): 226–39.

— (2003). A decade of independent Tajikistan: Some reflections. In M. Singh (Ed.), *India and Tajikistan: Revitalizing a traditional relationship* (pp. 29–46). New Delhi: Anamika Publishers.

Kavalski, E. (2003). The international socialization of the Balkans. *Review of International Affairs*, 2(4), 71–88.

—(2005a). The EU as a vehicle of ideational mobility: Setting normative appropriateness in the Baltics and in the Balkans. In C. F. Gicquel, V. Makarov, & M. Zolkos (Eds), *The challenge of mobility in the Baltic sea region* (pp. 95–115). Berlin: Berliner Wissenschaft Verlag.

—(2005b). The Balkans after Iraq, Iraq after the Balkans. . . Who's next? *Perspectives on European Politics and Societies*, 6(1), 103–27.

—(2006a). From the Western Balkans to the Greater Balkans Area: The external conditioning of "awkward" and "integrated" states. *Mediterranean Quarterly*, 17(3), 86–100.

—(2006b). "We Are the Hawks of Freedom:" Bulgaria's good fishing in the muddy waters of the Gulf. *Journal of Slavic Military Studies*, 19(1), 33–56.

—(2006c). Identity of peace: Framing the European security identity of the EU. In I. P. Karolewski & V. Kaina (Eds), *European identity: Theoretical perspectives and empirical insights* (pp. 91–112). Berlin: LIT Verlag.

—(2007a). The fifth debate and the emergence of complex international relations theory: Notes on the application of complexity theory to the study of international life. *Cambridge Review of International Affairs*, 20(3), 435–54.

—(2007b). Partnership or rivalry between the EU, China and India in Central Asia. *European Law Journal*, 13(6), 839–56.

—(2007c). Whom to follow? Central Asia between the EU and China. *China Report*, 43(1), 43–55.

—(2008a). *Extending the European security community: Constructing peace in the Balkans*. London: I. B. Tauris.

—(2008b). The complexity of global security governance. *Global Society*, 22(4), 423–43.

—(2008c). Venus and the porcupine: Assessing the EU-India strategic partnership. *South Asian Survey*, 15(1), 63–81.

Kavalski, E. (Ed.). (2009a). *China and the global politics of regionalization*. Farnham: Ashgate.

Kavalski, E. (2009b). Timescapes of security: Clocks, clouds, and the complexity of security governance. *World Futures*, 65(7), 527–51.

Kavalski, E. (Ed.). (2009c). *The "new" Central Asia: The regional impact of international actors*. London: World Scientific.

Kavalski, E. (2009d). Uncovering the "new" Central Asia: The dynamics of external agency in a turbulent region. In E. Kavalski (Ed.), *The "new" Central*

Asia: The regional impact of international actors (pp. 1–27). London: World Scientific.

—(2009e). India and Central Asia: The no influence of the "look north" policy. In E. Kavalski (Ed.), *The "new" Central Asia: The regional impact of international actors* (pp. 239–60). London: World Scientific.

—(2009f). The grass was always greener in the past: Re-nationalizing Bulgaria's return to Europe. In I. P. Karolewski & A. M. Suszycki (Eds), *Nationalism in contemporary Europe* (pp. 2219–44). Lanham, MD: Lexington Books.

—(2010a). *India and Central Asia: The mythmaking and international relations of a rising power*. London: I. B. Tauris.

Kavalski, E. (Ed.). (2010b). *Stable outside, fragile inside? Post-Soviet statehood in Central Asia*. Farnham: Ashgate.

Kavalski, E. (2010c). The international politics of fusion and fissure in the awkward states of post-Soviet Central Asia. In E. Kavalski (Ed.), *Stable outside, fragile inside? Post-Soviet statehood in Central Asia* (pp. 1–33). Farnham: Ashgate.

—(2010d). Playing the EU: The logic of mythmaking in Bulgaria's foreign policy towards Central Asia. *Mediterranean Quarterly*, 21(1), 101–21.

—(2010e). Shanghaied into cooperation: Framing China's socialization of Central Asia. *Journal of Asian and African Studies*, 45(2), 131–45.

Kavalski, E. & McCullock, M. R. J. (2005). Back to Althusius? Pre-Westphalian suggestions for a post-Westphalian world. *Atlantic Journal of World Affairs*, 1(1), 106–28.

Kavalski, E. & Zolkos, M. (2007). The hoax of war: The foreign policy discourses of Poland and Bulgaria on Iraq. *Journal of Contemporary European Studies*, 15(30), 377–93.

Kavalski, E. & Zolkos, M. (Eds). (2008). *Defunct federalisms: Critical perspectives on federal failure*. Aldershot: Ashgate.

Keats, J. (1970[1818]). In R. Gittings (Ed.), *The letters of John Keats*. Oxford: Oxford University Press.

Keay, J. (1994 [1977]). *When men and mountains meet: The explorers of the western Himalayas, 1820–75*. Oxford: Oxford University Press.

Kelstrup, M. & Williams, M. C. (Eds). (2000). *International relations theory and the politics of European integration: Power, security, and community*. London: Routledge.

Kent, A. (2007). *Beyond compliance: China, international organizations, and global security*. Stanford, CA: Stanford University Press.

Keohane, R. (2002). *Power and governance in a partially globalized world*. London: Routledge.

Khalid, A. (2006). Backwardness and the quest for civilization: Early Soviet Central Asia in comparative perspective. *Slavic Review*, 65(5), 231–51.

Kier, E. (1995). Culture and military doctrine: France between the wars. *International Security*, 19(4), 65–93.

Kinnvall, C. (2006). *Globalization and religious nationalism in India: The search for ontological security*. London: Routledge.

Kirchner, E. J. (2006). The challenge of EU security governance. *Journal of Common Market Studies*, 44(4), 947–68.

— (2007). Regional and global security. In E. J. Kirchner & J. Sperling (Eds), Global security governance (pp. 3-22). London: Routledge.

Kirchner, E. J. & Sperling, J. (Eds). (2007). *Global security governance*. London: Routledge.

Klein, B. (1988). Hegemony and strategic culture: American power projection and alliance defence politics. *Review of International Studies*, 14(1), 133–48.

Klein, J. T. (2004). Interdisciplinarity and complexity. *E:CO*, 6(1/2), 2–10.

Klein, Y. (1989). A theory of strategic culture. *Journal of Comparative Strategy*, 5(3), 3–23.

Knorr, K. (1977). Is international coercion waning or rising? *International Security*, 1(4), 92–110.

Koh, H. H. (1997). Why do nations obey international law. *Yale Law Journal*, 106(8), 2599–659.

Koldziej, E. A. (2005). *Security in international relations*. Cambridge: Cambridge University Press.

Korkmaz, V. (2010). The nexus of globalization and regionalism within Eurasian security: Shanghai cooperation organization' In A. Patnaik & Tulsiram (Eds), *Globalization and Eurasia*. New Delhi: Knowledge World.

Krahman, E. (2003). Conceptualizing security governance. *Cooperation and Conflict*, 38(1): 5–26.

— (2003a). National, regional, and global governance: One phenomenon or many. *Global Governance*, 9(1), 331–43.

—(2003b). Conceptualizing security governance. *Cooperation and Conflict*, 38(1), 5–26.

—(2005). American hegemony or global governance. *International Studies Review*, 7(3), 531–45.

Krasner, S. (1984). Approaches to the state. *Comparative Politics*, 16(2), 232–43.

Krastev, I. (2003). Bringing the state up. Paper presented at the conference "Interethnic Relations in the Western Balkans," Berlin, 12 September.

Krause, K. & Latham, A. (1998). Constructing non-proliferation and arms control: The norms of western practice. *Contemporary Security Policy*, 19(1), 23–54.

Kroenig, M., McAdam, M., & Webber, S. (2010). Taking soft power seriously. *Comparative Strategy*, 29(5), 412–31.

Kucera, J. (2011). India's Central Asian soft power. *The Diplomat*, 3 September.

Kulchi, Y., Fadin, A., & Sergeev, V. (1996). *Central Asia after the empire*. London: Pluto Press.

Kumar, R. (2008). India as a foreign policy actor: Normative redux. In N. Tocci (Ed.), *Who is a normative foreign policy actor? The European Union and its global partners* (pp. 211–64). Brussels: Centre for European Policy Studies.

Kurlantzick, J. (2006). China's charm: Implications of China's soft power. *Carnegie Policy Brief*, 47.

—(2007). *Charm offensive: How China's soft power is transforming the world*. New Haven, CT: Yale University Press.

—(2008). Monsters' ball. *New Republic*, 8 October.

Laffan, B., O'Donnell, R., & Smith, M. (1999). *Europe's experimental union*. London: Routledge.

Lak, D. (2005). *Mantras of change: Reporting India in a time of flux*. New Delhi: Penguin Viking.

—(2008). *The future of a new superpower*. New York: Viking.

Lal, R. (2006). *Understanding China and India*. Westport, CT: Praeger.

Lama, M. (2005). India's aid policy towards neighbours. In I. P. Kosla (Ed.), *Economic Diplomacy* (pp. 125–48). New Delhi: Konark.

Lambridis, P. & Koukoulis, T. (2005). The awakening of the red dragon. *Asia Europe Journal*, 3(4), 479–99.

Lambsdorf, O. (2006). China, India and Europe. Paper presented at the SAIS Center for Transatlantic Relations, 18 April.

Lampton, D. (2007). Alternative security and foreign policy futures for China. *Asia Policy*, 4(1), 7–15.

Lane, D. & Maxfield, R. (1995). Foresight complexity and strategy. *Santa Fe Institute Working Paper* 105.

—(1996). Strategy under complexity. *Long Term Change*, 29(2), 215–31.

Lanteigne, M. (2005). *China and international institutions: Alternate paths to global power*. London: Routledge.

Lantis, J. S. (2005). Strategic culture: From Clausewitz to constructivism. *Strategic Insights*, 4(10), 1–15.

Larsen, H. (2002). The EU: A global military actor. *Cooperation and Conflict*, 37(30), 283–302.

Lasswell, H. D. (1935). *World politics and personal insecurity*. New York: Free Press.

Latham, A. (1998). Constructing national security: Culture and identity in Indian arms control and disarmament practice. *Contemporary Security Policy*, 19(1), 129–58.

Lattimore, O. (1950). *Pivot of Asia: Sinkiang and the inner Asian frontiers of China and Russia*. Boston, MA: Little, Brown, and Company.

Lavenex, S. (2004). EU external governance in wider Europe. *Journal of European Public Policy*, 11(4), 680–700.

Lebow, R. N. (2010). *Forbidden fruit: Counterfactuals and international relations*. Princeton, NJ: Princeton University Press.

Lefkon, O. (2003). Culture shock: Bringing conflict prevention under the wing of UN development. . . and vice versa. *New York University Journal of International Law and Politics*, 35(1), 671–702.

Levy, J. S. (1994). Learning and foreign policy: Sweeping a conceptual minefield. *International Organization*, 48(2), 297–315.

Lewis, D. (2008). *The temptations of tyranny in Central Asia*. London: Hurst and Company.

Li, M. (2008). China debates soft power. *Chinese Journal of International Politics*, 2(2), 287–308.

Linklater, A. (2005). A European civilizing Process? In C. Hill & M. Smith (Eds), *International relations of the European Union* (pp. 367–87). Oxford: Oxford University Press.

Linz, J. & Stepan, A. (1996). Toward consolidated democracies. *Journal of Democracy*, 7(2), 14–33.

Lipschultz, R. (Ed.). (1995). *On security*. New York: Columbia University Press.

Liu, X. (2009). A misty cold war in the Himalayas: China's historical temperament in international relations. In Y. Hao, C. X. G. Wei, & L. Dittmer (Eds), *Challenges to Chinese foreign policy* (pp. 295–318). Lexington, KY: University Press of Kentucky.

Liu, X. R. (1996). *Western perspectives on Chinese higher education*. Madison, NJ: Farleigh Dickinson University Press.

Lloyd, S. J. (1997). Land-locked Central Asia: Implications for the future. *Geopolitics*, 2(1), 97–133.

Lo, B. (2008). *Axis of convenience: Moscow, Beijing, and the new geopolitics*. Washington, DC: Brookings Institution Press.

Loke, B. (2009). Between interest and responsibility: Assessing China's foreign policy and burgeoning global role. *Asian Security*, 5(3), 195–215.

Lynch, M. (2002). Why engage? China and the logic of communicative engagement. *European Journal of International Relations*, 8(2), 187–230.

Lynn, J. (2003). *Battle: A history of combat and culture*. Boulder, CO: Westview Press.

MacFarlene, S. N. (2004). Caucasus and Central Asia: Towards a non-strategy. *GCSP Occasional Paper Series* 37.

Mackinder, H. J. (1904). The geographical pivot of history. *Geographical Journal*, 23(4), 421–37.

Macmillan, A., Booth, K., & Trood, R. (1999). Strategic culture. In K. Booth & R. Trood (Eds), *Strategic cultures in the Asia Pacific* (pp. 3–28). London: Macmillan.

Magen, A. (2006). The shadow of enlargement: Can the European neighbourhood policy achieve compliance? *Columbia Journal of EuropeanLaw*, 12(2), 383–427.

Mahalingam, S. (2004). India-Central Asia energy cooperation. In K. Santhanam & R. Dwivedi (Eds), *India and Central Asia: Advancing the common interest* (pp. 111–43). New Delhi: Anamaya Publishers.

Mahan, A. T. (1900). *The problem of Asia and its effect upon international policies*. Cambridge, MA: John Wilson and Sons.

Mahapatra, C. (2005). The United States and the Asian powers. In R. R. Sharma (Ed.), *India and emerging Asia* (pp. 156–80). New Delhi: Sage.

Mair, P. (2004). The Europeanization dimension. *Journal of European Public Policy*, 11(2), 337–48.

Makinda, S. (2000). Reading and writing international relations. *Australian Journal of International Affairs*, 54(3), 389–401.

Manners, I. (2002). Normative power Europe: A contradiction in terms? *Journal of Common Market Studies*, 40(2), 235–58.

— (2006). Normative power Europe reconsidered. *Journal of European Public Policy*, 13(2): 182–99.

—(2006a). The European Union as a normative power. *Millennium*, 35(1), 167–80.

—(2006b). Normative power Europe reconsidered: Beyond the crossroads. *Journal of European Public Policy*, 13(2), 182–93.

Manners, I. & Whitman, R. (1998). Towards identifying the international identity of the European Union. *Journal of European Integration*, 10(2), 231–49.

Manohoran, N. (2003). Multiculuturalism in India: Diverse dots in a multiple mosaic. In M. Mekenkam, P. van Tongeren, & H. van de Veen (Eds), *Searching for peace in Central and South Asia: An overview of conflict prevention and peacebuilding activities* (pp. 326–35). Boulder, CO: Lynne Rienner, 2003.

Markell, P. (2003). *Bound by recognition*. Princeton, NJ: Princeton University Press.

Matveeva, A. (2006). *EU stakes in Central Asia*. Paris: EU Institute for Security Studies.
Maxfield, R. R. (1997). Complexity and organizational management. In D. S. Alberts & T. J. Czerwinski (Eds), *Complexity, global politics, and national security* (pp. 171–218). Washington, DC: National Defense University.
Mearsheimer, J. J. (2001). *The tragedy of great power politics*. New York: W. W. Norton.
Mehta, P. B. (2009). Still under Nehru's shadow? The absence of foreign policy frameworks in India. *Indian Review*, 8(3), 213–25.
Meierhenrich, J. (2004). Forming states after failure. In R. Rotberg (Ed.), *When states fail*. Princeton, NJ: Princeton University Press.
Menon, S. (2007). The challenges ahead for India's foreign policy. *World Focus*, 28(335/336), 389–91.
Menon, N. & Nigam, A. (2007). *Power and contestation: India since 1989*. London: Zed Books.
Mercer, J. (2010). Emotional beliefs. *International Organization*, 64(1), 1–31.
Meyer, C. O. (2005). Convergence towards a European strategic culture? A constructivist framework for explaining changing norms. *European Journal of International Relations*, 11(4), 524–9.
—(2007). *The quest for a European strategic culture*. Basingstoke: Palgrave Macmillan.
Meyer, K. E. (2003). *The dust of empire: The race for mastery in the Asian heartland*. New York: Public Affairs.
Meyer, K. E. & Brysac, S. B. (1999). *Tournament of the shadows: The great game and the race for empire in Central Asia*. Washington, DC: Counterpoint.
Migdal, J. S. (2004). State-building and the non-nation-state. *Journal of International Affairs*, 58(1), 17–46.
Milanovic, B. (1994). Why have communist federations collapsed? *Challenge*, 37(2): 61–5.
Minton-Beddoes, Z. (1998). A survey of Central Asia: A Caspian gamble. *The Economist*, 346(8054), 7 February.
Misra, K. P. (1981). Towards understanding nonalignment. *International Studies*, 20(1), 26–37.
Mitleton-Kelly, E. (2003). *Organizational complexity*. Turku: FFRC.
Mitra, S. K. (2003). The reluctant hegemon: India's self-perception and the South Asian strategic environment. *Contemporary South Asia*, 12(3), 399–412.
Mitzen, J. (2006). Anchoring Europe's civilizing identity: Habits, capabilities, and ontological security. *Journal of European Public Policy*, 13(2), 270–85.
Mohan, C. R. (2004). *Crossing the Rubicon: The shaping of India's new foreign policy*. Basingstoke: Palgrave Macmillan.
—(2006). Shaken by Shanghai. *Indian Express*, 18 June.
— (2007). Indian foreign policy. *World Focus*, 28 (335/336): 392–7.
—(2007a). Soft borders and cooperative frontiers: India's changing territorial diplomacy towards Pakistan and China. *Strategic Analysis*, 31(1), 1–23.
—(2007b). Indian foreign policy. *World Focus*, 28(335/336), 392–7.
Monnet, J. (1978). *Memoirs*. Garden City, NY: Doubleday and Co.
Montuori, A. (2005). The complexity of improvisation and the improvisation of complexity. *Human Relations*, 56(2), 237–55.

Moravcsik, A. (2004). In G. Lindstrom & B. Schmitt (Eds), *Lessons from Iraq* (pp. 185–94). Paris: EU Institute for Security Studies.

Morel, P. (2008). Shanghai Cooperation Organization. *EPC Event Report* S10/08, 18 February.

—(2009). Closer engagement with Central Asia. Interview of the EU Special Representative for Central Asia, published on the EU Council website, August.

—(2010). Statement of the EUSR for Central Asia for the media at Dushanbe, Tajikistan, 14 January.

Morgenthau, H. J. (1965). Vietnam: Shadow and substance. *New York Review of Books*, 16 September.

Morlino, L. (2009). Are there hybrid regimes? *European Political Science Review*, 1(2), 273–96.

Muni, S. D. (2003). India and Central Asia: Towards a cooperative future. In N. Joshi (Ed.), *Central Asia—the great game replayed: An Indian perspective* (pp. 11–121). New Delhi: New Century Publications.

Muni, S. D. & Mohan, C. R. (2005). India's options in a changing Asia. In R. R. Sharma (Ed.), *India and emerging Asia* (pp. 52–79). New Delhi: Sage.

Munro, R. H. (1994). The Asian interior: China's waxing spheres of influence. *Orbis*, 38(4), 585–605.

—(2006). China's relations with its neighbours. *International Journal*, 61(2), 320–8.

Murphy, C. N. (2000). Global governance: Poorly done and poorly understood. *International Affairs*, 76(2), 789–805.

Murray, M. K. (2008). *The struggle for recognition in international politics: Security, identity, and the quest for power*. Unpublished PhD Dissertation: The University of Chicago.

Murray, W. (1999). Does military culture matter. *Orbis*, 43(1), 27–42.

Myer, W. (2002). *Islam and colonialism: Western perspectives on Soviet Asia*. London: Routledge Curzon.

Naik, J. A. (1995). *Russia's policy towards India: From Stalin to Yeltsin*. New Delhi: MD Publications.

Nanclares, J. (2001). The federal elements of the European Union. *ZEUS*, 8(4), 595–626.

Narayanan, R. (2007). The Chinese discourse on the "rise of China." *Strategic Analysis*, 31(4), 645–63.

Narlikar, A. (2006). Peculiar chauvinism or strategic calculation? Explaining the negotiating strategy of a rising India. *International Affairs*, 82(1), 59–76.

Nayak, M. & Selbin, E. (2010). *Decentring international relations*. London: Zed Books.

Nayar, B. R. & Paul, T. V. (2003). *India in the world order: Searching for major power status*. Cambridge: Cambridge University Press.

Nel, P. (2010). Redistribution and recognition: What emerging regional powers want. *Review of International Studies*, 36(4), 951–74.

Nelken, D. (2006). Signaling conformity. *Michigan Journal of International Law*, 27(3), 933–72.

Nettle, J. P. (1968). The state as a conceptual variable. *World Politics*, 20(4), 559–92.

Neumann, I. (2001). Regionalization and democratic consolidation. In I. Zielonka & A. Pravda (Eds), *Democratic consolidation in Eastern Europe* (pp. 58–75). Oxford: Oxford University Press.

Nexon, D. H. (2009). *The struggle for power in early modern Europe: Religious conflict, dynastic empires, and international change*. Princeton, NJ: Princeton University Press.

Nincic, M. (2005). *Renegade regimes*. New York: Columbia University Press.

Niou, E. & Ordeshook, P. (1990). Stability in anarchic international systems. *American Political Science Review*, 84(4), 1207–34.

Norris, J. (2005). *Collision course: NATO, Russia and Kosovo* (Westport, CT: Praeger). In the current version there are plenty of typos and incomprehensible signs.

North, D. (1990). *Institutions, institutional change, and economic performance*. Cambridge: Cambridge University Press.

Nourzhanov, K. (2009). Changing security threat perceptions in Central Asia. *Australian Journal of International Affairs*, 63(1), 85–104.

—(2010). International democratic norms and domestic socialization in Kazakhstan: Learning processes of the power elite. In E. Kavalski (Ed.), *Stable outside, fragile inside? Post-Soviet statehood in Central Asia* (pp. 107–32). Farnham: Aldershot.

Nurgaliev, B. (2007). Interview with *Wenhuibao*. 22 January, available at <http://www.sectsco.org/html/01203.html>.

Nye, J. S. (1990). *Bound to lead: The changing nature of American power*. New York: Basic Books.

—(2004). *Soft power: The means to success in world politics*. New York: Public Affairs.

—(2008). *The powers to lead*. New York: Oxford University Press.

Öberg, P., Oskarsson, S., & Svensson, T. (2011). Similarity vs. homogeneity: Contextual effects in explaining trust. *European Political Science Review*, 3(3), 345–69.

Odysseos, L. (2007). *The Subject of coexistence: Otherness in international relations*. Minneapolis, MN: The University of Minnesota Press.

Ogden, C. (2011). International "aspirations" of a rising power. In D. Scott (Ed.), *Handbook of India's International relations* (pp. 3–13). London: Routledge.

Olcott, M. B. (1994). Ceremony and substance: The illusion of unity in Central Asia. In M. Mandelbaum (Ed.), *Central Asia and the world: Kazakhstan, Uzbekistan, Tajikistan, Kyrgyzstan, and Turkmenistan* (pp. 17–46). New York: Council on Foreign Relations Press.

Olsen, J. (2003). Europeanization. In M. Cini (Ed.), *European Union politics* (pp. 333–48). Oxford: Oxford University Press.

Ong, R. (2001). *China's security interests in the post-cold war era*. London: Routledge Curzon.

—(2005). China's security interests in Central Asia. *Central Asia Survey*, 24(4), 425–39.

Osterhammel, J. (1995). Mapping the field. In M. H. Hunt & N. Jun (Eds), *Toward a history of Chinese communist foreign relations, 1920s–1960s: Personalities and interpretive approaches* (pp. 129–61). Washington, DC: Woodrow Wilson Center.

Ovchinnikov, V. (2000). No need to fear the Russian tiger. *Rossiyskaya Gazeta*, 19 September.

Paine, S. C. M. (1996). *Imperial rivals: China, Russia, and their disputed frontier*. Armonk, NY: M. E. Sharpe.

Palat, M. K. (1994). Central Asia and South Asia: Structuring of a new relationship. *South Asian Survey*, 1(1), 49–57.

—(1999). The "romance" of the silk road. *The Hindu*, 9 January.

Paltiel, J. (2009). China regionalization policies: Illiberal internationalism or neo-Mancian benevolence? In E. Kavalski (Ed.), *China and the global politics of regionalization* (pp. 47–62). Farnham: Ashgate.

Pan, G. (2007). A Chinese perspective on the Shanghai cooperation organization. In "The Shanghai cooperation organization (pp. 45–58). *SIPRI Policy Paper* 17.

—(2009). The SCO's success in security architecture. In R. Huisken (Ed.), *The architecture of security in the Asia-Pacific* (pp. 33–44). Canberra, ACT: Australian National University.

Pandit, R. (2007). Indian forces get foothold in Central Asia. *The Times of India*, 18 July.

—(2008). Outpost at Tajikistan still on India's radar. *The Times of India*, 21 January.

Pant, G. (2005). Reform and resurgence: The trajectory of change in West Asia. In R. R. Sharma (Ed.), *India and emerging Asia* (pp. 181–205). New Delhi: Sage.

Paris, R. (2002). International peacebuilding and the "*mission civilsatrice*." *Review of International Studies*, 28(4), 637–56.

—(2004). *At War's End*. Cambridge: Cambridge University Press.

Parker, N. (2008). A theoretical introduction: Spaces, centers, and margins. In N. Parker (Ed.), *The geopolitics of Europe's identity: Centers, boundaries, and margins* (pp. 3–24). Basingstoke: Palgrave Macmillan.

Peerenboom, R. (2006). The fire-breathing dragon and the cute, cuddly Panda: The implications of China's rise for developing countries, human rights, and geopolitical stability. *Chicago Journal of International Law*, 7(1), 17–50.

Peimani, H. (1998). *Regional security and the future of Central Asia: The competition of Iran, Turkey, and Russia*. Westport, CT: Praeger.

Pempel, T. J. (2005). *Remapping East Asia*. Ithaca, NY: Cornell University Press.

Phinnemore, D. & Warleigh-Lack, A. (Eds). (2009). *Reflections on European integration: 50 years of the treaty of Rome*. Basingstoke: Palgrave Macmillan.

Pickering, P. M. (2007). *Peacebuilding in the Balkans*. Ithaca, NY: Cornell University Press.

Pickles, J. (2008). Conclusion: State, society, and hybrid post-socialist economies. In J. Pickles (Ed.), *State and society in post-socialist economies* (pp. 253–62). Basingstoke: Palgrave Macmillan.

Pierce, R. (1960). *Russian Central Asia, 1867–1917: A study of colonial rule*. Berkeley, CA: University of California Press.

Pillai, S. K. (2003). Border conflicts and regional disputes. In M. Mekenkam, P. van Tongeren, & H. van de Veen (Eds), *Searching for peace in Central and South Asia: An overview of conflict prevention and peacebuilding activities* (pp. 249–66). Boulder, CO: Lynne Rienner.

Pirie, N. W. (1937). The Meaninglessness of the terms life and living. In J. Needham & D. Green (Eds), *Perspectives on biochemistry* (pp. 11–22). Cambridge: Cambridge University Press.

Pomorska, K. (2007). The impact of enlargement: Europeanization of Polish foreign policy. *Hague Journal of Diplomacy*, 2(1), 25–51.

Poore, S. (2003). What is the context? *Review of International Studies*, 29(1), 279–84.

Postel-Vinay, K. (2008). The historicity of European normative power. In Z. Laïdi (Ed.), *EU foreign policy in a globalized world* (pp. 47–54). London: Routledge.

Pouliot, V. 2008. The logic of practicality: A theory of practice of security community. *International Organization*, 62(2), 257–88.

Press-Barnathan, G. (2005). The changing incentives of security regionalization: From 11/9 to 9/11. *Cooperation and Conflict*, 40(3), 296–312.

Prozorov, S. (2010). The other as past and present: Beyond the logic of temporal othering in IR theory. *Review of International Studies*, 37(3), 1273–93.

Puchala, D. (2003). *Theory and history in international relations*. London: Routledge.

Pye, L. (1967). *The spirit of Chinese politics*. Cambridge, MA: MIT Press.

—(1990). China: Erratic state, frustrated society. *Foreign Affairs*, 69(4), 56–74.

—(1995). Factions and politics of *guanxi*: Paradoxes in Chinese administrative and political behavior. *China Journal*, 31(1), 35–53.

Qin, Y. (2011). Rule, rules, and relations. *Chinese Journal of International Politics*, 4(2), 117–45.

Radaelli, C. (2003). The Europeanization of public policy. In K. Featherstone & C. Radaelli (Eds), *The politics of Europeanization* (pp. 27–56). Oxford: Oxford University Press.

Raddon, A. (2007). Timescapes of flexibility and insecurity. *Time & Society*, 16(1), 61–82.

Rai, V. & Simon, W. (2007). *Think India*. New York: Dutton.

Ramet, S. P. (2005). *Thinking about Yugoslavia: Scholarly debates about the Yugoslav break-up and the wars in Bosnia and Kosovo*. Cambridge: Cambridge University Press.

—(2007). *The liberal project and the transformation of democracy*. College Station, TX: Texas A&M University Press.

Ramo, J. C. (2007). *The Beijing Consensus*. London: Foreign Policy Center.

Rana, K. S. (2007). *Asian diplomacy: The foreign ministries of China, India, Japan, Singapore, and Thailand*. New Delhi: Oxford University Press.

Rashid, A. (1994). *The resurgence of Central Asia: Islam or nationalism*. London: Zed Books.

Raugh, H. B. (2004). *The Victorians at war, 1815–1914: An encyclopedia of British military history*. Washington, DC: ABC-CLIO.

Rhodes, R. A. W. (1996). The new governance. *Political Studies*, 44(4), 652–67.

Risse, T. & Sikkink, K. (1999). The socialization of international human rights norms into domestic practices. In T. Risse, S. C. Ropp, & K. Sikkink (Eds), *The power of human rights: International norms and domestic change* (pp. 1–38). Cambridge: Cambridge University Press.

Roach, S. S. (2011). Ten reasons why China is different. *Project Syndicate*, 27 May.

Roberts, A. (1991). A new age in international relations. *International Affairs*, 67(3), 509–25.

Rosemont, H. (2006). 'Two loci of authority: Autonomous individuals and related persons. In P. H. Hershock & R. T. Ames (Eds), *Confucian cultures of authority* (pp. 1–20). Albany, NY: SUNY Press.

Rosenau, J. (1979). Muddling, meddling, and modelling: Alternative approaches to the study of world politics in an era of rapid change. *Millennium*, 8(2), 130–44.

Rosenau, J. (Ed.). (1993). *Global voices*. Boulder, CO: Westview.

Rosenau, J. (1995). Governance in the twenty-first century. *Global Governance*, 1(1), 13–43.

Rosner, K. (2010). China scores again in energy: Russia and Central Asia. *IAGS Journal of Energy Security*, 12 January.

Roy, O. (2000). *The new Central Asia: Geopolitics and the birth of nations*. London: I. B. Tauris.

Ruggie, J. G. (1975). Complexity. In T. La Porte (Ed.), *Organized social complexity* (pp. 119–50). Princeton, NJ: Princeton University Press.

—(1993). Territoriality and beyond: Problematizing modernity in international relations. *International Organization*, 47(4), 139–74.

Rumelili, B. (2007). *Constructing regional community and order in Europe and Southeast Asia*. Basingstoke: Palgrave.

Rummel, R. (1976). *Understanding conflict and war*. Beverly Hills, CA: SAGE Publications.

Russett, B. (1993). *Grasping the democratic peace: Principles for a post-Cold War world*. Princeton, NJ: Princeton University Press.

Sabol, S. (2010). Turkmenistan: Flawed, fragile, and isolated. In E. Kavalski (Ed.), *Stable outside, fragile inside? Post-Soviet statehood in Central Asia* (pp. 175–94). Farnham: Ashgate.

Said, E. W. (1978). *Orientalism*. London: Vintage Books.

—(1994). *Culture and imperialism*. London: Vintage Books.

Saran, S. (2003). Present dimensions of Indian foreign policy. In A. Sinha & M. Mohta (Eds), *Indian foreign policy: Challenges and opportunities* (pp. 115–23). New Delhi: Academic Foundation.

Sasley, B. E. (2011). Theorizing states' emotions. *International Studies Review*, 13(3), 452–76.

Schäffer, S. & Tolksdorf, D. (2009). The eastern partnership: "ENP-plus" for Europe's eastern neighbors. *CA Perspectives* 4.

Schimmelfennig, F. (2000). International socialization in the "new Europe." *European Journal of International Relations*, 6(1), 109–39.

Schimmelfennig, F. & Sedelmeier, U. (Eds). (2005). *The Europeanization of Central and Eastern Europe*. Ithaca, NY: Cornell University Press.

Schmitt, J. (1997). Command and (out of) control: The military implications of complexity theory. In D. S. Albers & T. J. Czerwinski (Eds), *Complexity, global politics, and national security* (pp. 99–111). Washington, DC: National Defence University.

Schrim, S. A. (2010). Leaders in need of followers: Emerging powers in global governance. *European Journal of International Relations*, 16(2), 197–221.

Scobell, A. (2001). The Chinese cult of defence. *Issues and Studies*, 37(5), 100–27.

—(2002). *China and strategic culture*. Carlisle, PA: Strategic Studies Institute, US Army War College.

Scott, D. (2009). India's "extended neighborhood" concept: Power projection for a rising power. *India Review*, 8(2), 127–39.

Scott, W. (1958). Rationality and non-rationality of international attitudes. *Journal of Conflict Resolution*, 2(1), 8–16.

Sengupta, A. (2009). *Heartlands of Eurasia: The geopolitics of political space*. Lanham, MD: Lexington Books.

Shambaugh, D. (1994). The insecurity of security: The PLA's evolving doctrine and threat perceptions. *Journal of Northeast Asian Studies*, 13(1), 3–25.

—(2004/2005). China engages Asia: Reshaping the regional order. *International Security*, 29(3), 64–99.

Shambaugh, D. (Ed.). (2005). *Power shift: China and Asia's new dynamics*. Berkeley, CA: University of California Press.

Shams-ud-Din (1997). The new great game in Central Asia. *International Studies*, 34(3), 329–41.

Shams-ud-Din (Ed.). (2000). *Geopolitics and energy resources in Central Asia and Caspian region*. New Delhi: Lancer.

Shanghai Cooperation Organization Charter (2002). Available at: http://www.sectsco.org/html/00096.html.

Shanghai Cooperation Organization Concept on Combating Terrorism, Separatism, and Extremism (2005). Available at: http://www.ecrats.com/ru/docs/read/conception_shos_members.

Shanghai Cooperation Organization Convention on Combating Terrorism, Separatism, and Extremism, (2001). Available at: http://www.sectsco.org/html/00093.html.

Shanghai Cooperation Organization Declaration (2001). Available at: http://www.sectsco.org/html/00088.html.

Shanghai Cooperation Organization Protocol on the Establishment of the SCO-Afghanistan Contact Group (2005). Available at: http://www.hrichina.org/content/5226

Shanghai Cooperation Organization Scheme for Mutual Relations with Other International Organizations and States (2002). Available at: http://www.sectsco.org/html/00101.html.

Shannon, V. (2000). Norms are what states make of them. *International Studies Quarterly*, 44(2), 293–316.

Shapiro, M. & Bonham, M. (1973). Cognitive process and foreign policy. *International Studies Quarterly*, 17(2), 147–74.

Sharma, R. R. (1997). Indo-Russian relations in the emerging context. In M. Rasgotra & V. D. Chopra (Eds), *India's relations with Russia and China: A new phase* (pp. 65–74). New Delhi: Gyan Publishing.

—(2003). State-building in Tajikistan: problems and prospect. In M. Singh (Ed.), *India and Tajikistan: Revitalizing a traditional relationship* (pp. 67–100). New Delhi: Anamika Publishers.

—(2004a). Challenges to stability in Asia. *International Studies*, 41(3), 263–77.

—(2004b). Issues confronting Central Asia. *International Studies*, 41(4), 427–9.

—(2005). Asia's quest for identity and security. In R. R. Sharma (Ed.), *India and emerging Asia* (pp. 29–51). New Delhi: Sage.

—(2007). Political system and democratic discourse in Central Asia: A view from outside. In J. N. Roy & B. B. Kumar (Eds), *India and Central Asia: Classical to contemporary periods* (pp. 123–33). New Delhi: Concept Publishing.

Sheehan, M. (2005). *International Security*. Boulder, CO: Lynne Rienner.

Shi, Y. (2007). Great power politics in Central Asia today: A Chinese assessment. In E. Van Wie Davis & R. Azizian (Eds), *Islam, oil, and geopolitics: Central Asia after September 11*. Lanham. MD: Rowman and Littlefield.

Shih, C. (1990). *The spirit of Chinese foreign policy*. New York: St. Martin's Press.

—(1993). *China's just world*. Boulder, CO: Lynne Rienner.

—(2003). *Navigating sovereignty: World politics lost in China*. Basingstoke: Palgrave Macmillan.

Sil, R. & Katzenstein, P. (2010). *Beyond paradigms: Analytical eclecticism in the study of world politics*. New York: Palgrave Macmillan.

Singer, J. D. (1989). System structure, decision processes, and innocence of international war. In M. Midlarsky (Ed.), *Handbook of war studies* (pp. 1–12). Boston, MA: Unwin Hyman.

Singh, J. (1999). *Defending India*. New York: St. Martin's Press.

Singh, M. (2003). India and Tajikistan: A perspective for the 21st century. In M. Singh (Ed.), *India and Tajikistan: Revitalizing a traditional relationship* (pp. 197–204). New Delhi: Anamika Publishers.

Singh, N. (2006). *India: A rising power*. New Delhi: Authors Press.

Sinha, Y. (2004). India and Central Asia in the emerging security environment. In K. Santhanam & R. Dwivedi (Eds), *India and Central Asia: Advancing the common interest* (pp. 5–10). New Delhi: Anamaya Publishers.

Sjursen, H. (2006). The EU as a "normative" power: How can this be? *Journal of European Public Policy*, 13(2), 235–51.

Smith, M. (2009). Between "soft power" and a hard place: European Union foreign and security policy between the Islamic world and the United States. *International Politics*, 46(5), 596–615.

Smith, M. E. (2004). *Europe's foreign and security policy: The institutionalization of cooperation*. Cambridge: Cambridge University Press.

Smith, J. & Jenks, C. (2006). *Qualitative complexity: Ecology, cognitive processes and the re-emergence of structures in post-humanist social theory*. London: Routledge.

Snyder, J. L. (1977). *The Soviet strategic culture: Implications for limited nuclear options*. Santa Monica, CA: Rand Corporation.

—(1991). *Myths of empire: Domestic politics and international ambition*. Ithaca, NY: Cornell University Press.

Söderbaum, F. & van Langenhove, L. (Eds). (2006). *The EU as a global player: The politics of interrregionalism*. London: Routledge.

Song, W. (2011). Peaceful rise from the border: Chinese practice of diplomatic leadership in the Shanghai cooperation organization. In Y. Hao & B. K. P. Chou (Eds), *China's policies on its borderlands and their international implications* (pp. 47–68). London: World Scientific.

Sörensen, J. S. (2002). Balkanism and the new radical interventionism. *International Peacekeeping*, 9(1), 1–22.

Soucek, S. (2000). *A history of inner Asia*. Cambridge: Cambridge University Press.

Spakowski, N. (2009). National aspirations on a global stage: Concepts of world/global history in contemporary China. *Journal of Global History*, 4(4), 479–89.

Sperling, J., Kay, S., & Papacosma, S. V. (2003). *Limiting institutions? The challenge of Eurasian security governance*. Manchester: Manchester University Press.

Stacey, H. (2003). Relational sovereignty. *Stanford Law Review*, 55(4), 2029–59.

Stern, M. (2006). "We" the subject: The power and failure of (in)security. *Security Dialogue*, 37(2), 187–205.

Stoker, G. (1998). Governance as theory. *International Social Science Journal*, 155(1), 17–27.

Stuart-Fox, M. (2003). *A short history of China and Southeast Asia*. Crows Nest, NSW: Allen & Unwin.

Suganami, H. (2008). Narrative explanation and international relations: Back to basics. *Millennium*, 37(2), 327–56.

Sun, Z. (2004). New and old regionalism: The Shanghai cooperation organization and Sino-Central Asian relations. *Review of International Affairs*, 3(4), 600–12.

Suter, K. (2003). *Global order and global disorder*. Westport: Praeger.

Telò, M. (2006). *Europe: A civilian power?* Basingstoke: Palgrave Macmillan.

Teló, M. (Ed.). (2007). *The European Union and new regionalism*. Aldershot: Ashgate.

Teschke, B. (2003). *The myth of 1648*. London: Verso.

Tessman, B. F. (2009). The evolution of Chinese foreign policy: New incentives with slowing growth. *Asian Security*, 5(3), 296–318.

Tocci, N. (2008). Proliferating normative foreign policy: The European Union and Its global partners. In N. Tocci (Ed.), *Who is a normative foreign policy actor? The European Union and its global partners* (pp. 1–23). Brussels: Center for European Public Policy Studies.

Trenin, D. (2011). Challenges and opportunities: Russia and the rise of China and India. In A. J. Tellis, T. Tanner, & J. Keough (Eds), *Asia repsonds to its rising powers: China and India* (pp. 227–56). Washington, DC: National Bureau of Asian Research.

Tsoukalis, L. (2003). *What kind of Europe?* Oxford: Oxford University Press.

Tsygankov, A. P. (2007). Modern at last? Variety of weak states in the post-Soviet world. *Communist and Post-Communist Studies*, 40(1), 423–39.

Turner, S. (2011). China and Russia after the Russian-Georgian war. *Comparative Strategy*, 30(1), 50–9.

Udgaonkar, B. M. (1999). India's nuclear capability, her security concerns, and the recent tests. *Current Science*, 76(2), 154–66.

—(2001). The international dimension of national security: Some observations. *Strategic Analysis*, 24(10), 1773–94.

Upahyaya, P. (2009). Peace and conflict: Reflections on Indian thinking. *Strategic Analysis*, 33(1), 71–83.

USA Today (2005). China and Russia warn of world domination. 2 July.

Varma, P. K. (2004). *Being Indian*. New Delhi: Penguin Books.

Vennesson, P. (2010). Competing visions of the EU grand strategy. *European Foreign Affairs Review*, 15(1), 57–75.

Vermeersch, P. (2005). European Union enlargement and immigration policy. *Communist and Post-Communist Studies*, 38(1), 71–88.
Vucetic, S. (2011). Genealogy as a research tool in IR. *Review of International Studies*, 37(3), 1295–1312.
Wacker, G. (2011). China and its Central Asian neighbors. In Y. Hao & B. K. P. Chou (Eds), *China's policies on its borderlands and their international implications* (pp. 69–92). London: World Scientific.
Wæver, O. (1996). European security identities. *Journal of Common Market Studies*, 34(1), 103–32.
— (1997). *Concepts of security*. Copenhagen: Copenhagen University Press.
—(1997a). *Concepts of security*. Copenhagen: Copenhagen Political Studies Press.
—(1997b). After neo-medievalism: Imperial metaphors for European security. In J. P. Burgess (Ed.), *Cultural politics and political culture in post-modern Europe* (pp. 321–67). Amsterdam: Rodopi.
—(1998). Explaining Europe by decoding discourses. In A. Wivel (Ed.), *Explaining European integration* (pp. 100–46). Copenhagen: Copenhagen Political Studies Press.
—(2000). The EU as a security actor. In M. Kelstrup & M. C. Williams (Eds), *International relations theory and the politics of European integration* (pp. 250–94). London: Routledge.
—(2002). Identity, communities, and foreign policy. In L. Hansen & O. Wæver (Eds), *European integration and national security* (pp. 20–49). London: Routledge.
—(2004). 10x10. *Tidsskriftet Politik*, 4(7), 1–5.
Wallerstein, I. (1996). *Open the social sciences*. Stanford, CA: Stanford University Press.
Waltz, K. (1979). *Theory of international politics*. Reading, MA: Addison-Wesley.
—(1997). Evaluating theories. *American Political Science Review*, 91(4), 913–17.
Wang, F. (2005). Preservation, prosperity, and power: What motivates China's foreign policy. *Journal of Contemporary China*, 14(45), 669–94.
Wang, G. (1996). *The revival of Chinese nationalism*. Leiden: Institute for Asian Studies.
Wang, Y. (2011). *Harmony and war: Confucian culture and Chinese power politics*. New York: Columbia University Press.
Warikoo, K. (Ed.). (1995). *Central Asia: Emerging new order*. New Delhi: Har-Anand Publications.
Warikoo, K. (2003). The Afghanistan crisis and Tajikistan. In M. Singh (Ed.), *India and Tajikistan: Revitalizing a traditional relationship* (pp. 145–54). New Delhi: Anamika Publishers.
Warkotsch, A. (2006). The European Union and democracy promotion in bad neighborhoods: The case of Central Asia. *European Foreign Affairs Review*, 11(4), 509–15.
Webber, M. (2007). *Inclusion, exclusion, and the governance of European security*. Manchester: Manchester University Press.
Webber, M., Croft, S., Howorth, J., Terriff, T., & Krahman. E. (2004). The governance of European security. *Review of International Studies*, 30(10), 3–26.
Weiss, T. (2000). Governance, good governance, and global governance. *Third World Quarterly*, 21(5), 795–814.

Wendt, A. (1992). Anarchy is what states make of it. *International Organization*, 46(2), 391–425.
—(1999). *Social theory of international politics*. Cambridge: Cambridge University Press.
—(2003). Why a world state is inevitable: Teleology and the logic of anarchy. *European Journal of International Relations*, 9(4), 559–64.
Wenger, E. C. & Snyder, W. M. (2000). Communities of practice: The organizational frontier. *Harvard Business Review*, 78(1), January–February, 139–45.
White, B. (2000). *Understanding European Union Foreign Policy*. Basingstoke: Palgrave Macmillan.
White, D. M. (1971). Power and intention. *International Organization*, 65(3), 749–59.
White Paper (2000). *White paper on China's national defence*. Available at: http://www.china.org.cn/english/2791.htm, 16 October.
Whiting, A. S. (1989). *China eyes Japan*. Berkeley, CA: University of California Press.
Whiting, A. S (1998). Forecasting Chinese foreign policy: IR theory vs. the fortune cookie. In T. W. Robinson & D. Shambaugh (Eds), *Chinese foreign policy* (pp. 506–523). Oxford: Clarendon Press.
Whitman, J. (2005). *The limits of global governance*. London: Routledge.
Wilkinson, C. (2007). The Copenhagen school on tour in Kyrgyzstan: Is securitization theory useable outside Europe? *Security Dialogue*, 38(1), 5–25.
—(2010). International agency in Kyrgyzstan: Rhetoric, revolution, and renegotiation. In E. Kavalski (Ed.), *Stable outside, fragile inside? Post-Soviet statehood in Central Asia* (pp. 133–56). Farnham: Aldershot.
Williams, M. C. (2007). *Culture and security*. London: Routledge.
Wimbush, S. E. (2011). Great games in Central Asia. In A. J. Tellis, T. Tanner, & J. Keough (Eds), *Asia repsonds to its rising powers: China and India* (pp. 259–84). Washington, DC: National Bureau of Asian Research.
Wivel, A. (2004). Small EU member states after enlargement: A new context of foreign policy-making', paper presented at the "Workshop on Small States," University of Iceland, 17–18 September.
Wolfers, A. (1962). *Discord and collaboration: Essays on international politics*. Baltimore, MD: John Hopkins University Press.
Womack, B. (2008). China as a normative foreign policy actor. In N. Tocci (Ed.), *Who is a normative foreign policy actor? The European Union and its global partners* (pp. 265–300). Brussels: Center for European Policy Studies.
Wood, S. (2011). Pragmatic power EUrope? *Cooperation and Conflict*, 46(2), 242–61.
Wood, J. & Dupont, B. (Eds). (2006). *Democracy, society and the governance of security*. Cambridge: Cambridge University Press.
Xing, G. (2001). China and Central Asia. In R. Allison & L. Jonson (Eds), *Central Asian security: The new international context* (pp. 152–72). London: Royal Institute for International Affairs.
Yan, X. (2011). International leadership and norm evolution. *Chinese Journal of International Politics*, 4(2), 233–64.
Yazdani, E. (2008). The European Union and Central Asia. *International Studies*, 45(3), 247–55.

Youngs, R. (2002). *The European Union and the promotion of democracy: Europe's Mediterranean and Asian politics*. Oxford: Oxford University Press.

Yunker, J. (2004). Effective global governance without effective global government. *World Futures*, 60(7), 503–33.

Zaman (2011). SCO: India, Pakistan to become full members, Turkey—dialogue partner, Afghanistan—observer, 4 November.

Zaman, R. U. (2009). Strategic culture: A "cultural" understanding of war. *Comparative Strategy*, 28(1), 68–88.

Zhang D. (2005). Interview with the *Zhonghuayingcai* magazine. Available at: http://www.sectsco.org/html/00468.html, 25 May.

—(2006a). Generalizing Experience, Deepening Cooperation. Available at: http://www.sectsco.org/html/01007.html, 14 May.

—(2006b). Interview with the *Oriental Weekly*. Available at: http://www.sectsco.org/html/01008.html, 6 September.

Zhang, F. (2009). Regionalization in the Tianxia? Continuity and change in China's foreign policy. In E. Kavalski (Ed.), *China and the global politics of regionalization* (pp. 19–32). Farnham: Ashgate.

Zhang, Y. (2001a). System, empire, and state in Chinese international relations. *Review of International Studies*, 27(1), 43–63.

—(2001b). Problematizing China's security: Sociological insights. *Pacifica Review*, 13(3), 242–53.

Zhang, Y. & Tang, S. (2005). China's regional strategy. In D. Shambaugh (Ed.), *Power shift: China and Asia's new dynamics*. Berkeley, CA: University of California Press.

Zhao, H. (2003). The Shanghai cooperation organization. *China and Eurasia Forum Quarterly*, 4(3), 105–23.

Zheng, B. (2005). China's "peaceful rise" to great power status. *Foreign Affairs*, 84(5), 18–24.

Zhou, Y. (2004). *China's diplomacy*. Beijing: China Intercontinental Press.

Zielonka, J. (2007). *Europe as empire: The nature of the enlarged European Union*. Oxford: Oxford University Press.

Zolkos, M. (2005). *Conceptual analysis of the human rights and democracy nexus*. Copenhagen: Copenhagen Political Studies Press.

Index